高等院校经济管理类专业应用型系列教材

经贸函电

Business Correspondence

刘颖　吕雪　主　编
王曦　熊霞　副主编

清华大学出版社
北　京

内 容 简 介

本书由三篇十三章内容构成。第一篇讲述了外贸函电写作基本知识及电子通信方式，并着重介绍了电子邮件在函电中的运用。第二篇以外贸业务流程发展为线索，介绍了建立业务关系、资信调查、询盘与发盘、还盘与接受、订单及履行、信用证及其他支付方式、包装和装运、保险、索赔与理赔等各环节的函电撰写。第三篇用完整的外贸业务流程的函电范例，帮助读者从整体上把握外贸函电在实际业务中的运用。同时，对外销员考试中的外经贸英语部分进行详细解析。

本书可供国际经济与贸易、商务英语专业的学生、外贸工作者学习，也可供所有需要与外商进行有效沟通的从业人员自学或参考。

图书在版编目（CIP）数据

经贸函电/刘颖，吕雪主编. --北京：清华大学出版社，2014（2019.8重印）
高等院校经济管理类专业应用型系列教材
ISBN 978-7-302-36457-3

Ⅰ. ①经… Ⅱ. ①刘… ②吕… Ⅲ. ①对外贸易－英语－电报信函－写作－高等学校－教材
Ⅳ. ①H315

中国版本图书馆 CIP 数据核字（2014）第 091240 号

责任编辑： 刘翰鹏
封面设计： 宋　彬
责任校对： 袁　芳
责任印制： 李红英

出版发行： 清华大学出版社
网　　址： http://www.tup.com.cn，http://www.wqbook.com
地　　址： 北京清华大学学研大厦 A 座　　**邮　　编：** 100084
社 总 机： 010-62770175　　**邮　　购：** 010-62786544
投稿与读者服务： 010-62776969，c-service@tup.tsinghua.edu.cn
质量反馈： 010-62772015，zhiliang@tup.tsinghua.edu.cn
课件下载： http://www.tup.com.cn，010-62795764
印 装 者： 北京九州迅驰传媒文化有限公司
经　　销： 全国新华书店
开　　本： 185mm×260mm　　**印　　张：** 18.5　　**字　　数：** 422 千字
版　　次： 2014 年 9 月第 1 版　　**印　　次：** 2019 年 8 月第 4 次印刷
定　　价： 36.00 元

产品编号：058706-01

随着经济全球化的不断深入及经贸领域的变革，社会对涉外经贸人才提出了更高的要求，需要他们系统地掌握经济学基本原理，通晓国际经济贸易知识和惯例，能熟练运用计算机进行业务操作，并能熟练运用专业英语与外商进行有效沟通。

本书由三篇十三章内容构成。第一篇对外贸函电写作基本知识及电子通信方式进行概述，并结合实践发展趋势着重介绍电子邮件在函电中的运用。第二篇以外贸业务流程发展为线索，介绍了建立业务关系、资信调查、询盘与发盘、还盘与接受、订单及履行、信用证及其他支付方式、包装和装运、保险、索赔与理赔等各环节的函电撰写。该篇各章节由学习目标、专业背景知识介绍、写作技巧、样函、焦点词汇及短语、常用语句、练习等模块构成。同时，各章节皆配有样函译文、练习参考答案及 PPT。第三篇为经贸函电实用部分，提供完整的外贸业务流程的函电范例，帮助读者从整体上把握外贸函电在业务中的实际运用。同时，对外销员考试中的外经贸英语部分进行详细解析。本书力争反映当今世界进出口业务的现实和最新变化，通过例文真切反映交易的实际过程，从而培养学习者的实际应用能力，贴近学习者的就业需求。

本书可供国际经济与贸易、商务英语专业的学生、外贸工作者学习，也可供所有需要与外商进行有效沟通的从业人员自学或参考。

本书由武汉东湖学院经济学院、武汉东湖学院外语学院、汉口学院经济学院、中国地质大学江城学院经济学院共三所高校的四个学院的教师共同研究编写。武汉东湖学院经济学院刘颖老师和武汉东湖学院外语学院吕雪老师担任主编；汉口学院经济学院王曦老师、中国地质大学江城学院经济学院熊霞老师担任副主编。

本书各章内容及电子资源的编写分工是：刘颖编写第一～四章、第十二章、第十三章，并与吕雪共同编写第五～七章，王曦编写第八章、第九章，熊霞编写第十章、第十一章。全书由刘颖负责拟定大纲并统稿。

在本书编写过程中，参考了一些教材、著作和文献，引用了学术期刊上的最新研究成果的一些观点。在此，向上述教材、著作和文献的原作者表示衷心的感谢！

本书受篇幅所限，将样函译文、习题参考答案采用电子文件免费提供给读者使用，并附有国际经济组织的名称、国内外港口汇总表以供参考，为授课教师提供PPT。这些学习资料均可以在清华大学出版社网站下载。

由于作者水平有限，书中难免有不足之处，恳请同行和读者批评、指正！

刘 颖

2014年6月

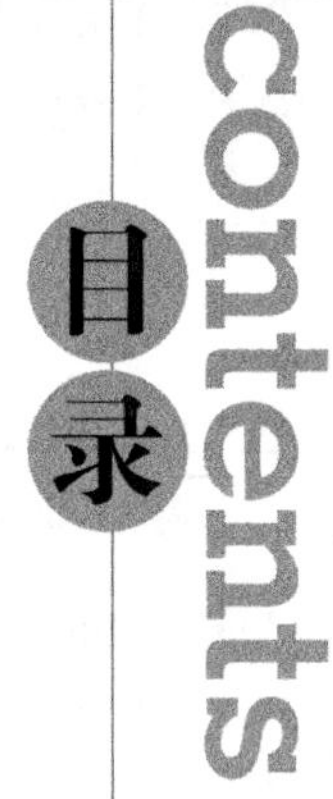

第一篇　英文商务信函写作概述
Brief Introduction to the Business Letters Writing

第二篇 常用外贸信函
Business Letters for Frequent Occasions

第三篇 经贸函电实用部分
Practical Usage of Business Correspondences

第一篇

英文商务信函写作概述

Brief Introduction to the Business Letters Writing

Unit 1
Fundamentals of Writing English Business Letter
外贸函电写作基本知识

1.1 Study Aim(学习目标)

(1) 了解外贸函电的写作要求和基本原则。

(2) 了解英式商务信函与美式商务信函的差异。

(3) 掌握信函构成及信函格式,能根据已知信息熟练编写信函。

1.2 Introduction(专业背景知识介绍)

外贸函电又称商务英语函电或英文商务信函,是在对外经济贸易活动中以英语为载体而进行的函电往来。外贸函电是商家、厂家与客户之间用于联系业务、咨询商情、沟通商情、订购出售、索要价款的主要途径和工具。在对外经贸活动中,外贸函电以信函、电报、电传、传真、电子邮件等通信方式传递信息。随着现代信息技术的发展,电报及电传的使用已日趋减少,电报可以说已绝少使用,电子邮件因其不断提升的快捷性和保密性受到商界人士的青睐。但不论如何,信函仍是商业信息交换的基础。因此,撰写英语商务信函是外贸函电知识的重要内容。

外贸函电的作用主要有两个。一是用以索取信息或传递信息,联络与沟通感情,处理商务交流中相关事宜。在对外贸易活动中,从事外贸业务的公司之间远隔重洋,他们之间的业务往来往往利用函电这种通信工具来建立纽带。互相不能晤面的公司往往通过函电去判断对方的业务能力及服务水平,一封得体的函电可为建立一个重要的业务关系铺平道路。相反,如果函电词不达意,就可能引起误会,甚至引发矛盾,造成客户资源流失。二是作为买卖双方交易磋商过程的法律依据。大部分外贸函电都具有公文的性质,尤其是在发盘、接受、订购等重要外贸活动环节中,函电作为专业性书面记录,具有法律效力。同时,作为具有法律效力的专业书面记录,函电还可在当事方发生交易争端时作为判定依据。

按照不同的分类方式,我们可将外贸函电分为不同的类别。按文体正式程度和内容重要性,外贸函电可分为正式函件和便函。正式函件用以陈述外贸业务活动中具有实质性意义的事项,对交易内容、交易方式和交易利益产生实际影响。正式函件通常在函件正文有标题,并在信函结尾处需加盖出信单位的公章。便函用于陈述一般性和礼节性事项,有利于联络双方感情,加强相互了解,为挖掘潜在业务关系打下基础。便函通常不要求在函件正文设标题,同时,在信函结尾处无须加盖出信单位的公章。

从外贸业务内容和商务操作角度,外贸函电发挥着沟通买卖双方的媒介作用,涉及外贸业务中的各个环节。以信用证方式交易下的外贸业务流程为例,涉及的函电类型分别为建立业务关系函(Establishing Business Relations)、资信调查函(Status Enquiry)、询盘函(Enquiry)、发盘函(Offer)、还盘函(Counter-offer)、接受函(Acceptance)、订购函(Orders)、装运函(Shipment)、保险函(Insurance)、付款函(Terms of Payment)、索赔和理赔函(Claim and Settlement)等函件。

1.3 Foundation for Writing English Business Letters (英文商务信函写作基础)

要写好外贸英文商务信函并非易事,写信人需要具备以下写作基础。

(1) 精通英语

英文商务信函是一种具有独特语言风格的外贸专业信函。不同于一般的日常英语,它还包括一些特殊的专业贸易用语、缩略用法等。同时,一般日常英语的部分词汇短语在用于外贸函电写作时,会出现词义和用法的变化。因此,写信人不但应具备扎实的英语基础,同时还要掌握外贸函电写作中特殊的基本术语、写作格式,以及专业表述方式。

(2) 通晓外贸理论和实务

在外贸业务活动中,函电的内容主要涉及进出口业务的具体操作。因此,写信人应充分掌握对外经济交往中的必备知识,包括国际贸易理论和政策、进出口贸易各环节的具体操作实务、相关国际惯例和商务法规。

(3) 通晓商务沟通的艺术

国际商务往来的对象是人,撰写外贸函电最终是为了达到某种商业目的。要写出一封好的函电,写信人应充分考虑写信对象的身份、地位、立场、商业目标及磋商让步空间,甚至思量其性格特征。根据所掌握的信息,站在对方的角度思考问题,运用商务沟通的艺术,在函电的语言、行文、遣词造句上做出适当的安排。

1.4 Guidelines of Writing English Business Letters—Seven "C" (英文商务信函写作原则——7C 原则)

为了达到商务沟通的目的,在撰写外贸函电时需掌握七大写作原则,通常被简称为7C 原则。

1. Clearness(清楚)

清楚原则是指收信人收到信函时可以完全了解写信人要表达的意思,不会产生误解。

这就要求写信人头脑清楚、条理清晰、表达准确。在无损信函完整性和礼貌性的前提下，写信人应使用平实、简单、直接的词句，且所有的词句都应能够非常清晰明确地表现真实的意图，避免双重意义的表达。

(1) 避免用词错误。

例如：As to the steamers sailing from Hong Kong to San Francisco, we have bimonthly direct services.

此处 bimonthly 有歧义：可以是 twice a month 或者 once two month。故读信者无法清楚地认定写信人要表达的意图。可以改写为：

① We have two direct sailings every month from Hong Kong to San Francisco.

② We have semimonthly direct sailing from Hong Kong to San Francisco.

(2) 注意词语所放的位置。

例如：

① We shall be able to supply 10 cases of the item only.

② We shall be able to supply 10 cases only of the item.

此处 only 的位置不同，修饰的对象分别为 the item 及 10 cases，导致两个句子的含义不同。前者表达只对于这件物品，我们能够提供 10 箱。其他的物品我们提供的数量并非 10 箱，强调这件物品我们在提供数量上很特殊，而不一定是表达仅仅提供 10 箱而不能提供更多了，only 修饰 the item，表明这件东西提供的数量和其他的东西提供的数量有所区别；后者表达了这件物品我们只能提供 10 箱，数量上不能再供应了，only 修饰 10 cases，强调数量上的局限性。

(3) 注意句子的结构。

例如：

① We sent you 5 samples yesterday of the goods which you requested in your letter of May 20 by air.

② We sent you, by air, 5 samples of the goods which you requested in your letter of May 20.

显然，第二句的句子结构比第一句的句子结构更加清晰合理。

2. Conciseness(简洁)

简洁是指不影响信函的礼貌性的前提下，用最精练的语言表达最完整的内容。简洁使信函更加简明有力。商务英语信函的格式要简明扼要，语言要通俗易懂，内容要精练丰富。这就要求写信者在行文过程中尽量选用易懂、朴素的词汇，采用简洁，直接的句子。

(1) 尽量使用简洁的表达方式。

例如：

① We wish to acknowledge receipt of your letter...可改为：We appreciate your letter...

② Enclosed herewith please find two copies of...可改为：We enclose two copies of...

(2) 同义短句和单词的换用。

例如：

① enclosed herewith 可更换为 enclosed；

② at this time 可更换为 now；

③ due to the fact that 可更换为 because；

④ a draft in the amount of $1000 可更换为 a draft for $1000。

3. Correctness（准确）

英语商务信函与买卖双方的权利、义务、利益、企业形象息息相关，是缮制各种商业单据的依据和进行商业活动往来的重要凭证。准确无误是英语商业信函写作中最为重要的原则。准确原则不仅仅指单词拼写、标点符号无误，语法使用、结构格式正确，还应确保信函所涉及的信息、数字表达言之确凿。因此，在进行商业英语信函写作中应反复审核相关信息，如收信人的职称、姓名、地址、交货时间、地点、货物品质、颜色、尺码、单价、总价、包装等，同时要特别注意某些单词的使用。

例如：某月下旬可笼统地表达为 the last ten days period of a month，但由于某些月份共有 31 天，因此，如 7 月下旬则应表达为 the last eleven days period of July，而不是 the last ten days period of July。

又如，The vendor shall deliver the goods to the vendee by June 15。此句中用到介词 by，应理解为卖方应该在 6 月 15 日前，包括 6 月 15 日当日将货物交付给买方，by 也可以翻译为“不迟于 6 月 15 日”。而如果要表达在 6 月 15 日前，不包括 6 月 15 日当日，则应将 by 换成介词 before。

再如，某些词汇在一般语境中和在外贸函电中使用时，词义及词性用法有很大的差异。如果无视这些差异，在阅读和撰写外贸函电时极易产生歧义，对业务的磋商和展开会造成严重的影响。下表选择了几个有代表性的词汇，对比在一般语境和外贸函电撰写中的不同含义和用法，见表 1-1。

表 1-1　词汇在一般语境和外贸函电中的不同

词　汇		一般语境中	外贸函电中
名词	coverage	覆盖	所投保的险种、险别
	document	文件	单证
	literature	文学	书面材料
	offer	提议	发盘、报盘
	quotation	引用，引用的话语	报价
动词	offer	提议，提供	发盘、报盘
	quote	引用	报价
	cover	将……盖上	给（货物）投保
形容词	particular	具体的	（名词）详细情况、具体细节
	subject	易受到/需经过	以……为准，以……为条件
介词	with	随着……，与……	向……（投保、索赔、下订单等）

另外，正确使用标点符号有助于清晰、准确地传达信息。如果不加考虑，随意使用，有时就会使意思混乱，不知所云，甚至有可能造成经济损失。下面，将就英文商务信函中常用的几种标点符号的规范使用作相应说明。

（1）逗号。逗号用于隔开并列的词、短语或分句。使用逗号时应注意以下几个问题。

① 如果三个或三个以上的词或词组排列在一起时，最后两个词或词组之间用 and 或 or 连接，在 and 或 or 之前加上逗号更规范。如：reports, proposals, and manuals are the responsibility of the technical-writing department; the advertising department handles brochures, catalogs, and press kits。

② 句首的介词短语后，如果此短语有五个以上单词，一般应该用逗号隔开。如：After collecting the samples in the area, the investigators came back again to the workshop to test the purity of the goods.

③ 句子的独立成分或插入语要用逗号隔开。如：Obviously, the mistake has been overlooked by the local merchants.

（2）冒号。冒号有两个作用：一是分条列项；二是解释阐明。冒号前面应该是一个完整的分句，比较下面两个句子。

① In our group everyone was asked to do the following works: collect evidences, analyze and write a research report.

② In our group everyone was asked to: collect evidences, analyze and write a research report.

句子②的冒号前的部分不是一个完整的分句，使用不规范。

（3）分号。分号的含义介于句号和逗号之间，表示一个句子语法结构完整，而内容还不完整，需要进一步解释。分号可以用句号来替换，如果把第二个分句的头一个字母大写，分号前后的两个句子都可以变成独立的句子。但这些句子中的句号不能用逗号替换；如果用逗号，则要用连接词。如：

① We loaded the machine into the truck within the stipulated period of time; however, the snow forced us to delay the transportation.

② We loaded the machine into the truck within the stipulated period of time. However, the snow forced us to delay the transportation.

③ We loaded the machine into the truck within the stipulated period of time, the snow forced us to delay the transportation.

相较之下，句子③的标点符号是不准确的。

（4）括号。括号有两个作用：一是补充说明；二是对上下文加以评论或解释。写作时应考虑括号标点符号应放在括号内还是括号外。如果括号内的部分只是整个句子的一部分，则标点符号应放在括号外。比较以下两句，②句更为规范。

① The investigation shows the goods are not up to the standard. (See Figure 3-2 for a complete record of our findings.)

② The investigation shows the goods are not up to the standard. (See Figure 3-2 for a complete record of our findings.)

注意：括号内如果用感叹号或问号，则应保留。如：The three of them （you can't believe it!） share precisely the same type.

（5）破折号。破折号能让句子结构一目了然，意思相应清楚准确。有时，还能起到强调的作用。如：

① Other raw materials are stored there, too—dolomite（白云岩）, limestone（石灰石） and soda ash（苏打灰）.

② To emphasize it once again, we are making use of technology for the benefit of the people—not pursuing technology for its own sake.

（6）连字符。连字符连接两个或两个以上的单词，一起构成复合词，连字符号前后不应空格。作用是将意义表达清楚，避免混淆或歧义。比较以下两句：

① They have decided to have three week-long rest.

② They have decided to have three-week long rest.

①句表示三次时间为一周的休息，②句表示一次时间为三周的休息。

（7）所有格符号。所有格符号也称撇号，常用作名词所有格。构成数字、字母和缩写词的复数时，是否加撇号，要根据具体情况而定。如：Bob got two A's and three B's. 此处如 A 和 s 之间不加"'"，则表意不清，读音会误认为是单词 As。

以"s"结尾的多音节名词的所有格，不管单复数，只在名词后加"'"，而不加"'s"。而以字母"s"结尾或以"s"音结尾的单音节名词的所有格依然要加"'s"。如：The companies's joint efforts have been proved successfully. 以及 The boss's marketing research report had been forwarded to the Board of Directors. 。

两个并列名词的所有格表示一个含义，只在后一个名词后加"'s"；如果表示两个含义，则在两个名词后都加"'s"。如：Jenny and Lucy's program has been approved, but Peter's and Bob's haven't. （Jenny 和 Lucy 两人共同提出的计划，而 Peter 和 Bob 两人分别提出一个计划。）

4. Concreteness（具体）

具体原则是指信函中涉及的内容要言之有物，信息要翔实具体、丰富生动，表达要完整。商务信函写作中注意避免类似：soon, at an early date, good, nearly 等笼统的、含混不清的表达，应尽量运用具体的事实和数字进行说明。

例如：I will send the samples to you soon. 就不如 I will send the samples to you in two weeks. 如果能再具体，那就更好了，例如 I will send the samples to you next Monday.

又如，与 These bikes ride lightly. 相比，These forever brand bikes weigh 10 kilos each and are comfortable to ride. 更为具体明确。

再如，Please send your check full month. 可写为 Please send your check for ＄200 before Jan 2,2013. 后者能更好地提醒对方支票的金额和发送支票的时间期限。

5. Courtesy（礼貌）

为了建立、保持一个友好贸易关系，商务英语信函往来一般要注意遵循礼貌原则，以礼待人。一封礼貌的信函可以加深与已有客户的业务关系,也有助于结交新的业务伙伴。在商务活动中,及时是礼貌之首。一个好的国际商务人员会在第一时间对信函进行回复,以示礼貌。此外,在撰写商务信函时,遵守国际商务往来惯例;尊重对方风俗习惯;语言表达要客气有分寸,避免使用命令口气;多用友好、肯定的语气,尽量用委婉语气指出对方不尽如人意的地方,尽量避免使用可能激怒和伤害对方的言辞或语气,尽可能站在客户的角度上,考虑对方的愿望和背景,做到互利互惠。礼貌原则不仅体现在使用 Please、Thanks you 等词汇上,而且要在字里行间体现我方的礼仪和风尚,做到不卑不亢、得体大方。

例如:

(1) We insist on a prompt answer to our letter.

We would appreciate your answering this letter promptly.

(2) To start the scheduling process, please describe your availability for meetings during the second week of the month.

Could you let me know what times you'd be free for a meeting the second week of the month.

很显然,以上两组表达含义相同的句子中,第二句的表达都比第一句显得礼貌。

6. Consideration(体谅)

体谅是指发信人尽可能以对方利益为出发点,站在对方的立场周到、细致地考虑问题,在分析对方会如何理解信息的基础上,提供其所需要的信息。简而言之,体谅原则就是要做到移情于对方,多为对方着想。此外,体谅意味着要坚持用肯定而非否定的态度行文。体谅原则是商务交往中为了促成交易所使用的一种技巧。

例如,"You earn 2 percent discount when you pay cash. We will send you the brochure next month."与"We allow 2 percent discount for cash payment. We won't be able to send you the brochure this month." 相比,前者是站在对方的角度看问题,并尽可能使用肯定的方式来进行描述。

又如,与 We are shipping your order of September 21 this afternoon 相比,The two dozen Corning Ware starter sets you ordered will be shipped this afternoon and should reach you by September 28 给对方提供了所需要的具体信息,并站在对方的角度来看待该问题。

再如,与 We are happy to extend you a credit line of $5000 相比,You can now charge up to $5000 on your American Expression card 就顾及了对方的情感。

7. Completeness(完整)

商务信函应该力求完整。一封完整的商务信函不仅可能会带来预期的结果,还可能建立更好的商务关系。一封完整的商业信函应该是把对方提出的问题逐一回答,并对自己要表达的重要信息说明清楚完全。比如答谢来信时,最好提及上封信的日期、主要内容,甚至编号。又如,接受对方的报盘时根据是什么(如报价单、信件等),因为接受函具有法律效应,表明双方已经成交该业务,此信发出后,对方收到,即对双方都有约束力。如果不完整,有漏洞,就有可能引起不必要的纠纷。信函的完整性有助于建立良好的企业形象,节省双方的商务往来时间而达到预期的效果,避免因为重要信息不全而引起不必要的延迟和纠纷。

例如,Our product has won several prizes 显得内容单薄,没有充分的说服力,而 Our Hair Washing Machine has won first prizes in four national contests within the past three years 则提供了具体的产品名称、具体时间、具体的奖项和数量,给对方提供关于我方产品更为完整的信息,并且更具有说服力。

1.5 Parts and Layout of English Business Letter (信函的内容构成及格式)

英文商务信函给读信者留下的第一印象通常决定了这封信函是否确实会被阅读,同时它也决定了读信者对信函内容的反应。因此,写信人必须能够通过恰当地安排好信函的段落和格式,使其有效地传达自己的想法。

1. The Content of the Letter(信函的内容构成)

通常来说,英文商务信函的内容由标准部分和可选部分共同构成。标准部分,由 7 部分构成,是一封规范的英文商务书信必备的部分,包括:

(1) 信头(Letter Head)
(2) 日期 (Date)
(3) 封内名称和地址 (Inside Name and Address)
(4) 称呼(Salutation)
(5) 正文(Body of the Letter)
(6) 结尾敬语(Complimentary Close)
(7) 签名(Signature)

可选部分包括以下 7 部分,写信人可根据具体情况酌情选择使用,包括:

(1) 参考编号(Reference Number)
(2) 经办人(Attention)
(3) 事由(标题)(Subject)
(4) 辨认代号(Identification Mark)
(5) 附件 (Enclosure)
(6) 抄送(The Carbon Copy to ××)
(7) 附言(Postscript)

按照在信函中出现的先后顺序,各部分内容写作要求如下。

(1) Letter Head(信头)

信头也称为信笺抬头,由寄信公司的名称、地址和邮编号码、电话号码、传真号码、电报挂号、网址、E-mail 地址等构成。使用信头的目的是使收信人一目了然,知晓信函来自何处,便于回信和查阅。

实际使用中,大部分公司会事先专门印制有信头的信笺纸,除了包括惯常的内容,有的信头还包含公司商标、公司负责人的姓名及职务职称等。当我们撰写英文商务信函时,可直接使用这种信笺纸。信头通常位于信纸的最上端,居中或居于右上方。

信头的写法有并列式和斜列式两种。在并列式信头中,各行内容开头要左对齐,比较常用。例如:

CHINA NATIONAL LIGHT INDUSTRUAL
PRODUCTS IMP. & EXP. CO., LTD.
No. 912 Section Jinsong, Chaoyang District,
Beijing, 100021 China
Tel: 0086-10-6774774 Fax: 0086-10-6772315
http://www.chinalight.com.cn
E-mail: info@chinalig.com.cn

斜列式信头,各行内容开头逐次向右移两三个字母。例如:

CHINA NATIONAL LIGHT INDUSTRUAL
  PRODUCTS IMP. & EXP. CO., LTD.
    No. 912 Section Jinsong, Chaoyang District,
      Beijing, 100021 China
        Tel: 0086-10-6774774
          Fax: 0086-10-6772315
            http://www.chinalight.com.cn
              E-mail: info@chinalig.com.cn

(2) Date(日期)

日期是写信或打字时的日期。在英文商务信函写作中,日期是至关重要的一个部分。日期决定着一个合同是否生效,订单是否执行,交易是否按时付款等。因此,英文商务信函中的日期绝不能被遗漏或被写错。日期通常写在信头下方 2 ~ 4 行的位置,顶边写在信纸的左边或右边。撰写日期时要注意以下几点。

① 避免完全用数字来表示日期,如 7/11/2012。因为日期的英式写法是日、月、年;美式写法是月、日、年。全部用数字来表示日期,可能因在不同的国家理解不同,造成误解。

② 年份应完全写出,不能用(94)代替(1994),同时,年份前通常要加逗号。

③ 月份要写英文名称,不能用数字来代替,第一个字母要大写,但可以用缩写。

④ 日期可用基数词或序数词,为了避免可能出现的错误,最好使用基数字。例如,5 May,2011(英式写法);May 5,2011(美式写法)。

(3) Reference Number(参考编号)

为了便于书信的存档和查阅,避免混淆,写信人可在日期上方,或与日期平齐靠左的位置打印上参考编号,后接冒号。参考编号一般可分为 Your Ref.(你方编号)和 Our Ref.(我方编号)。

（4）Inside Name and Address（封内名称和地址）

封内名称和地址是收信人的名称和地址。一般是列在信笺的左上方，沿左页边线写起，低于日期位置2行，也分为并列式和斜列式两种，但应与信头的书写格式保持一致。同时，封内地址与信封上收信人的名称和地址写法相同。

在信纸上设置封内名称和地址部分是为了便于外贸函电的准确便捷应用。对发信人而言，便利有两点：一是发信时可与信封地址相互对照，避免放入信封时发生差误；二是发信后便于准确归档，便于以后查找。对收信人而言，便利也有两点：一是收信人读信时，如发现信封名称地址与封内名称地址不符，可以知晓是放入信封时发生错误，将信返回；二是收信后如信封与信函分离原信仍能保持完整，便于查阅。

封内名称和地址的书写次序是，先写收信人姓名（称呼语 + 全名）、头衔和单位名称，再写单位的地址。英文信函的地址一般包含四个部分，各项内容单独成行，从小到大分别是门牌号码和街（路）名、城市、县、州（省）名及邮政编码（Post Code 或 Zip Code）、国别名。例如：

Lin Fang

Vice President

Beijing Metal Co.

234 East lane

Beijing, 100021

The People's Republic of China

在撰写封内名称和地址时，应注意以下事项。

① 书写收信单位名称时，应特别尊重对方的习惯，不能随意增删公司名称前的冠词The，也不能随意改用全称及缩写，如 Company 与 Co. 之间不能互换，否则会被认为是不礼貌的行为。

② 注意缮写邮政编码，以确保信函能迅速送达收信人。对于美国地址，通常在城市名称后面写州名和邮区号。

③ 注意不要遗漏国名，即使信函是寄送到大城市的，因为同一名称的城市可能有好几个。如“London”这样有名的大城市，在世界上也有两个，一个在英国，一个在加拿大。加上国名，以免误寄。且国名通常使用正式的全称。如“中国”，规范的写法是“The People's Republic of China”，而不是“China”。

（5）Attention（经办人）

如果收函人为某单位，而发函人希望某人或某部门特别注意并直接收到该信函时，则可以加上“For the attention of...”或“Attention...”，该部分一般放在封内地址与称呼之间。例如：

Richard Thomas & Baldwins Ltd.,

151 Gower Street

London, SC7 6DY, England

Attention Mr. Cave

or　For the attention of Purchasing Manager

(6) Salutation(称呼)

称呼是写信人对收信人的一种称谓,是指信件开头对收信人的客套称呼用语。其位置是在封内地址的下面空两行,从信纸左边顶头写,每个词的开头字母要大写,称呼末尾处的符号,英国人多用逗号,美国人和加拿大人则多用冒号。

在英文信函中,类似于"阁下"、"先生"等类礼貌性称谓,常用 Dear Sir,此处 Dear 纯属公务上往来的客气用法,也可以使用 Gentlemen,以复数形式出现,前不加 Dear,是 Dear Sir 的复数形式;称呼男性姓名时,应在其前面加 Mr.。若称呼多位男性,则在姓名前加 Mr. 的复数形式 Messrs.。对一般以人名为名称的公司和企业常用这种称呼,例如 Messrs. Black and Brothers。在英文信函中,称呼女性,可以按其实际婚姻状况,在其姓名前加 Dear Miss 或 Dear Mrs.;另外,不论该女性结婚与否,我们都可以用 Madam 进行称呼。

写给收信人的信,也可用头衔、职位、职称、学位等再加姓氏或姓氏和名字进行称呼。常见的有 Professor(缩写为 Prof.),Doctor(缩写为 Dr.),General(缩写为 Gen.)。例如:Prof. Tim Scales。

对于无具体收信人姓名,可用 Dear Sir or Madam 称呼收信者,也可以使用 To these who may be concerned 称呼收信者,译为"至启者"或"敬启者"。

(7) Subject(事由(标题))

为了节省时间,便于收件单位或个人快速将函电传递到相关部门或个人及时处理,可在信函正文开头加上事由或标题,其表示方式可以为"Subject"或"Re"字样,也可不加任何单词,直截了当开头。为了便于读信人快速找到事由,通常将事由部分标上下划线。事由写在称呼语下面 2 行,一般是在信笺中间位置,事由要简单扼要,一般可用商品名称、数量、信用证或合同号等作为事由。

例如:

Subject: General Agency Appointment

Re: ZHONG HE V.0063E. TRIU 9551882

PURCHASING SILK PAINTINGS

(8) Body of the Letter(正文)

正文是商务函电的主体,是表明一封信函优劣的关键,在书写正文时应注意把握英文商务信函写作原则——7C 原则。正文通常由开头语、主体部分和结尾语构成。

开头语没有固定的格式,但习惯上先用客套的语句把收到对方来信的日期、主题及简单内容加以综合叙述,使对方一目了然,明白这是答复哪一封去信的。如果是第一次通信,也可以利用开头语作必要的自我介绍,并表明目的要求。开头语一般与主体部分分开,自成一节,要求简单明了。

主体部分可按中心思想分段,一个中心为一段。若信函内容在一页内无法叙述完全,可采取续页的做法。需要续页时,应在前一页最后一行的右边写 to be continued,续页上端应注明收信人名称、日期和页数。为了避免第一页与第二页、第三页在发信时误置,在续页时不要用印有信头的信纸,此处名称可尽量缩写,如 Page 2, The Universal Trading Co., Ltd. Jan. 7, 2011。

结尾语一般用来总结本文所谈的事项,提示对收信人的要求,如“希望来信来函订货”、“答复询问”等,另外也附加一些略带客套的语气。主体部分结束后,另起一段写结尾语。

(9) Complimentary Close(结尾敬语)

结尾敬语是写信人在信函的结尾的客套语,相当于中文结尾中用的“敬上”、“谨启”等。常用的结尾敬语: Sincerely yours, Sincerely, Cordially yours, Yours sincerely, Yours truly, Yours cordially, Very truly yours, Respectfully yours。

通常,表示敬意的结尾敬语和称呼是前后匹配的。

如: Dear Sirs,—Faithfully yours(英式)

Gentlemen:—Yours truly(美式)

需要注意的是,结尾的谦称后必须加逗号。表 1-2 列举了英语函电中与称呼相匹配的结尾敬语的用法。

表 1-2 英语函电中与称呼相匹配的结尾敬语的用法

称呼(Salutation)		结尾敬语(Complimentary close)	备注(Remarks)
男性(Male)	女性(Female)		
Sir Sirs	Madam Mesdames	Yours respectively Yours very respectively	下级对上级十分正式的称呼和敬语
Dear Sir Dear Sirs	Dear Madam Mesdames	Yours faithfully Faithfully yours	英国的标准用法
Gentlemen	Ladies	Yours truly Truly yours	美国的普遍用法
Dear Mr. Smith My dear Mr. Smith	Dear Mrs. Smith Dear Miss Smith Dear Ms. Smith My dear Mrs. Smith	Yours sincerely Yours cordially Yours very sincerely Yours very cordially	用于互相熟悉的私人函,有时也用于业务函

(10) Signature(签名)

在结尾敬辞下面,应将发信人单位的名称用大写打出,然后加上写信人的手写签名及打印出的写信人签名、职位及(或)部门。常见的职位有: Chairman of the Board of directors(董事长),President 或 General Manager(总经理),Director(董事),Stand Director(常务董事),Manager(经理),Head of Department(职员),Manageress(女经理),Head of a Department(处长),Section chief(科长)等。

需要指出的是,写信人如要代表企业单位或代理签署时,应在结尾敬辞下打印出全部大写的企业单位名称,然后才签署,以表明该信不是以写信人个人身份写的,信函所述事宜均由企业单位负责。如:

Yours faithfully,

for TOYOTA MOTOR (CHINA) INVESTMENT CO., LTD.

Li Zhengru

Li Zhengru

Project Manager (Beijing)

(11) Identification Mark(辨认代号)

辨认代号可提供产生信函的信息资料,以识别信函的口述人和秘书或打字员,一般是由其姓名的第一个字母组成。在两组辨认代号中间,通常用冒号或斜线分开。例如: JE: TS, JE/TS, je: ts,缮打在签名下方的第三行左边边缘线上。

(12) Enclosure(附件)

如信函带有附件,应在正文中指出,同时在信函末尾,即签名下方注明 Encl. 或 Enc. ,如果附件不止一项,应写成 Encls. 或 Encs. 。例如:

Enclosure(s)

Enclosure: One Cope of Invoice

Enclosures 4

Encl.

Encls.

(13) The Carbon Copy to ××(抄送)

如信函有抄送第三方及相关人的必要,则在信尾注明,写法有两种。

一是 CC (CC to, C. C. , 复数时打 CCs),其后接抄送单位或人名称、地址。这种抄送函件不但抄送其他有关单位,同时使对方也知道已抄送其他单位。

二是 BCC (Blind Carbon Copy,隐蔽抄送)。这种抄送只有收函人自己清楚,其他收函人均不知道已收到该函副本。

(14) Postscript(附言)

当信函已打妥,但发现仍有内容没写完,需要进行补充,此时则可在信末签名下面几行的左方,与正文齐头,打上"P. S. "(Postscript)符号,然后写上要补充的内容。应该注意:在正式的信函中,附言应尽量避免,如果时间允许,最好重打信函。

2. The Format of the Letter(信函的格式)

撰写一封沟通效果良好的英文商务信函,写信人除了要恰如其分地撰写语句和段落外,还要安排好信函的格式。英文商务信函常用的格式有四种,分别是缩行式(The indented form)、齐头式(The block form)、修正齐头式(The modified block form)和混合式(Semi-block style with indented paragraphs)。

(1) The indented form(缩行式)

缩行式信函的信头和封内地址每逢换行时,下一行要比上一行往右缩进 2 ~3 个字母的位置;日期放在信纸的右上端,结尾敬语、签名放在中间偏右下方,事由一般居中;正文每一段的第一行都从左边空白边缘往右缩进 3 ~5 个字母的位置,其他各行都是从左边顶头写;段落之间要空 1 或 2 行。注意,同一封信中的缩格数应该统一,如信头和封内地址缩 3 格,正文也应该缩 3 格。如下文所示。

Messrs. William & Sons

58 Lancastor House

Manchester, England

Our Ref. No.: ac0021

Your Ref. No.: jk0021

March 20, 2009

The National Transport Co.

120 Broadway Street

Rangoon, Burma

Dear Sirs,

Re: Lab Instruments

Your firm has been recommended to us by Messrs. Charles Evans Ltd., Birmingham England, with whom we have done some business for the past two years.

We are thinking of getting a supply of instruments. Please furnish us with a catalogue, price list and brochure, if available.

We are looking forward to your early reply.

Yours faithfully,

Messrs. William & Sons

H. Smith

H. Smith
Manager

(2) The block form(齐头式)

齐头式也称为平头式。在齐头式信函中,凡是用打字机打上去的每一行字,包括日期、封内地址、事由和结尾敬语,都是从左边的空白边缘打起,一律不缩进。但信头有时也可置中央,各段间应空1或2行,以示分段。如下文所示。

EL Mar Trading Company

16 Main Street

Fresno, California

U. S. A.

Tel: 123456

Cable Address: ELMAR FRESNO

Our Ref. No.: KMP/DE

Your Ref. No.: JKP/DE

8 January, 2009

International Investment Ltd.

77 Pearl Road

Swanton, Manchester

England

Gentlemen,

We thank you for your quotation NO. 1234 on 5000pcs of plastic speaker.

Reverting to the 10 lots of speaker stand which arrived here per M/V Orient' on October 30, in the same hold, we have to inform you that among them, six cartons of different sizes arrived in a broken and mixed condition because their packing was not sufficiently strong and their plastic hoops broken in transit.

Since it was most difficult to assert them, inconveniences and losses occurred. Though such unfortunate things have also occurred before and you were notified to that effect in time, the present case shows that our comments were ignored, for no improvement in packing has been made.

Therefore, we must have your promise to take effective measures to improve your packing before we could make this new order with you.

We await your reply.

Yours faithfully,
Allen Inc.

James Smith

James Smith
Manager

(3) The modified block form(修正齐头式)

修正齐头式除了日期、结尾敬语和签名部分外,其他用打字机打上去的部分每行开头都与左边空白边缘看齐。信头由于事先印就,一般居中。事由一般居中。

M. D. Ewart & Co. ,LTD.
36 Tower Street
Tronto 4, Canada

August 22, 2009

Our Ref. No.: SWE/119
Your Ref. No.: M.306/0038

China National Metals& Minerals
Import & Export Corporation
P. O. Box No. 65
Beijing
People's Republic of China

Dear Sirs,

Order No KAB/1884 100 Dozen mixers

We are in receipt of your letter of June 15 informing us that the captioned goods have been shipped per S. S. "Fengqing", and thank you for your invoice NO. B31170 in triplicate.

With regard to the packing for mixers, you say that you have taken up the matter with the competent departments, and are of the opinion that packing in cartons will prevent skillful pilferage; such cartons are well protected against moisture; They are light and convenient to handle, etc. After discussing the matter with our clients, we find that your comments sound quite reasonable. However, we can't be sure how things will prove to be until the first lot of goods packed in such cartons arrives.

We are of the opinion that if the result of packing in cartons turns out to the satisfaction of our clients, you may continue using this packing in future.

However, in case of the result not being so, we are afraid that this will considerably affect the development of business between us.

You may rest assured that in our mutual interest we shall do everything possible to give you our full cooperation.

Yours faithfully,

Liu Mei

Liu Mei
M. D. Ewart & Co. , LTD.

(4) 混合式(Semi-block style with indented paragraphs)

混合式信函的特点是正文的每一段落的第一行采用缩行式;除信头、日期、结尾敬语和签名部分外,其他部分采用齐头式。

Office of the Attorney
AAA Company
123 Main Street
Centerville, IL666
U. S. A.

April 21, 2009

President, Billboard Inc.
999 Broadway
Metropolis
U. S. A.

Dear Sir,

We value your long-term relationship with us.

A review of your account shows that some time has passed since you last made payment to us. If there is some difficulty you are facing that is causing this, we would like the opportunity of working matters out with you. If there is the result of oversight, we would appreciate early remittance.

We look forward to hearing from you in the near future.

Your truly,

H. Smith

H. Smith

Manager
AAA Company

在书写英语商务信函的时候,必须谨记:选定一种格式,坚持使用,不能在行文中途改用别的格式。布局好的信件是双方交易的好的开始。一封布局优雅、端庄匀称的信件，会留给人一种良好的印象，促进双方的进一步往来，直至交易达成。

1.6 Addressing Envelopes（信封的写法）

用于进行跨国商务沟通的经贸函电，其信封的书写不同于国内信函信封的写法。与封内地址的写法一致，信封的写法可使用齐头式或缩行式。分别如图 1-1、图 1-2 所示。

图 1-1 英文信封（Envelope）的写法（Block Format 齐头式）

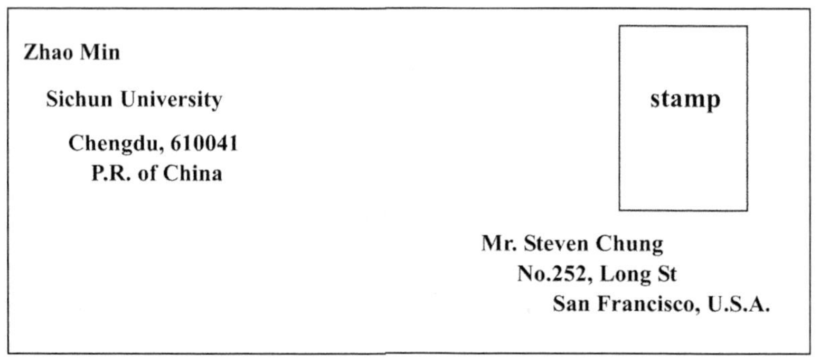

图 1-2 英文信封（Envelope）的写法（Indented Format 缩行式）

（1）寄信人的名字和住址写在信封的左上角，且务必与封内地址在形式和标点上完全一致；收信人的名字和住址写在信封的中下偏右的位置。在信封的右上角贴上邮票。

（2）寄信人通常不会自称 Mr.，Mrs. 或 Miss.，但是在收信人的姓名前则必须加上尊称 Mr.，Mrs. 或 Miss. 以示礼貌。

（3）寄信人和收信人的住址的写法与中文信函信封的写法相反。英文地址的书写顺序是由小到大：第一行写寄信人的门牌号码、街道名称，注意门牌号码和街道名称之间要加逗号；第二行先写城市名称，再写省或州名称，往右空两个字母的位置，再写上邮编。对于寄往国外的信件，第三行写出寄信人所在国家的名称。以寄往美国的信件为例，信封上的邮编(zip code),在美国州名之后以五位数阿拉伯数字表示,前三位数代表州或都市,后两位数表示邮区,至于邮政区号 10027 的念法是 one double o two seven。

(4) 住址中内容常用简写表示,使用比较多的简写有 No. 表示号(Number),Rm. 表示 Room (室),F 表示 Floor(楼),Aly. 表示 Alley(弄),Ln. 表示 Lane(巷),Rd. 表示 Road (路),St. 表示 Street (街),Sec. 表示 Section(段),Dist. 表示 District(区),Ave. 表示 Avenue(大道),Prov. 表示 Province(省)等。

(5) 如要说明信件由何种方式递送或信件为何种类别,一般在信封正面的左下角进行标注(Remarks)。常用到的标注有 By Air Mail、Via Air Mail、Par Avion(航空邮件)、Registered(挂号邮件)、Ordinary Mail(平信)、Express(快递邮件)、Immediate、Urgent(急件)、Printed Matter(印刷品)、Parcel Post(包裹邮件)、Photo Enclosed(内有照片)、Sample (样品)。如系私人信函或密件,必须让收信人亲自开启而不要他人拆阅的,可在信封正面的左下角标注(remark)为:Private(私人信)、Personal(个人信)、Confidential(机密信)。如怀疑信件能否送交收信人,可在信封最下边标明:If undelivered please return to ×××,即:如无法投递,请退交×××。

(6) 如信件需由别人或单位转交给收信人,则需在转交人前面加上 C/O(= care of 由……转交)后接转交人的姓名地址。例如,某人托李娜转交一封信给李明,可表示为:

Li Ming
C/O Li Na
318 Doswell Avenue
Fort Arkinson, Wisconsin
The United States of America

1.7 The Opening Sentences and Closing Sentences (常用开头语和结尾语)

1. Opening Phrases & Sentences Generally Used In Business Letters(商业书信常用开头语)

(1) 特此奉告等。

To inform one of; To say; To state; To communicate; To advise one of; To bring to one's notice (knowledge); To lay before one; To point out; To indicate; To mention; To apprise one of; To announce; To remark; To call one's attention to; To remind one of; etc.

We are pleased to inform you that …

We have pleasure in informing you that …

We have the pleasure to apprise you of …

We have the honor to inform you that (of) …

We take the liberty of announcing to you that …

We have to inform you that (of) …

We wish to inform you that (of) …

We think it advisable to inform you that …

We are pleased to have this opportunity of reminding you that (of) …

We take the advantage of this opportunity to bring before your notice…

Please allow us to call your attention to…

Permit us to remind you that (of)…

May we ask your attention to…

We feel it our duty to inform you that (of)…

(2) 为(目的)奉告某某事项。

The purpose of this letter is to inform you that (of) …

The purport of this line is to advise you that (of) …

The object of the present is to report you that …

The object of this letter is to tell you that …

By this letter we Purpose to inform you that (of) …

Through the present we wish to intimate to you that …

The present serves to acquaint you that …

(3) 惠请告知某某事项等。

Please inform me that (of) …

Kindly inform me that (of) …

Be good enough to inform me that (of) …

Be so good as to inform me that (of) …

Have the goodness to inform me that (of) …

Oblige me by informing that (of) …

I should be obliged if you would inform me that (of) …

I should be glad if you would inform me that (of) …

I should esteem it a favor if you would inform me that (of) …

I will thank you to inform me that (of) …

You will greatly oblige me by informing that (of) …

We shall be obliged if you will inform us that (of) …

We shall be pleased to have your information regarding (on, as to; about) …

We shall deem it a favor if you will advise us of …

We shall esteem it a high favor if you will inform us that (of) …

(4) 特确认,本公司某月某日函件等。

We confirm our respects of the 10th May …

We confirm our letter of the 10th of this month …

We confirm our last letter of the 10th June …

We had the pleasure of writing you last on the 10th of this month …

We confirm our respects of the 10th June …

We confirm the remarks made in our respects of the 10th July …

We confirm the particulars of our enquiry by telephone of this morning …

In confirming our telegram of this morning, …

Confirming our respects of the 10th May, …

Confirming our last of the 10th June, …

(5) 贵公司某月某日函电,敬悉等。

We have pleasure in acknowledging receipt of your esteemed favour of the 3rd May …

We are pleased to acknowledge receipt of your favor of the 1st June …

We have to acknowledge receipt of your favor of the 5th July …

Your letter of May 5 was very welcome …

Your letter of April 10 gave me much pleasure …

Your esteemed favor of 7th May was duly received by us …

Your favor of the 5th June is duly to hand …

Your favor of the 10th is to (at) hand …

We are in due receipt of your favor dated the 7th June …

We are in receipt of your letter of the 7th July …

We are in possession of your letter of the 5th April …

We have duly received your favor of the 5th March …

Your letter of yesterday's date is duly to (at) hand …

Your esteemed communication of yesterday's date is just to (at) hand …

We thank you for your favor of the 5th May …

We are obliged for your letter of the 5th May …

Many thanks for your latter of the 5th June …

Very many thanks for your letter of May 5 …

In acknowledging receipt of your letter of the 5th June, …

Your favor of the 5th May has just reached me …

Your favor of the 5th May is duly received …

Your favor of the 5th May is now before me …

Your promised letter under date (of) the 5th June has just reached us …

(6) 特回答贵公司某月某日函所叙述有关事项等。

I have the pleasure of stating, in answer to your inquiry of the 4th inst, that …

In reply to your letter of the 5th of May, I have to inform you that (of) …

I hasten to answer your inquiry of the 15th May, by stating that …

We are in receipt of yours of the 5th June, in reply to which we are pleased to state that …

In reply to yours of the 10th May, relative to…, I would say that …

I am in receipt of your favor of the 7th May, and in response I inform you that (of) …

In response to your letter of 10th May, I wish to say that …

In answer to your favor of the 5th May regarding... I reply as follows: ...
Answering your letter of the 8th of February, I would say that ...
In reply to your letter of February 8th, I inform you that (of) ...
Replying to yours of the 8th of February regarding..., I would say that ...
Replying to your favor under date of February 8th, I say that ...
(7) 非常遗憾,我们奉告您关于……
We regret to inform you that (of) ...
We are sorry to have to draw your attention to ...
We regret to have to say that ...
We regret to advise you that ...
We very much regret to announce you that ...
It is most regrettable that we have to inform you that (of) ...
It is with our greatest regret that we must inform you that (of) ...
To our greatest regret we must herewith inform you that (of) ...
It is a matter for regret that I have to inform you that (of) ...
It is to be regretted that I must inform you that (of) ...
It is with regret and reluctance that we have to inform you that (of) ...
It gives us a deep sorrow that we have to announce you that ...
It causes me much sorrow to have to say that ...
I feel sorry for having to announce you that ...
I express my sorrow for announcing you that ...
(8) 当我们得悉……甚为遗憾等。
We are very sorry to hear (know) that...
We are grieved to hear of (about) ...
We are indeed sorry to hear that ...
We very much regret to hear that ...
We regret to hear of (that) ...
It is with great regret that we just learn that ...
Much to our regret we have heard that ...
We regret to receive your information re ...
We regret that we have been informed that (of) ...
To our deep regret we were informed that (of) ...
(9) 我们对于您某月某日来函的询价,深表谢意等。
We thank you very much for your inquiry of the 10th of May...
I thank you for your inquiry of the 10th May...
We are very much obliged by your enquiry dated the 10th May...
We are indebted to your inquiry under date (of) the 10th May for...
I thank you for your inquiry of July 10...

Thanks for your kind enquiry of May 5...

(10) 兹函附某某,请查收等。

Enclosed please find...

Enclosed we hand you...

We enclose herewith...

Herewith we have the pleasure to hand you...

We have pleasure in enclosing herewith...

We take the liberty to enclose herein...

We are pleased to enclose herewith...

We are pleased to hand you enclosed...

(11) 遵照某月某日来函指示等。

In accordance with the instructions given (contained) in your favor of the 10th May...

According to the directions contained in yours letter of the 6th May...

According to the instructions given in your letter under date of the 10th of last month...

In conformity with (to) your instructions of the 10th June ...

Pursuant to your instructions of May 10...

(12) 关于详情,下次叙述等。

I will write you particulars in my next.

Particulars will be related in the following.

I will relate further details in the following.

I will inform you more fully in my next.

I will go (enter) into further details in my next.

(13) 如下列所记,如附件所述等。

As stated below,...

Annexed hereto, ...

Attached you will find...

As shown on the next page...

As indicated overleaf...

As at foot hereof, ...

Sent with this, ...

As the drawings attached, ...

As shown in the enclosed documents, ...

As already mentioned, ...

As particularized on the attached sheet, ...

As detailed in the previous letter, ...

(14) 因电文不太明确等。

Your telegram just received is quite unintelligible.

Please repeat your wire on receipt of this, stating your meaning more clearly.

Your telegram is not clear; explain the third and fourth words.
Your telegram is unintelligible; repeat more fully in plain language.
Your cable is not clear, repeat, using the codes agreed upon (on).
We cannot understand your telegram; state the code used and which edition.
Your telegram is not signed with cipher as agreed on; confirm if correct.
We cannot trace the code you used; please repeat the telegram in plain words.
Your telegram is too short to be understood. Please repeat it more fully.
The telegram was vague (pointless), and they requested them to explain in plain words.

2. Closing Phrases & Sentences Generally Used in Business Letters(英文商业信函常用结束语)

(1) 我们盼望于近日内接获回信等。
We hope to receive your favor at an early date.
We hope to be favored with a reply with the least delay.
We await a good news with patience.
We hope to receive a favorable reply per return mail.
We await the pleasure of receiving a favorable reply at an early date.
We await the favor of your early (prompt) reply.
A prompt reply would greatly oblige us.
We trust you will favor us with an early (prompt) reply.
We trust that you will reply us immediately.
We should be obliged by your early (prompt) reply.
Will you please reply without delay what your wishes are in this matter?
Will you kindly inform us immediately what you wish us to do?
We request you to inform us of your decision by return of post.
We are waiting (anxious to receive) your early reply.
We thank you for the anticipated favor of your early reply.
We should appreciate an early reply.
We thank you in anticipation of your usual courteous prompt attention.
We thank you now for the courtesy of your early attention.
We hope to receive your reply with the least possible delay.
Kindly reply at your earliest convenience.
Please send your reply by the earliest delivery.
Please send your reply by messenger.
Please reply immediately.
Please favor us with your reply as early as possible.
Please write to us by tonight's mail, without fail.
May we remind you that we are still awaiting your early reply?

May we request the favor of your early reply?

A prompt reply would help us greatly.

A prompt reply will greatly oblige us.

Your prompt reply would be greatly appreciated.

Your prompt attention to this matter would be greatly esteemed.

We look forward to receiving your early reply.

We thank you now for this anticipated courtesy.

As the matter is urgent, an early reply will oblige.

We reply on receiving your reply by return of post.

(2) 回信请用电报等。

We await your reply by telegraph.

Please wire reply to our telegram of this morning.

We are anxiously awaiting your reply by telegram.

Please arrange for your telegraphic reply, or long distance call, to reach us before noon on Monday.

Cable reply immediately, using Western Union Code.

Please acknowledge by wire the receipt of these instructions.

Please do not fail to telegraph your reply immediately on receipt of this letter.

Please telegraph your decision without delay as we have offers waiting.

Please telegraph reply immediately, our offices will be open until 9 p. m.

Oblige us by replying by telegram before noon tomorrow, as we have another offer.

Inform us by telegram of your lowest quotations.

Wire me at the Grand Hotel. Yokohama, before noon.

Wire in time for us to write you in reply by 7 p. m. mail.

Telegraph me from Osaka before noon stating your telephone numbers.

Kindly reply me by wire (telegraphically).

We should be pleased to have you telegraphically reply us.

(3) 关于某某事项,谨表谢意等。

Please accept our thanks in advance for your usual kind attention.

Please accept our thanks for the trouble you have taken.

We are obliged to you for your kind attention in this matter.

We are greatly obliged for your trial order just received.

We wish to assure you of your appreciation of your courtesy in this matter.

We thank you for your order just received.

We thank you for the special care you have given to the matter.

We tender you our sincere thanks for your generous treatment of us in this affair.

Allow us to thank you for the kindness extended to us.

We are very sensible of your friendly services on our behalf, for which please accept our sincere thanks.

(4) 请原谅我的回信延迟等。

Please excuse my late reply to your very friendly letter of March 1.

I hope you will forgive me for not having written you for so long.

I hope you will excuse me for not having replied to you until today.

I humbly apologize you for my delay in answering to your kind letter of May 5.

I have to (must) apologize you for not answering your letter in time.

I must ask you to kindly accept our excuses, late as they are.

(5) 我们对您的关照,谨致谢意等。

We request you to accept our warmest thanks for the anticipated favour.

We thank you in advance for the anticipated favour.

(6) 我们时刻不忘尽我们所能,为您服务等。

We assure you of our best services at all times.

We shall spare no efforts in endeavoring to be of services to you.

We shall be pleased to be of service to you at all times.

(7) 请原谅给您添了麻烦等。

We hope you will pardon us for troubling you.

We regret the trouble we are causing you.

I regret the trouble it caused you.

We trust you will excuse us for this inconvenience.

We wish to crave your kind forbearance for this trouble.

We solicit your forbearance for such an annoyance.

We trust you will overlook this botheration, which we exceedingly regret.

Kindly excuse me for troubling you in this matter.

(8) 请宽恕某某事项等。

Please excuse this clerical error.

We tender you our apology for the inconvenience this error may have caused you.

We request you to accept our regret for the error of our clerk.

We greatly regret that we have caused you such a inconvenience.

We wish to express our regret for the annoyance this mistake has caused you.

We frankly admit we were at fault and we are anxious to repair the consequences.

(9) 请多加关照等。

We solicit a continuance of your valued favour.

We solicit a continuance of your confidence and support.

We hope we may receive your further favour.

We hope to receive a continuance of your kind patronage.

We request you to favour us with a continuance of your kind support.

We solicit a continuance of your kind patronage.

(10) 如有机会,我们必会报答您等。

It would give us a great pleasure to render you a similar service should an opportunity occur.

We wish to reciprocate the goodwill.

We shall on a similar occasion be pleased to reciprocate.

We hope to be able to reciprocate your good offices on a similar occasion.

We are always ready to render you such or similar services.

We shall at all times be willing to reciprocate such or similar favour.

We shall be happy to have an opportunity of reciprocating to you on a similar occasion.

(11) 今天我已经讲完应报告事项等。

With nothing further to add today.

Without anything further for the present.

With nothing further for the present.

Without anything more to communicate for today.

Without more to write you by this mail.

Without further to advise you today.

We have no more (nothing further) to tell (inform) you today.

3. Words, Phrases & Clauses Used in Business Letters(商业英文书信中所使用的词语)

(1) 贵函

Your letter; Your favour; Your esteemed letter; Your esteemed favour; Your valued letter; Your valued favour; Your note; Your communication; Your greatly esteemed letter; Your very friendly note; Your friendly advice; Yours.

(2) 本信,本函

Our (my) letter; Our (my) respects; Ours (mine); This letter; These lines; The present.

(3) 前函

The last letter; The last mail; The last post; The last communication; The last respects (自己的信); The last favour(来信).

(4) 次函

The next letter; The next mail; The next communication; The letter following; The following.

(5) 贵函发出日期

Your letter of (the) 5th May; Your favour dated (the) 5th June; Yours of the 3rd July; Yours under date (of) the 5th July; Your letter bearing date 5th July; Your favour of even date(AE); Your letter of yesterday; Your favour of yesterday's date; Your letter dated yesterday.

(6) 贵方来电、电传及传真

Your telegram; Your wire; Your cablegram(从国外); Your coded wire(密码电报); Your code message; Your cipher telegram; Your wireless telegram; Your telex; Your Fax.

(7) 贵方电话

Your telephone message; Your phone message; Your telephonic communication; Your telephone call; Your ring.

(8) 通知

(Noun)

Advice; Notice; Information; Notification; Communication; A report; News; Intelligence; Message.

(Verb)(通知,告知)

To communicate (a fact) to; To report (a fact) to...on; To apprise (a person) of; To let (a person) know; To acquaint (a person) with; To intimate (a fact) to; To send word; to send a message; To mail a notice; To write (a person) information; To give notice(预告); To break a news to(通知坏消息); To announce(宣布).

(9) 回信

(Noun)

An answer; A reply; A response.

(Verb)

To answer; To reply; To give a reply; To give one's answer; To make an answer; To send an answer; To write in reply; To answer one's letter.

(特此回信)

Reply to; Answering to; In answer to; In reply to; In response to.

(等候回信)

To await an answer; To wait for an answer.

(收到回信)

To get an answer; To favor one with an answer; To get a letter answered.

(10) 收讫,收到

(Noun)

Receipt(收到); A receipt(收据); A receiver(领取人,取款人); A recipient(收款人).

(Verb)

To receive; To be in receipt of; To be to (at) hand; To come to hand; To be in possession of; To be favored with; To get; To have; To have before (a person); To make out a receipt(开出收据); To acknowledge receipt(告知收讫).

(11) 确认

To confirm; Confirming; Confirmation; In Confirmation of(为确认……,为证

实……)；A letter of confirmation(确认函或确认书).

(12) 高兴，愉快，欣慰

To have the pleasure to do；To have the pleasure of doing；To have pleasure to do；To have pleasure in (of) doing；To take (a) pleasure in doing (something)；To take pleasure in doing (something)；To be pleased to (with)(by)；To be delighted at (in)(with)；To be glad to (of)(about)；To be rejoiced in (at).

(13) 随函附件

Enclose；Enclose please find.

(14) 迅速，立刻

Urgently；Promptly；Immediately；With all speed；At once；With dispatch；With all dispatch；With the quickest possible dispatch；With the least possible delay；As soon as possible；As quickly as possible；As promptly as possible；At one's earliest convenience；At the earliest possible moment；At an early date；Without delay；Without loss of time；Immediately on receipt of this letter；By express messenger；By Special messenger；By special delivery；By express letter.

(15) 回信

By return；By return of post；By return of mail；By return of air-mail.

(16) 依照

According to；Agreeably to；Conformably to；Pursuant to；In accordance with；In conformity with (to)；In obedience to；In deference to；In compliance with；In agreement with；In pursuance of.

(17) 就……，关于

About；Regarding；Concerning；As to；As regards；With regard to；In regard to；(of)；Respecting；Relative to；In connection with；Referring to；With reference to；In reference to；Re.

(18) 期满到期及应付之款

To be due；To fall due (become) due(日期将到)；Duly(正时，及时)；In due course (依照顺序).

(19) (每个，按照，通过)

Per(=by, through) rail. (post, mail, steamer)(通过铁路、邮政、轮船)

Per pro. =by proxy (由代理)

Per annum (=yearly，每年)

Per man, per capital (=per head，依照人数，每一人)

Per piece (每一个，每一件)

(20) 表示抱歉(冒昧做了某事)

To take the liberty of doing something；To take the liberty to do something；To take the liberty in doing something.

(21) 甚感遗憾，请包涵

To regret；To be sorry；To be chagrined；To be mortified；To be vexed；To regret to say; To be sorry to say; To one's regret; To feel a great regret for; To express regret; To be regretted; To be a matter for regret; To be regrettable; To be deplorable.

(22)(我们)对于……甚感荣幸

To have the honor of doing (being); To have the honor to do (be); To do one (oneself) the honor of doing (being); To esteem (regard) it as a high honor to do (be); To appreciate the honor to do (be); To feel honored to do (be); To owe one a debt of honor to do (be); To be honored with doing (being) something; To honor one with doing (being) something.

(23) 请

Please; Kindly; Be good enough; Be kind enough; Have the kindness.

(24) 感谢,衷心感谢等

To thank; To be (feel) thankful; To be (feel) grateful; To be obliged; To be indebted; To esteem (it) a favor (privilege); To give (tender, return) one's thanks; To express one's gratitude (appreciation); To tender one's sincere thanks for; To be overwhelmed with gratitude.

(25) 请照顾等

(Noun)(请吩咐)

Command; Order; Service.

(Verb)(服务)

To command; To order; To serve; To be at one's service; To render service to one; To do one a service; To be of service to one.

1.8 Dissimilarities in Letter Writing (英式商务信函与美式商务信函的差异)

英式商务信函与美式商务信函在写法上有许多不同之处,如遣词、信封格式、书信格式、称呼、结尾客套语、日期的写法等均有所不同。具体介绍如下:

(1) 英语商务信函与美式商务信函在遣词方面存在着一定的差异。一般来说,英语商务信函较为保守,许多英国人喜欢用老式书信体,用词较为正式,而美国书信语言比较有活力,格式也较为简便。因此,当我们通信的对象在英国或其旧殖民地国家时,应使用严谨正式的英式英语信函;如果写信的对象在美国或美国势力范围内的地区时,应使用灵活的美式英语信函。虽然,英式英语的语言文化在长期发展中也在不断发生变化,但总地来说,两者间的差异是十分明显的。

(2) 英语商务信函与美式商务信函信封写法不同。信封上收信人的姓名、地址,英式商务信函多用缩行式,美式商务信函多用平头式。发信人的姓名、地址,英式商务信函写在左下角,美式商务信函写在左上角。航空信函的空邮字样"AIRMAIL"、"VIA AIR MAIL"、"BY AIR MAIL",英式商务信函写在信封左上角,美式商务信函则写在贴邮票处的下方。

(3) 英语商务信函与美式商务信函通常惯用的书信格式不同。英语商务信函的信函格式是缩行式或混合式,美式商务信函的信函格式是平头式或改良平头式。

(4) 英语商务信函与美式商务信函撰写称呼惯用的方式不同。英式一般用 Dear Sirs,美式一般用 Gentlemen。称呼后一般要使用标点符号,英式采用逗号(comma),美式用分号(colon)或冒号。在英文书信中要使用敬语,最普遍的敬语是 Mr.、Mrs. 和 Miss.(用于未婚女性)。在称呼中对收信人的敬称,英式商务信函常使用 Mr.、Mrs.、Messrs.,均不加缩写句点,相反的趋向于自由化的美式商务信函需加缩写句点如 Mr.、Mrs.、Messrs.。

(5) 在信函的结尾客套语方面,英式商务信函和美式商务信函使用习惯各不相同,典型的英式写法是 Yours sincerely(熟人或知道对方姓名),Yours faithfully(不知对方姓名)等,而美式写法则习惯把"Yours"放在后面,成为 Sincerely yours,Faithfully yours 等。

(6) 在表达日期时,英式商务信函是按日-月-年的顺序,如 25 July, 2012。美式商务信函是按月-日-年的顺序,如 July 25, 2012。国际通用的日期格式是按日-月-年顺序排列的。

另外,部分常见的词汇在英式英语和美式英语中对应的词义有所差异,具体如表 1-3 所示。

表 1-3 部分常见词汇在英式英语和美式英语中对应的词义差异

Am. E 美式英语	Br. E 英式英语	词义
ad	advert	广告
ale	beer/bitter	淡色啤酒
apartment	flat	一套公寓房间
automobile	motor-car	骑车
baggage	luggage	行李
bathrobe	dressing-gown	浴衣、睡衣
bathtub	bath	浴缸
battery	accumulator	蓄电池
bill-fold	wallet	皮夹
bill(money)	banknote, or note	钞票
billboard	boarding	招贴板
billion	1000 million	十亿
biscuit	scone	甜饼
blank	form	空白表格
bucket	pail	提桶
bulletin-board	notice-board	布告栏
cab-stand	cab-rank	出租汽车停车处
can	tin	罐头
candy	sweets	糖果
chain-store	multiple-shop	联合商店

续表

Am. E 美式英语	Br. E 英式英语	词　义
check	bill	账单
city hall	town hall	市政厅
common stock	ordinary shares	普通股
consent decree	agreed verdict(courts)	最后达成的裁决
cop	bobby	警察
corn	maize	玉米
corporation	limited liability company	有限公司
cracker	biscuit	饼干
custom-made	bespoke	定做的
daylight-saving time	Summer time	夏令时
dessert	sweet course	甜食
distributor	stockist(of merchandise)	销售者
district(legislative)	division	区域
dock	wharg	码头
domestic malis	inland mails	国内邮件
down-town	the City	市中心
drawers(men's)	pants	短裤
drug-store	chemist's shop	药店
elevator	lift	电梯
eraser	Indian rubber	橡皮
filling-station	petrol-pump	加油站
first floor	ground floor	一楼
flashlight	torch	手电筒
gasoline	petrol	汽油
hardware	ironmongery	五金
Inc.	Ltd.	有限(公司)
information bureau	inquiry office	问讯处
line up	queue up	排队
long distance	trunk	长途电话
lumber	timber	木材
mail	post	邮件
molasses	treacle	糖浆
movie theatre	cinema	电影院
napkin	serviette	餐巾
necktie	tie	领带
newsdealer	news-agent	报刊经销人
newsstand	kiosk	报摊

续表

Am. E 美式英语	Br. E 英式英语	词　义
notions	fancy goods	精巧的花色小商品
one-way ticket	single ticket	单程车票
overcoat	greatcoat	大衣
pantry	larder	食品储藏室
parking lot	car park	停车处
peanut	monkey nut	花生
pen point	nib	笔尖
period	full stop	句号
race track	race course	跑道
radio	wireless	无线电
railroad	railway	铁路
schedule(railroad)	time table	(铁路)时刻表
sedan	saloon-car	轿车
sell out	sell up	售完
sidewalk	pavement	人行道
soft drinks	minerals	软饮料
spool	reel	卷轴
store	shop	店铺
subway	underground	地铁
suspenders	braces	长裤吊带
telephone booth	call box	电话亭
ticket-office(railroad)	booking office	(铁路)售票处
toilet	lavatory/closet	厕所
trolley/street car	tram/tram-car	有轨电车
truck	lorry	卡车
undershirt	vest/singlet	汗衫
windshield	wind-screen	(汽车等)挡风玻璃

1.9 Exercise(练习)

1. Please rewrite the following date for standard business letters.

(1) 6/5/08

(2) 10-9-09

(3) 8 June 2010

(4) Oct. 28, 07

(5) Jan. 13. 2006

2. Address the following information into in English envelop.

发信人：宣传公司

地址：美国 米特罗波利斯 百老汇 999 号 邮区号：NY222, U. S. A.

收信人：李明先生(总经理) 收　中西部进出口公司

地址：美国芝加哥东十街 12 号,邮区号 IL56789

3. Arrange the following in proper form as they should be set out a letter. 请将以下商业书信的组成部分按其正确格式排置成一封完整信函(使用修正齐头式)。

(1) Sender's name: China National Light Industrial Products Import & Export Corporation. Shanghai Branch

(2) Sender's address: 128 Huchun Road, Shanghai, China

(3) Sender's cable address: INDUSTRY SHANGHAI

(4) Sender's telex address: 33054 INDUS CN

(5) Date: March 23, 2014

(6) Receiver's name: H. G. Wilkinson Company, Limited

(7) Receiver's address: 245 Lombart Street, Lagos, Nigeria

(8) Salutation used: Dear Sirs,

(9) Subject matter: Sewing Machines

(10) The Message:

(11) We thank you for your letter of March 16 enquiring for the captioned goods.

(12) The enclosed booklet contains details of all our Sewing Machines and will enable you to make a suitable selection.

(13) Complimentary close: Yours faithfully,

Unit 2 Electronic Communication Way

电子通信方式

2.1 Study Aim(学习目标)

(1) 了解电报、电传、传真、电子数据交换、电子邮件等五种电子通信方式各自的优缺点。

(2) 掌握电子邮件的格式、内容构成、文体特点。

2.2 Introduction(专业背景知识介绍)

随着现代化信息技术的不断发展,各企业的往来函电的方式也越来越多,人们可以使用电报、电传、传真、电子数据交换,及电子邮件等多种方式进行经济贸易交流。当今电报、电传的使用已经很少见,对传真的使用也日益减少,使用最多的是电子邮件和电子数据交换。下面介绍电报、电传、传真、电子数据交换、电子邮件的特点,并详细介绍目前使用最为广泛的电子邮件的格式、内容构成、文体特点。

1. Telegraph(电报)

电报是最早的、可靠的即时远距离通信方式,它是19世纪30年代在英国和美国发展起来的。电报信息通过专用的交换线路以电信号的方式发送出去,该信号用编码代替文字和数字,通常使用的编码是莫尔斯编码。

(1) 电报的分类

电报在交易磋商中曾经被广泛使用,直到目前为止,电报也是合同法规定的书面合同形式之一。电报按不同的角度,可以有不同的分类:按地区分,电报可分为国内电报和国际电报;按业务分,电报可分为政务电报、私务电报、局务电报和新闻电报;按传递时间快慢,电报可以分为普通电报与加急电报;按所用文字和电码分,可分为明码电报、商用成语电报、商用密码电报和罗马字电报。下面就明码电报与商用密码电报、普通电报与加急电报、公务电报与私务电报三组直接对应的电报类型进行介绍。

① 明码电报与商用密码电报

电报对某些电文的传递,不是直接拍发和接收的,尤其是汉字书写的电文,需将文字译成可用电信号传达的电码后才能用发报机向外拍发。电码有全社会共同约定的,也有个别人或集团之间互相约定的。全社会共同约定的电码供公众公开使用,叫明码;由个别人或集团之间互相约定的电码,主要用于保密活动,所以叫密码。商用密码电报是采用商务密码写成的电报。以下为以明文电报和商务密码电报实例。

明文电报实例:

Date of dispatch: July 10, 2009

TEXTILES SHANGHAI

YTLXJAN24 1000DZ JACQUARD CTTNBTHTWL K25225 ACCEPTED SHPAMTAPR ASPERTERM AGRDUPON ORDER 10245 AIRED PLSCNFM ANDSEND S/CASAP

商用密码电报实例:

Date of dispatch: June 10, 2008

ALICO KAPACHI ACME

OSONM SEWINGMACHINE JB3-1 IGBYE

MACHINERY CN HEFEI

电文解密如下:

OSONM = Refer to your telegram of 27th inst.

SEWINGMACHINE JB3-1 = Sewing Machine JB3-1

IGBYE = impossible to accept, best we can do is to renew our offer firm subject to reply here by Friday our time

公众日常拍发和接收的电报,都是明码电报。如今明码电报的翻译工作,一般是由电信局的业务人员来进行,发报人将拟好的电文按邮电局规定的手续写好后交付业务人员就可以了,收报人收到的已经是业务人员根据接收的电码译成文字的电文了。

② 普通电报与加急电报

普通电报又称平电,与加急电报的区别在于传递的时间长短。就我国电报传递的条件来讲,普通电报一般在2~8个小时之内可以收到。但是,普通电报夜间停送,如果事情特别紧急,普通电报的速度不能满足需要时,就须发加急电报。加急电报比普通电报速度更快,收费也相应提高,办理发报手续时须写明“加急业务”,并按“加急业务”交费。

③ 公务电报与私务电报

电报依其内容来分,首先可分为公务电报和私务电报两大类。公务电报是为公事而拍发的,公务电报稿的写作属公文文种。私务电报是个人生活交际及经济活动中常用的,这类电报稿的写作属于应用文范围。贸易函电电报属于私务电报。

(2) 电报的计费方法

国际商业明文电报是按字数、分地区计费的,凡是一个组合不超过10个字码,包括英文字母、阿拉伯数字及电报中能使用的有关符号连在一起,按一个计费字计算,超过20个字码的按两个字计费,以此类推。因此汉译英时,首先注意运用英语中最基本、最常见的拼合词;另外,注意电文中没有标点符号,必须使用时,则用文字代替,如COMMA代替“,”。

(3) 函电电报范例

中文电报形式:

信用证 SB5864①已照改②请竭力在月底前发货③。

翻译要点评析:

① 信用证 SB5864。信用证在英文中有缩写形式即 L/C,SB5864 是信用证号,因此可译为 L/CSB5864。

② 已照改。这是典型的完成时态。由于英文电报中用分词代替现在进行时或将来时两个时态,用过去分词代替完成时态或被动语态(以及定语从句),因此可用 amend 的过去分词形式 amended。

③ 月底前发货。根据时态,这是一个将来时,因此可用 ship 的现在分词形式 shipping,月底前 by the end of the month 缩写为 ENDOFMONTH。

英文电报形式:

L/CSB5864 AMENDED ACCORDINGLY ENDEAVOUR SHIPPING ENDOFMONTH

2. Telex(电传)

电传(Telex)是 Teleprinter Exchange(电传机交换)或 Teletypewriter Exchange(电传打字电报机)的缩略词,一般取第一个词的头三个字母 Tel 和后一个词的头两个字母 ex 合在一起,简称 Telex。Telex 已经成为国际通用的名称。虽然在当今的国际贸易业务中,使用电传的几率比较小,多用传真代替,但由于电传的保密性要高于传真,因此,仍然为一些商务部门使用。

(1) 电传内容特点和计费标准

电传的内容全部使用大写字母;相当于电话通信,比书信快捷;信息传送准确,保真度高;电传的缩略字数量很大,而且具有一定规律性和创造性;可随时使用。

电传方式的计费标准有 2 种:一种是用户电传,按每次发报时间的长短计费;另一种是专线电传,每天 24 小时,双方可以随时直接联系,按月或按年收费。

(2) 电传的组成部分

电传一般分为三个部分:第一部分包括发报人、收报人的电传号码和回呼号码(Answer back);第二部分为电传正文;第三部分是重复发报人和收报人的电传号码和回呼号码。下面我们以实例来分析电传各组成部分。

86161 COSAD CN ①

884424 WSLTD G ②

12.6.84 MAC/MAY 13 ③

TO: PENAVICO × × × ④

FM: SOCEAN SHIPPING LTD. LDN ⑤

MT. "W" ⑥

RYTLX DATED 7/6 RE. PROFORMA DISBT OWNERS ARRANGING REMITTANCE ACDGLY REVERTING WITH DETAILS. RE. INCOME TAX VSL LOADING FOR SINGAPORE WITH GROSS FRT INCOME USD 155000

THERE4 FRT TAX TO PAY USD 6238. 75. RYTLX 8/6 LDO PRICE NOTED THANKS PLS ARRANGE SUPPLY 30TONS LDO ON ARRIVAL QINGDAO AS VSL RUNNING EXTREMLY SHORT OF DIESEL. PLS CFM. CFM. COSTS OF LDO N FRT TAX USD 6238. 75 ARE ALSO BEING REMITTED ALONG WITH DISBT FUND. ⑦

THANKS N RGDS ⑧

SOCEAN SHIPPING

AS AGENTS FOR OWNERS ⑨

884424 WSLTD G ⑩

86161 COSAD CN ⑪

电传说明：

①86161 是收报人的电传号码，COSAD 是收报人的回呼号码（Answer-back Code），CN 是国名代号。

②884424 是发报人的电传号码，WSLTD 是发报人的回呼号码，G 是国名代号。

③为发报日期及电传案号。

④为收报人的电报挂号或改用收报人的名称、地址等。

⑤为发报人的名称、地址。

⑥为电传标题。

⑦为电传正文。

⑧为结尾敬语。

⑨为发报人的名称，相当于信函的最后签署。

⑩是②的重复。

⑪是①的重复。

如果需要更正电传内容，对于即刻发错的内容，其纠正办法是接着错误的词连续打 5 个 X，然后空 1 个，再接着打更正的词，如：...HAS EBBXXXXX BEEN READY FOR...。

（3）电传写作的基本原则

① 留主舍次，即保留中心词，而舍去无关紧要的虚词。如：

We have not received your telex of October 12, 2003 可缩略为 UR TLX OCT12 NOT RECEIVED。

② 短词代替长词，单词代替短语，短语代替从句。如：

We have received your telex of the 15th in which you offered us 50 metric tons of rice. 可转换为 UR TLX 15TH OFFERING US 50 RICE。

③ 用现在分词表示将来时，用过去分词表示完成时态或被动语态，并省略相对应的助动词和其他成分。如：

The L/C was established on October 3 可转换 L/C ESTABLISHED OCT3。

④ 灵活使用前后缀。如：

We can obtain orders. 可转换为 ODR OBTAINABLE。

（4）电传常用缩略语的构词规律

① 由两个或两个以上单字所组成的某些短语和专有名词词组中主要单字，各取其第

一个字母。如:

PRC = the People's Republic of China

FYG = for your guidance

ASAP = as soon as possible

SHEEIU = Sundays and holidays excepted even if used

② 保留某些单字的第一个字母和最后一个字母。如:

YR = your

FM = from

MR = Mister

DO = Ditto

③ 保留第一个音节法。

a. 保留第一个音节及第二个音节的第一个字母(或第二个音节同发音之辅音组),即某些单字的前几个字母。如:

ABBR = abbreviation

ADV = advise

DOC = document

CERT = certificate

COMM = commission

b. 保留第一音节及后面全部字音或重要辅音。如:

ALRDY = already

RECVD = received

UNQT = unquote

DESTN = destination

④ 保留字音法。

保留重要字音或全部字音,但第一音节第一字母,无论是辅音还是元音一律保留。如:

RPT = repeat

ACPT = accept

MGR = manager

CNTR = container

⑤ 多音节的字,用省字号"'"代替被省略的字母。如:

ADT'L = additional

D'CULT = difficult

O'SEAS = overseas

S'HAI = shanghai

⑥ 某些多音节的字具有相同的第一字母和相同的最后字母,在省略字母时,多保留几个辅音字母,用以区别。如:

QLTY = quality

QNTY = quantity

ATTN = attention

ADDN = addition

⑦ 简化某些字的字尾。如：

LOADG = loading（以“G”简化-ing）

DISCHARGD = discharged（以“D”简化-ed）

SHIPT = shipment（以“T”简化-ment）

COMMN = commission（以“N”简化-ion）

⑧ 按照某些字母的发音来组成缩写字。如：

V = we

R = are

U = you

N = and

OZ = ounce

NITE = night

LITE = light

THRU = through

⑨ 利用阿拉伯数字代替与之具有相同发音的音节。如：

2 = too

B4 = before

THERE4（T4）= therefore

⑩ 保留第一音节和第二音节。如：

AVE = avenue

MEMO = memorandum

AUTO = automobile

PARA = paragraph

⑪ 保留第一音节、第二音节及第三音节第一个辅音字母。如：

APPROX = approximate

IMMED = immediate

IRRESP = irrespective

ORGAN = organization

⑫ 保留最后一个音节全部，其他音节取其重要辅音或全部辅音字母（重音在最后音节时，通常按照此方法缩写）。如：

ADRSEE = addressee

GTEE = guarantee

MTIME = meantime

YDAY = yesterday

⑬ 单词首字母组合中间加分隔符。如：

C/O = Care of

C/O = Chief Officer

B/L = Bill of Lading

S/O = Shipping Order

⑭ 以“X”或“Z”代替某些字母的字头或字尾。如：

XMAS = Christmas

PAX = passenger

FAX = facsimile

BIZ = business

WZ = with

3. Fax(传真)

传真是一种现代化的通信方式,将文字、图表、相片等记录在纸面上的静止图像,通过扫描和光电变换,变成电信号,经各类信道传送到目的地,在接收端通过一系列逆变换过程,获得与发送原稿相似记录副本的通信方式,称为传真。

(1) 传真的使用方法

传真操作简便,发信人只要把写好的信函及相应的附件,轻轻插入传真机文件输入口,拨通对方的传真机号码,对方回复后,按“开始”(有的是“发送”)按钮就完成了信息传输。

(2) 传真的主要内容

传真的内容主要由三部分构成：第一部分为题头,内容包括收发传真双方的基本情况,先写收件人(To)情况,再写发件人(From)以及发送传真日期与传真页数;第二部分为主题与正文;第三部分为结尾。

一般情况下,公司有专门的传真用纸,上面已印上了公司的地址、电话、传真号。日期、对方电话和传真号只要填好即可。传真实例如下：

CRYSTAL LOGISTICS LTD.

Vicarage Drive, Barking, Essex 1g117NA

Telephone: 081-55132235 Fax: 081-55132221

No. of Pages: 2

To: Mr. Huang Hua-qiang　　Fax: 0086265958000

COSCO SHANGHAI INT'L FREIGHT CO. ,LTD.

From: John Smith

CRYSTAL LOGISTICS LTD

Date: 3rd March 2006

CC: Sue Prazer

EXEL LOGISTICS

Dear Mr. Huang,

RE: ZHONG HE V. 0063E. TRIU 9551882

5c/s 917kg7.57m^3, YUNHE V.0030E, CBHU9733042, 2c/s853kg5.91m^3

The above-mentioned shipments have been loaded onto COSCO regular service and are bound for Qingdao port via Shanghai. Crystal Logistics have notified you that we pay for the T/S fee + on carriage charge to Qingdao.

This morning I received a phone call form the shipper who has expressed dissatisfaction with our service. Apparently the British consulate has been in contact with your goods shipper about the transshipment formalities. They have told the shipper in the U. K. that the goods must move under Bond (for which they have to pay USD 1500) to Qingdao. Since the shipper has paid the on carriage to Qingdao to Crystal Logistics, COSCO Freight Shanghai must take this cargo, after clearing at Shanghai, to Qingdao CFS.

Please advise us if there are any problems with the usual method of shipping to Qingdao.

Best Regards,

John Smith

(3) 传真的优点

与电传相比,传真具有下列优点。

① 速度快捷。传真机传输信息载体(文字或符号)的速度是每秒最高达9600bps,传输一页1000字的信息,约需时30~60秒,而电传则需12~13分钟,比电传快10倍以上。

② 费用低廉。传真的计费方法与电传相同,都是按时计费,两者的费率也基本相近。传真传输信息快得多,省时,产生费用自然比电传低得多。

③ 真迹传输。传真可以把原件复制得一模一样传送出去。文字、图片、表格、相片、签字、手迹等都可以传送,无所不可,而电传只能传输文字,且仅限于中文(四码)、英文、法文以及罗马字。而正本信用证、正本租约、正本提单、正本合约(协议)等重要的、篇幅较长的文件都可以通过传真原样传给对方,电传则无法办到。

④ 文体自由。书写传真文稿,同书写信函一样自由自在,不必在省字上下功夫,不必像写电报电传那样字字推敲,也不必考虑多用缩写字。

4. EDI(电子数据交换)

电子数据交换(EDI)(Electronic Data Interchange)是企业和企业之间进行电子商务的常用方式。EDI是用户的计算机系统之间的对结构化的、标准化的商业信息进行自动传送和自动处理的过程。换句话说,电子数据交换(EDI)是指借助于计算机技术和网络技术,将贸易过程中的票证单据、按统一格式在网上传输,以提高贸易运作效率,降低成本。由于使用EDI可以减少直到最终消除贸易过程中的纸面单证,因而EDI也被俗称为"无纸贸易"。EDI可以用于商业机构、非营利机构、政府之间传送订单、合同、发票、保险单、海关申报单、账单、库存报表等文件。

(1) EDI的特点

① EDI的使用对象是不同的组织之间,EDI传输的企业间的报文,是企业间信息交

流的一种方式；

② EDI 所传送的资料是一般业务资料，如发票、订单等，而不是指一般性的通知；

③ EDI 传输的报文是格式化的，是符合国际标准的，这是计算机能够自动处理报文的基本前提；

④ EDI 使用的数据通信网络一般是增值网、专用网；

⑤ 数据传输由收送双方的计算机系统直接传送、交换资料，不需要人工介入操作；

⑥ EDI 与传真或电子邮件的区别在于传真与电子邮件，需要人工的阅读判断处理才能进入计算机系统。人工将资料重复输入计算机系统中，既浪费人力资源，也容易出现错误，而 EDI 不需要再将有关资料人工重复输入系统。

随着社会的发展和科学技术的进步，交易磋商的书面形式会越来越丰富。书面磋商形式的创新与变化极大地促进了无纸贸易的实现，跨行业、跨国境交易的开展，及商业惯例的标准化，都会给交易磋商的方式与规则带来极大的冲击。

(2) 电子数据交换技术

EDI 的基础是信息，这些信息可以由人工输入计算机，但更好的方法是通过条码和射频标签快速准确地获得数据信息。

在电子商务的发展过程中，传统的 EDI 作为主要的数据交换方式，对数据的标准化起到了重要的作用。但是传统的 EDI 有着相当大的局限性，比如 EDI 需要专用网络和专用程序，EDI 的数据难以人工识读等。为此，人们开始使用基于 Internet 的电子数据交换技术——XML 技术。

XML 自从出现以来，以其可扩展性、自描述性等优点，被誉为信息标准化过程的有力工具，基于 XML 的标准将成为以后信息标准的主流，甚至有人提出了 eXe 的电子商务模式(e 即 enterprise，指企业，而 X 则就指的是 XML)。XML 的最大优势之一就在于其可扩展性，可扩展性克服了 HTML 固有的局限性，并使互联网一些新的应用成为可能。

5. E-mail(电子邮件)

电子邮件(E-mail 或 e-mail、Email)是 electronic mail 的缩写。电子邮件是目前互联网上应用最广泛的服务，被称作"因特网应用之母"。电子邮件是指通过电信网络以电子手段传送和接收的信息，它是在传统邮件的巨大进步，也可以说，它是在普通邮件的基础上实现电子化。

(1) 电子邮件的优点

电子邮件的优点众多，它既具有普通邮件的功能，又解决了传统邮件传递速度慢的问题，同时它的费用也比较低廉。我们可以把电子邮件的优点列举如下。

① 速度快捷

与传统信函形式相比，电子邮件最突出的特点是其送达的速度非常快捷。根据收发地距离的远近，传统国内信函，一般需要三天，甚至一周左右的时间才能送达，国际邮件需要的时间更长。如果在长途运送的过程中，作为商务磋商的重要信函丢失，则会给交易双方带来难以预计的恶果。而电子邮件的发送只需要轻按鼠标，简单几秒钟就完成了传统邮件的长途跋涉。由于电子邮件的快捷性，从 20 世纪 90 年代开始，它就已经成为主要的交流媒介。

② 可保存

电子邮件可以像文件一样被保存下来,同时还可以作为记录使用。经过数值化处理的电子邮件可以方便地进行检索、加工、编辑和重新利用。而传统的通信媒体都不具备这个特点。

③ 高效率

电子邮件与传统邮件相比,除了以上提到的快捷性和可保存性,还具有高效率的特点。编辑一封电子邮件,可以一次同时发给多人,免去了重新书写和复印的辛苦,大大提高了人们的工作效率,缩短了商务运作周期。根据专业人士的统计,商务电子邮件在68%的情况下是一件多发,而传统邮件只有17%的情况是一件多发。另外,电子邮件既可以传递文字,也可以传递声音、图片、视频,这使得商务沟通更加高效。

④ 成本低廉

不论是通过电报,还是电传方式联络商业客户,要想把交流内容表述清楚,都需要较长的书写内容,从而造成通信的高额费用。如果换用及时性较强的另一种交流方式——电话,则要考虑高额的越洋电话费的问题。然而,电子邮件帮助广大有需求的商户解决了这个问题。只要支付网络运营费,有时候可能需要支付电子邮件账户的费用,就可以随时发送电子邮件,而这种费用是一般的商户都承担得起的。

⑤ 保密性强

传统的电话沟通方式很容易被人旁听,传统书信也可能在传递过程中被人为窃密,甚至篡改。而电子邮件弥补了电话和传统书信的不足,具有极高的保密性。

(2) 发送电子邮件的必备条件

电子邮件是运行在因特网上的一种服务,因此发送电子邮件的第一个必备条件就是用户能够登录因特网。因特网服务提供者为其用户提供电子邮件的地址,并告诉用户如何设置自己的电子邮件客户端或浏览器来收发邮件。

2.3 Writing Skills(写作技巧)

正是基于电子邮件运用的广泛性和普适性,下面就电子邮件的格式、内容设置、文体特点、写作技巧进行介绍。

1. 电子邮件的格式

电子邮件一般由三部分组成:邮件头(E-mail head)、正文(message content)和签名(signature)。

邮件头包括寄件人(From)的邮件地址(计算机自动输入)、收件人(To)的邮件地址(发件人输入)、抄送(Cc)(发件人输入被抄送者邮件地址)、主题行(Subject)(发件人输入)、日期(Date)(计算机自动输入)。有时候,邮件头中还有暗送(Bcc),被暗送者也能收到邮件,但他们的名字不会出现在邮件头中,所以他们处于匿名状态。

Cc 是 carbon copy 的缩写,而 Bcc 是 blind carbon copy 的缩写。有时候出于礼貌,在

Cc 栏添加某些人的邮件地址,这些人需要知道邮件主题,但未被请求就邮件内容做出反应。他们只需做到心中有数。Bcc 栏用时需谨慎,因为如上所述,这一栏的人可以看到 To 和 Cc 栏内的人的姓名,而自己的姓名却不会被这些人看见。

此外,邮件头中常有附件(Attachments)。做附件的目的是避免邮件太长,影响发邮件的速度等,因此先做好一个文件(file),然后在发邮件之前,将此文件附加上去,它被称为"附件"。

发送电子邮件的一般格式为:

To:(收件人)	johnny@yahoo.com
CC:(抄送)	
BCC:(密件抄送)	
Subject:(主题)	Pricelist

……………………………………………………………………………………………
……………………………………………(正文)

一般收到电子邮件的格式与发送邮件的格式有所不同,多了"发件人"和"日期":

From:(发件人)	yangminyi@hotmail.com
Date:(日期)	28 Febrary 2006 12:34:58
To:(收件人)	johnny@yahoo.com
Subject:(主题)	Pricelist

……………………………………………………………………………………………
……………………………………………(正文)

在发送电子邮件时,如果只需要发送附件,我们可以按以下格式:

To:(收件人)	johnny@yahoo.com
CC:(抄送)	
BCC:(密件抄送)	
Subject:(主题)	Attachment

W

Catalog.doc

(1.2MB)

2. 内容设置

(1) 地址栏(To)。电子邮件的地址,包括写信人地址、收信人地址、抄送收信人地址、密送收信人地址,这四部分无须填写繁杂的邮政地址,只需填入相应的电子邮件地址即可,而且并非每一项都要填,若收信人只有一个,就不需填写其他收信人的电子邮件地址,处理比一般信件要简单得多。

(2) 主题摘要(Subject)。邮件的标题应当简洁明了。邮件标题是邮件主要内容的浓缩,是读者浏览信箱时决定是否阅读该邮件的根据。简洁明了的主题内容可起到索引的作用,便于收件者以后在大量的邮件中查出相关的邮件。邮件标题选择得合适与否将影响到读者处理信件的效率。因此,为了确保收信人能及时阅读邮件,邮件的标题不仅要引人注目,而且应该言简意赅。另外,标题应该用名词短语或动名词短语,如:"Your Meeting in California","Your Order","Mrs. Jones","Weekly Sales Meeting"等标题使信息明确、一目了然。

(3)称呼(Salutation)。商务英文电子邮件通常用较正式的称呼,如:Dear + 对方的姓氏,有时可以省去 Dear,直呼对方的名或姓,或者用随意的称呼,如:"Hi,Johnson","Hi,Davis"等。若不能确定收件人是哪一位,可用这样的表达,如:"Dear Sirs","Dear Madam or Sir"或"To whom it may be concern"等。

(4)正文部分的写法。涉外商务电子邮件的正文书写格式绝大多数采用齐头式。齐头式是指正文中各部分都从每行的左边开始,这种格式便于打字和节省时间,提高工作效率。但有时笔者也可以选择缩进。如果选择缩进,则每段缩进的距离应该一致。若段落之间的缩进出现不一致,极易使函电显得潦草与不整洁。大多数商业函电都是段内单倍行距,而段与段之间是双倍行距。如果信函的内容较短,也可以在段内使用双倍行距,而在段落之间使用双倍,甚至三倍行距。

正文是电子邮件的主要部分,大多把话题分成几个小主题,每个小主题一段,每段一般只有一两句话,正文由两三个或三四个简短的段落构成。

正文首段开头通常有两种情况:第一种情况是感谢收件人。如果是在回复客户的询问,一般应该以感谢开头。例如,如果有客户想了解本公司,就可以类似"Thank you for contacting ABC Company."的方式开头。如果此人已经回复过一封邮件了,就可以类似"Thank you for your prompt reply."或是"Thanks for getting back to me."的方式开头。以感谢的方式开始商务电子邮件,使读者感到比较亲近舒服,而且显得更礼貌。

第二种情况是直接表明写信意图,说明写信主题和目的,建立良好的基调。这种开头适用于第一次与主动发送电子邮件给对方的情况。例如,"I am writing to enquire about..."或是"I am writing in reference to ..."在电子邮件开头澄清写信来意十分重要,这样才能更好地引出邮件的主要内容。另外,在行文中要注意语法,拼写和标点符号,保持句子简短明了,同时句意前后一致。

正文的结束语以简短的表达方式为主,表达友好祝愿,给读者留下明确、完整的主题意向,希望对方给予答复。再次感谢收信人并加上些礼貌语结尾。如"Thank you for your patience and cooperation."或"Thank you for your consideration."开始接着写,"If you have any questions or concerns,don't hesitate to let me know."及"I look forward to hearing from you."结束。

(5)敬意结尾(Complimentary Closing)。表示客套和礼节,措辞应恰当。通常用"Best Regards","Best Wishes",或使用"Good day to you"等表示美好祝愿的词组作为敬意结尾,使得电子邮件更趋向随意体(casual style)。

(6)签名(Signature)。通常是寄件者在信函的敬意结尾下面写上自己的姓名。因为电子邮件是在电脑上打出来的,所以不能像传统的外贸信函那样可用手签。

(7) 附件(Enclosure)。电子邮件中如果带有与邮件内容相关的附件,可用 Word、Excel 等软件编写成文件报表或扫描各种形式发票、订单或报价单等,并在邮件中说明具体文件的名称及份数等,以便对方确认。

(8) 附言(Postscript)。打好邮件后,若发现需要补充某些内容,可在签名下方注明 P. S. 再附上补充的内容。但补充的内容不宜太多,常常是一两句话。若补充的内容很多,则需另写一封邮件,以免喧宾夺主。

3. 文体特点

由于电子邮件具有速度快、使用方便、价格便宜、内容形式多样等诸多优点,因此成为现代商务活动适用函电进行沟通和交流的主要工具。据统计,全球有 90% 以上的国际贸易商人每天使用英语电子邮件进行业务交流。然而,由于商务活动交流环境和传递方式等语境因素的改变,外贸电子邮件的语篇特征和行文方式发生了很大的变化。下面以一封询盘函为例,将传统函电形式与电子邮件形式的内容进行对比。

传统信函形式。

Re: Exporting Sweater

Through the courtesy of the Commercial Counselor of your Embassy in London, we have your name and address. We take the liberty of writing to you with a view to enter into business relations with you.

We wish to inform you that we are dealing with the export of sweater with good quality and competitive price and in a position to accept orders according to the customer's samples.

In order to give you a general idea of our products, we are airmailing you under separate cover our latest catalogue for your reference. We will make you a firm offer for the goods as soon as we receive your specific inquiry.

We are looking forward to your early reply.

Yours faithfully,

电子邮件形式。

E-mail: Sweater

I'm glad to know u import sweaters.

We export sweaters with good quality and competitive price. For more information pls visit our web, www. ××× . com. If u are interested, we'll send u the price list.

Look forward to yr reply.

Bst rgds,

以两种形式表达相同的写作意图,区别显而易见。电子邮件简洁、口语化、网络语言化,表述质朴、自然、清楚,如"I'm glad to know u import sweaters."。而且使用了网络上常用的简写,如: u = you。很显然,电子邮件对双方来说都更加省力、省时,而且由于网络的即时传递,电子邮件的语言显得亲切,更能拉近双方的距离,更有助于增加双方的联系和交流。根据外贸电子邮件的语境,语体特征和写作特点,总结通过电子邮件方式撰写外贸函电的文体特点。

（1）回复迅速及时、内容更加简洁。由于是商务活动，又是在网上即时性的交流，要求速度快、效益高，给买家的回复要迅速及时；否则，可能会因为落在其他卖家之后而失去商机。所以，除了要像传统信函那样“正确、完整、具体、清楚”，还需要回复迅速及时，内容更加简洁。例如邮件中“I'm glad to know u import sweaters.”比信件中冗长的套语（Through the courtesy of the Commercial Counselor of your Embassy in London, we have your name and address.）要简洁得多。

（2）标题鲜明。在大量电子邮件充斥邮箱的今天，标题就显得异常重要，如果标题没有内容，或不能引起收信人的关注，很有可能被当成垃圾邮件删除。邮件主题应该鲜明，吸引对方打开并阅读邮件。

（3）朴实、人性化。由于电子邮件的即时性，拉近了发件人和收件人之间的距离，使用起来比传统书信更加方便、快捷，双方交流时热情而友好，很像两个朋友之间面对面交谈那样，简单、自然，比信件更加朴实、人性化，例如，If yr price and delivery date are good enough, we'll place a large order with u. 显然就比 Should your price be found competitive and delivery date acceptable, we intend to place a large order with you. 朴实而亲切，在向对方提出要求或表达歉意时，更容易让对方接受。

（4）更加口语化，是以口语和书面语为主体的网络语体。口语化和网络语言化电子邮件属于网络语言，具有电子语篇中网络英语的一些特征。网民中比例最大的是35岁以下的年轻人，他们大多高学历，高素质，而且思想活跃、新潮，乐于创新，他们的文字活泼、自由、亲切、简洁，特别贴近生活，因此电子邮件还具有口语化和网络语言化的特点。词汇层面常常使用缩略词，如：u = you, rgds = regards 等。语句层面常使用缩略语、省略句和口语。如：I'm = I am（缩略语）；If so, contact me today（省略句），I was very happy to get yr E-mail（口语）。在电子邮件中使用聊天式的网络用语，交流更人性化。如：How are u doing? Have a good nice day!

比较常见的缩写如下：

缩写	原文	意思
A/O	at once	立刻
AOB	Any other business	其他事
ASAP	As soon as possible	尽快
BCC	blind carbon copy	密送
B/cuz	because	因为
BIZ	business	商务
BTW	By the way	顺便提一下
CC	Carbon copy	抄送
Conf.	Confidential	机密
FAQ	frequently asked question	常见问题
F2F	face to face	相对/面对面
HV	have	有/用以构成完成式，表示已经……
HVB	have been	已经

IOW	In other words	换句话说
INFO	information	信息
IMM/IMMD	immediate	立刻的,直接的
Imho	In my humble opinion	依我拙见
MKT	market	市场
MGR	manager	经理
OIC	oh, I see	我已知晓
Pls.	Please	请
PS	Postscript	附言
rgds	regards	问候
SPEC	specifications	规格
TIA	thanks in advance	提前感谢
TKS, THKS	thanks	感谢
TDY	today	今天
TTYL	talk to you later	以后再谈
UR	you are	您是
VG	very good	非常好
VR	we are	我们是
WRT	With regard to	关于
yr	your	您的
2	to/too	朝向/也
4	for	为了

2.4 Specimen Letters（样函）

Letter 1:

Dear Mr. Beirut,

Agency for Teaching Aids

At the beginning of this month, I attended the Harrogate toy fair. While there, I had an interesting conversation with Mr. Douglas Gage of Edutoys plc about selecting an agency for our teaching aids.

Douglas described your dynamic sales force and innovative approach to marketing. He attributed his own company's success to your excellent distribution network which has served him for several years. We need an organization like yours to launch our products in the UK. Our teaching aids cover the whole field of primary education in all subjects . Our patented "Matrix" math apparatus is particularly successful. You may have reservations about American teaching aids suiting your market. This is not a problem since we have a complete range of British English versions. I enclose an illustrated catalogue of our British English editions for your information. Please let me have your reactions to the material. I shall be in London during the first two weeks of October. Perhaps we could arrange a meeting to discuss our proposal.

Yours truly,
Fred Jackson

Letter 2:

Dear Mr. Jackson,

Agency for Teaching Aids

Many thanks for your letter and enclosures of 12 September. We were very interested to hear that you are looking for an UK distributor for your teaching aids.

We would like to invite you to visit our booth, no. 46, at next month's London Toy Fair, at Earl's court, which starts on 2 October. If you would like to set up an appointment during non exhibit hall hours please call me. I can then arrange for our sensor staff to be present at the meeting. We look forward to hearing from you.

Yours truly,
Jone Beirut

Letter 3:

Dear Mr. Allen,

Establishment of Business Relations

We understand from our trade contacts that your company has reestablished itself in Beirut and is once again trading successfully in your region. We would like to extend our congratulations and offer our very best wishes for your continued success.

Before the war in Lebanon, our companies were involved in a large volume of trade in our textiles. We see from our records that you were among our best customers.

We very much hope that we can resume our mutually beneficial relationship now that peace has returned to Lebanon. Since we last traded, our lines have changed beyond recognition. While they reflect current European taste in fabrics, some of our designs are specifically targeted at the Middle Eastern market.

As an initial step, I enclose our illustrated catalogue for your perusal. Should you wish to receive samples for closer inspection, we will be very happy to forward them. We look forward to hearing from you.

Yours faithfully,
Martin Bush

Letter 4:

Dear Mr. James,

Thank you for your order No. 464 of 20 September. The models you selected from our showroom went out today under my personal supervision.

The package is being air freighted to you on swiss air. The relevant documentation is enclosed. I enjoyed meeting you and hope that this order represents the beginning of a long and prosperous relationship between our companies. The next time you visit us, please let me know in advance so that I can arrange a lunch for you with our directors.

Sincerely yours,
Michael Clinton

Letter 5:

Ladies/Gentlemen:

From the latest issue of Computer World we have learned about your Business Guide software package for IBM-compatible PCs. We would like to find out more information about the package because we think it might be appropriate to the needs of our customers.

Would you mind answering the following questions?

Is the program an integrated package, or does it come in several modules?

Can the user switch form function to function without down-loading?

Can the user customize the billing periods?

Is there any provision for security?

What is the price of the software?

If you have a brochure that describes the package, we would appreciate your sending it along.

Sincerely yours,
SHEN Husheng (Mr.)
Import Manager

Notes(注释)

1. enclose *v.* 随函附寄
2. enclosure *n.* 附件
3. illustrated catalogue 含有插图的目录
4. teaching aids 教学器材
5. mutually beneficial relationship 互惠的业务关系
6. long and prosperous relationship 长期繁荣的业务关系
7. IBM-compatible PCs 兼容机
8. module *n.* 模块

2.5 Common Mistakes or Improper Factors in Business E-mail (商务电子邮件的常见错误或不当)

(1) 主从句主语不一致。例如:

① Deciding to offer the most competitive quotation, our report was updated to include USD 100000 for new equipment. 我们觉得提供最有竞争力的报价,所以将报告中的新设

备报价更新为 10000 美元。

应改为：Deciding to offer the most competitive quotation, we have updated our report to include USD 10000 for new equipment.

② Standing on the observation deck, the whole city can be seen. 站在观光塔上，整个城市尽收眼底。

应改为：Standing on the observation deck, you can get a bird's-eye view of the whole city.

（2）中国式的英语。例如：This is my heart word. 这是我的心里话。

应改为：These words are from the bottom of my heart. 或 These are my heartfelt words.

（3）句子零碎。句子与分句之间应该用连词连接，或用适当的标点符号（分号或句号）隔开，不能用逗号隔开，或将零碎的分句组合成主从句。例如：The committee decided to table the last bill. Because of our previous objections. 因为大家之前的反对，委员会决定搁置最后一份议案。

应改为：The committee decided to table the last bill because of our previous objections.

（4）句子前后人称不一致。

① 人称的单复数形式不要混乱。例如：An authorized person must sign their names on the contract.

应改为：An authorized person must sign his names on the contract.

② 动词与主语要呼应。例如：This is one of the agency functions that is underestimated. 这就是代理作用被低估的一个例子。

应改为：This is one of the agency functions that are underestimated.

2.6 Common English Patterns in E-mail（邮件英语常用句型）

（1）I am writing to confirm/enquire/inform you... 我写信是要确认/询问/通知您……

（2）With reference to our telephone conversation today... 关于我们今天在电话中的谈话……

（3）In my previous E-mail on October 5... 先前在 10 月 5 日所写的信……

（4）As I mentioned earlier about... 如我先前所提及关于……

（5）As indicated in my previous E-mail... 如我在先前的信中所提出……

（6）As we discussed on the phone... 如我们上次在电话中的讨论……

（7）as you requested/per your requirement... 按照您的要求……

（8）In reply to your E-mail dated April 1, we decided... 回答您在 4 月 1 日写的信，我们决定……

（9）This is in response to your E-mail today. 这是针对您今天早上来信的回复。

（10）As mentioned before, we deem this product has strong unique selling points in

China. 如先前所述,我们认为这个产品在中国有强有力且独一无二的销售特色。

(11) As a follow-up to our phone conversation yesterday, I wanted to get back to you about the pending issues of our agreement. 追踪我们昨天在电话中所谈,我想答复您关于我们合约的一些待解决的议题。

(12) I received your voice message regarding the subject. I'm wondering if you can elaborate i. e. provide more details. 我收到您关于这个主题的留言。我想您是否可以再详尽说明,也就是再提供多一点细节。

(13) Please be advised/informed that... 请被告知……

(14) Please note that...请注意……

(15) We would like to inform you that...我们想要通知您……

(16) I am convinced that...我确信……

(17) We agree with you on... 我们同意您在……

(18) With effect from 4 Oct., 2008...从2008年10月4日开始生效……

(19) We will have a meeting scheduled as noted below...我们将举行一个会议,时间表如下……

(20) I am delighted to tell you that... 我很高兴地告诉您……

(21) We are pleased to learn that... 我们很高兴得知……

(22) We wish to notify you that... 我们希望通知您……

(23) Congratulation on your... 恭喜您关于……

(24) We are sorry to inform you that... 我们很抱歉地通知你……

(25) Due to circumstances beyond our control...由于情况超出我们所能控制……

(26) It would be difficult for us to accept... 我们很难接受……

(27) Unfortunately I have to say that, since receiving your enquiries on the subject, our decision has not changed. 很不幸地,我必须这么说,自从收到您关于这个货物的询盘,我们的决定一直都没有改变。

(28) We would be grateful if you could...我们会很感激,如果您可以……

(29) I could appreciate it if you could... 我会很感激,如果您可以……

(30) Would you please send us... 可否请您寄给我们……

(31) Your prompt attention to this matter will be appreciated. 您能立即注意此事,我们将非常感激。

(32) Please give us your preliminary thoughts about this. 请让我知道您对于这件事情初步的想法。

(33) Could you please let me know the status of this project? 我可以知道这个计划的进度吗?

(34) I would appreciate it very much if you would send me your reply by next Monday. 如果能在下周一前收到您的答复,我将非常感激。

(35) Hope this is OK with you. If not, let me know by E-mail ASAP. 希望您对此没有问题,如果不行,请利用电子邮件尽快让我知道。

（36）Could you please send me your replies to the above questions by the end of June? 请您在6月份前答复我上述问题好吗？

（37）May I have your reply by April 1, if possible? 如果可能，我可否在4月1日前收到您的答复？

（38）If you wish, we would be happy to... 如果您希望，我们很乐意……

（39）Please let me know if there's anything I can do to help. 如果有任何我方可以帮得上忙的地方，请让我方知晓。

（40）If there's anything else I can do for you on/regarding this matter, please feel free to contact me at any time. 对于这件事，如果还有任何我能帮得上忙的地方，请不要客气，随时与我联络。

（41）If you want additional recommendations on this, please let us know and we can try to see if this is possible. 关于此事，如果您需要额外的建议，请让我们知道，我们会尝试看看是否可能。

（42）I'm just writing to remind you of... 我只是写信来提醒您……

（43）May we remind you that... 我们想要提醒您……

（44）I am enclosing...我方附上……

（45）Please find enclosed... 请查阅附件……

（46）Attached hereto ... 附件是关于……

（47）Attached please find the most up-to-date information on/regarding/concerning... 附上关于某某的最新资料……

（48）Attached please find the draft product plan for your review and comment. 附上产品计划书的草稿，请审查及评价。

（49）If you have any further questions, please feel free to contact me. 如果您有任何问题，请不要客气与我联络。

（50）I hope my clarification has been helpful. 希望我的说明是有帮助的。

（51）Please feel free to call me at any time, I will continually provide full support. 请随时跟我联络，我会持续地提供全程支持。

（52）Please let me know if this is suitable. 请让我知道这是否恰当。

（53）We look forward to hearing from you soon. 我们期待很快能得到您的回复。

（54）Hope this is clear and we are happy to discuss this further if necessary. 希望上述说明很清楚，如有必要，我们很乐意进一步讨论。

（55）I look forward to receiving your reply soon. 我期待很快能收到您的回复。

（56）Looking forward to receiving your comments in due course. 期待在预期的时间收到您的反馈。

（57）I'll keep you posted. 我会与您保持联络。

（58）Please keep me informed on the matter. 请随时让我知道这件事的进展。

（59）I would like to apologize for... 我想就……道歉……

（60）I apologize for the delay in ... 对于……的耽搁，我深感抱歉。

(61) We are sorry for any inconvenience caused. 对于产生的任何不便,我们感到抱歉。

(62) I am sorry for any inconvenience this has caused you. 对于造成您的任何不便,我方感到抱歉。

(63) We apologize for not replying you earlier. 对于未能早一些回信给贵方,我们感到抱歉。

(64) I'm really sorry about this. 关于这件事,我真的很抱歉。

(65) Sorry, I'm late in replying to your E-mail dated Monday, April 1. 抱歉,太迟回复您在4月1日(星期一)发给我的邮件。

(66) We apologize for the delay and hope that it doesn't inconvenience you too much. 我们为耽搁道歉,希望不会给您带来太多的不便。

(67) Hoping that this will not cause you too much trouble. 希望不会为您带来太多的麻烦。

(68) Thank you for your help. 谢谢您的帮助。

(69) I appreciate very much that you... 我非常感激你……

(70) I truly appreciate it. 我真的很感激。

(71) Thank you for your participation. 谢谢您的参加。

(72) Thank you so much for inviting me. 非常感谢您邀请我。

(73) Your understanding and cooperation is greatly/highly appreciated. 很感激您的理解及合作。

(74) Your prompt response will be most appreciated. 很感激您快速的答复。

(75) Once again, thank you all for your commitment and support. 再一次感谢您的承诺及支持。

(76) Thanks for your input/clarification/message. 谢谢您的投入/澄清/信息。

(77) Any comments will be much appreciated. 对于您的任何建议,我将非常感激。

(78) Thank you very much for everything you've done for me. 谢谢您为我做的一切。

(79) I would appreciate your kindest understanding with/regarding this matter. 我很感激您对这件事情的理解。

(80) Please accept our thanks for the trouble you have taken. 有劳贵方,不胜感激。

(81) We are obliged to thank you for your kind attention in this matter. 不胜感激贵方对此事的关照。

(82) We tender you our sincere thanks for your generous treatment of us in this affair. 对贵方在此事中的慷慨之举,深表感谢。

(83) We thank you for the special care you have given to the matter. 贵方对此悉心关照,不胜感激。

(84) We should be grateful for your trial order. 如承试订货,不胜感激。

(85) We should be grateful for your furnishing us details of your requirements. 如承赐示具体要求,不胜感激。

(86) It will be greatly appreciated if you will kindly send us your samples. 如承惠寄样品，则不胜感激。

(87) We shall appreciate it very much if you will give our bid your favorable consideration. 如承优惠考虑报价，不胜感激。

(88) We are greatly obliged for your bulk order just received. 收到贵方大宗订货，不胜感激。

(89) We assure you of our best services at all times. 我方保证向贵方随时提供最佳服务。

(90) If there is anything we can do to help you, we shall be more than pleased to do so. 贵公司若有所需求，我公司定尽力效劳。

(91) It would give us a great pleasure to render you a similar service should an opportunity occur. 我方如有机会同样效劳贵方，将不胜欣慰。

(92) We spare no efforts in endeavoring to be of service to you. 我方将不遗余力为贵方效劳。

(93) We shall be very glad to handle for you at very low commission charges. 我方将很愉快与贵方合作，收费低廉。

(94) We have always been able to supply these firms with their monthly requirements without interruption. 我方始终能供应这些公司每月所需的数量，从无间断。

(95) We take this opportunity to re-emphasize that we shall, at all times, do everything possible to give you whatever information you desire. 我们借此机会再次强调，定会尽力随时提供贵方所需的信息。

(96) We are always in a position to quote you the most advantageous prices for higher quality merchandise. 我们始终能向贵方提供品质最佳的产品，报价最为优惠。

(97) This places our dealers in a highly competitive position and also enable them to enjoy a maximum profit. 这样可以使我方经营者具有很强的竞争力，还可获得最大的利润。

(98) We solicit a continuance of your confidence and support. 恳请贵方继续给予信任，大力支持。

2.7 Focal Words(焦点词汇及短语)

(1) E-mail(electronic mail) *n.* 电子邮件

E-是 electronic 的缩写，“电子的，因特网上的”，这是随着因特网的出现而出现的一个新词素。如：

E-commerce/E-business 电子商务

E-world 网上世界

E-frontier 网上前线

E-health 网上保健

E-retail(E-tail) 网上零售

E-life 网上生活

(2) forward *adj*. 前部的,向前的,前进的,远的

Our cabin was in forward part of the ship. 我们的舱位在船的前部。

adv. 向前;提出

At the meeting he brought forward the question of pricing. 在会议上他提出了定价问题。

vt. 送发,寄去;转交

Would you be so kind as to forward my letter? 你能帮我寄封信吗?

forwarding *n*. 运送,运输业;转运

a forwarding merchant 转运商

a forwarding station 发送站

look forward to 盼望

(3) under *prep*. 在……之下,根据

The products you are interested in come under the scope of our trade activities. 你方欲购的产品属于我们的经营范围。

Under this installment plan, one-third is paid in cash. 按此分期付款计划,1/3 付现。

Under CIF terms the seller is under obligations to effect insurance. 按 CIF 条款要求,卖方有责任投保。

The seller has to raise the price under the pressure of rising costs. 在成本上涨的压力下,卖方不得不提高价格。

under the signature of 经……签名

under the name of 以……的名义

under the pretext of 以……为借口

(4) for

①(表示目的)为;替;给;对

Our prices were calculated without insurance for any special risks. 我们的价格计算不包括任何特殊险别的保险费用。

There is little or no demand at present for this article. 目前对该商品无需求。

②(表示对象、用途)为;对于;供;适合于

for you reference 供您参考

for you information 供您参考;有消息说

for you inspection 供您审查

for you perusal 供您细阅

for you attention 供您处理

for our file(record) 供我备档

the goods not for sale 非卖品

the latest date for shipment 最迟装运期

③ 表示因为;由于

Thank you for your interest in our products. 感谢贵方对我方产品感兴趣。

Our products are well known for their fine quality. 我们的产品因优质而闻名遐迩。

④ 表示交换;替代

Enclosed is a check for $50000 in payment of your commission. 随函寄去5万美元支票一张,以支付贵方的佣金。

We have for years been agents for your firm here. 我们多年来是贵公司在此地分公司的代理。

⑤ 其他用法

The first steamer available this month will sail for London. 本月第一艘轮船将开往伦敦。

The insurance amount will be for 110% of the invoice value. 保险金额为发票金额的110%。

For our part, we'll do our best to make everything smooth sailing. 就我们方面来讲,我们将尽力使一切顺利发展起来。

2.8 Exercise(练习)

1. Multiple choice.

(1) We hope to receive your quotation with details ________ the possible time of shipment.

A. to include B. to be include

C. including D. being included

(2) We must point out that ________ your L/C reaches us before the end of this month, we shall not be able to effect shipment within the stipulated time limit.

A. if B. unless C. in case D. in case of

(3) Payment is to be made ________ sight draft drawn under an irrevocable letter of credit.

A. on B. upon C. against D. for

(4) ________, we require payment by L/C.

A. If business is resulted B. If business is materialized

C. If business finalizes D. If business results

(5) We regret ________ unable to accept your terms of payment as mentioned in your last mail.

A. to be B. being C. to D. for being

(6) Pens are packed 12 pieces ________ a box and 200 boxes ________ a wooden case.

A. to, in B. in, to C. to, to D. to, of

(7) Will you please ________ to take out All Risks insurance for us on the following consignment?

A. help B. arrange C. cover D. insure

(8) Please insure ________ invoice value plus 10%.

A. for B. with C. at D. against

(9) We will refund the premium ________ you ________ receipt of your debit note.

A. to, upon B. with, upon C. to, at D. with, at

(10) Would you please draw ________ us ________ sight for above-mentioned amount?

A. for, in B. against, with C. on, at D. to, at

2. Put the following English phrases into Chinese or Chinese phrases into English.

(1) 电子商务
(2) 网上业务
(3) 网址,网站
(4) 万维网
(5) 以互联网为基础的
(6) B2B
(7) B2C
(8) EDI
(9) online directory
(10) E-trade

3. Translate the following Chinese sentences into English using the words or phrases in the brackets, and translate the following English sentences into Chinese.

(1) 我们经营这类商品已经有20多年的历史了。(to handle/in the line)
(2) 我们能供应式样各异、尺码齐备的鞋。(a wide range of)
(3) 如果你们需要,我们可以提供一些石油。(to offer)
(4) Our silk has long been a best seller at your end.
(5) Your letter of May 10 has been transferred to us for attention from our Head Office in Beijing.
(6) This product is being marketed in all European countries.

4. Translate the following letter into English.

(1)

亲爱的艾明先生:

收到您4月22日的来信和订单,不胜感激。

自从贵方两年前自我方订货以后,我方的商品价格同其他供应商一样有所提高,但是您一定会很高兴,因为我方打算按以前的价格供货。随函附上新的产品目录和价目表,其中有几种不错的最新产品和最新价格。

我方会及时通知您订货的进展最新情况。如果贵方急于与我方联系,可以发传真到5483321。当然也欢迎贵方像以前那样来电或电传。

谨上

莱斯特·本姆斯坦因

销售总监

(2)

亲爱的奥古斯塔托先生:

感谢您的 HT-200-96 号订单。我们注意到你要求 35% 的折扣。

事实上,我们给您的报价跟其他的供应商比起来已经很优惠了。另外,我们现在的商业利润已经很微薄了,所以现在我们能给客户的最大折扣不能超过 25% 。

但是,考虑到我们两个公司之间的长期合作关系,如果您同意将订货量提高到×××,我们就准备提供给您 30% 的折扣。我们希望您能接受这个绝好的条件,本月 10 日之前条件不变。

我们盼望得到你的订单。

谨上

耿书英

出口经理

■ 第二篇 ■

常用外贸信函

Business Letters for Frequent Occasions

Unit 3

Establishing Business Relations

建立业务关系

3.1 Study Aim(学习目标)

(1) 熟悉建立业务关系的操作步骤,知晓获得潜在客户名址的渠道。

(2) 掌握建立业务关系的常用句型。

(3) 掌握建立业务关系函写作基本要点。

(4) 掌握建立业务关系函的书写方式,并能回复建立业务关系函。

3.2 Introduction(专业背景知识介绍)

客户是企业的"衣食父母",因此,从事国际商务活动的企业应尽力寻找新客户以扩展业务,同时维护与本企业有长期业务往来的老客户的关系。与潜在客户建立业务关系成为商务活动中至关重要的一步。如何挖掘有实力的潜在客户,从何种渠道获得潜在客户的名称和地址,以及如何用一封诚挚礼貌的函电给对方留下好的第一印象,打动潜在客户,是从事国际商务活动的工作者应该熟练掌握的技巧。

1. 寻找国外潜在客户的渠道

由于国际商务活动的进口方和出口方远隔千山万水,通常双方可通过以下渠道查找到潜在客户的名称和地址。

(1) Web 网络

(2) Banks 银行

(3) Commercial counselor's office 商务参赞处

(4) Chamber of commerce in foreign countries 商会

(5) Trade directory 商行名录、同业名录

(6) Advertisements 商业广告

(7) Attendance at the trade fairs and exhibitions held at home and abroad 参加国内外商品交易会和展览会

(8) Mutual visit by trade delegations and groups 贸易代表团队互访

(9) Business house of the same trade 同业商行

(10) Agents 公司代理商

(11) Branch office or representative abroad 国外分公司或代理处

(12) Market investigation 市场调查

2. 建立业务关系函的写作提示

(1) 出口商撰写建立业务关系函一般由以下几个部分组成。

① 说明本企业是从何种渠道获知对方名址的,并表明写信意图;

② 做一个简要的自我介绍,介绍本企业的经营范围和产品,可附寄公司简介、商品目录、价目表、小册子等参考材料,以便对方全面了解我方的信息;

③ 表明本企业希望对方做出的反应,以及本企业将如何行动;

④ 表达对与对方合作或早日收到答复的期望。

(2) 进口商撰写建立业务关系函一般由以下几个部分组成。

① 告诉对方是如何获知其名称和地址的;

② 对本企业经营的业务和市场的状况做一个简要的介绍;

③ 告知对方本企业的进口意图,以及希望对方做出的反应;

④ 有关本企业的资信状况有何资信证明人;

⑤ 对合作和答复的期盼。

书写建立业务关系函时,应该清晰、简洁、得体、礼貌,表现出本企业的商业信誉,给对方留下好印象。

3. 回复建立业务关系函的写作提示

根据对方来函的要求和本企业的经营意图撰写回复函,应注意回复函应及时、礼貌,以便给对方留下好印象。在同意与对方建立业务关系的情况下,可撰写回复函表达同意建立业务关系,并附送相关资料,或期待来访;在不同意与对方建立业务关系的情况下,可婉言谢绝对方建立业务关系的请求,及时说明谢绝原因,如表明正在履行其他合约不便接纳业务,或请客户征询其他公司等,从而为今后可能的交易留下余地。

3.3 Writing Skills(写作技巧)

建立业务关系的信函的写作步骤及常见表达方式如表 3-1 所示。

表 3-1 建立业务关系的信函的写作步骤及常见表达方式

写作步骤	表达方式
1. 说明信息来源(告知对方你从何种渠道得知对方公司的情况)	We learned from the Commercial Counselor's Office of our Embassy in your company that you are interested in Chinese handicraft.(我们从我国驻贵国大使馆的商务参赞处得知,您对中国工艺品很感兴趣。)

续表

<table>
<tr><th>写 作 步 骤</th><th>表 达 方 式</th></tr>
<tr><td rowspan="2">1. 说明信息来源(告知对方你从何种渠道得知对方公司的情况)</td><td>Mr. Jacques, Head of Arcolite Electric AG, has recommended you to us as a leading importer in Korea of lightweight batteries for vehicles. (雅克先生,Arcolite 电气股份公司的主管,将您作为一家主要的韩国汽车轻型电池的进口商推荐给我们。)</td></tr>
<tr><td>We have obtained your name and address from China Council for the Promoting of International Trade that you are in the market for Chinese handicraft. (我们从中国贸促会获得您的名址,以及您想购买中国工艺品。)</td></tr>
<tr><td rowspan="3">2. 说明去函目的</td><td>In order to expand our products into South America, we are writing to you to seek cooperate possibilities. (为了拓展我们的产品在美国南部的发展,我们给您写信寻求合作的可能性。)</td></tr>
<tr><td>We are writing to you to establish long-term trade relations with you. (我们写信给您是想与您建立长期的业务联系。)</td></tr>
<tr><td>We wish to express our desire to enter into business relationship with you. (我们愿与贵方建立业务关系。)</td></tr>
<tr><td rowspan="4">3. 本公司简介(可包含产品介绍)</td><td>We are state-owned corporation handling light industrial products. (我们是国有公司,经营轻工业产品。)</td></tr>
<tr><td>We are exporters of high reputation, engaged in exportation of the following articles. (我们是声誉卓著的出口商,经营下列商品的出口业务。)</td></tr>
<tr><td>We are a leading company with 30 years' experience in exporting household electric appliances and are closely connected with large manufactures in our country. (我公司具有 30 年的家用电器出口经验,并且与我国大生产商建立密切联系。)</td></tr>
<tr><td>Our Chinese silks are made of pure silk materials and in traditional skills. They feel soft, comfortable, durable and have enjoyed great popularity in the world market. (我们的中国丝绸使用纯丝材料,运用传统技能制成。丝绸柔软、舒适、耐用,在国际市场上享有很高的声望。)</td></tr>
<tr><td rowspan="2">4. 表达与对方合作及早日收到回复的愿望</td><td>For your information (consideration, reference), we enclose a copy of our recent catalogue. (我们随函附上一份我们的最新的目录,供您参考。)</td></tr>
<tr><td>Thank you for your proposal and hope to work with you to our mutual advantage. (感谢您的建议,希望在今后的工作中能与您互利。)</td></tr>
</table>

回复建立业务关系的信函的写作步骤及常见表达方式如表 3-2 所示。

表 3-2　回复建立业务关系的信函的写作步骤及常见表达方式

写作步骤	表达方式
1. 感谢对方对本公司的兴趣	We have received your letter with thanks.（感谢收到贵方来函。）
	We thank you for your interest in our product.（感谢贵方对我方产品的兴趣。）
2. 表示同意与对方建立业务关系	We shall be very glad to enter into business relations with you.（我们将非常高兴与贵方建立业务关系。）
	Your wish of establishing business relations coincides with ours.（贵方建立业务关系的愿望与我们不谋而合。）
3. 或者，说明谢绝与对方建立业务关系的理由	We currently have the sole agency for another computer company. Under the terms of the contract, we are barred from stocking any other company's products. The sole agency comes under review in one year's time.（我们现在正为另一家电脑公司担任独家代理，根据合约条款，不得销售别家电脑公司的产品。该代理权将于一年后期满。）
	We regret to say that we do not manufacture clothing but only produce silk and supply textiles as a wholesaler and a manufacture.（很抱歉本公司只是生产丝绸面料，供应纺织品的批发商和制造商，并不制造成衣。）
4. 表示将采取进一步的行动，或今后合作的可能性	We are sending you our catalogue and pricelist.（我们将给贵方寄去我们的目录和价格表。）
	We shall be very glad to have your specific inquiry.（我们将很高兴得到贵方的具体询价。）
	Then please contact us and we may be able to consider your new products.（届时请再联系我方，也许可以考虑贵方产品。）

3.4 Specimen Letters（样函）

Letter 1:

Dear Sirs,

We owe your name and address to the Commercial Counselor's Office of the Swedish Embassy in Beijing who have informed us that you are in the market for textiles.

We avail ourselves of this opportunity to approach you for the establishment of trade relations with you.

We are a state-operated corporation, handling both the import and export of textiles. In order to acquaint you with our business lines, we enclose a copy of our Export List covering the main items suppliable at present.

Should any of the items be of interest to you, please let us know. We shall be glad to give you our lowest quotations upon receipt of your detailed requirements.

In our trade with merchants of various countries, we always adhere to the principle of equality and mutual benefit. It is our hope to promote, by joint efforts, both trade and friendship to our mutual advantage.

We look forward to receiving your enquiries soon.

Yours faithfully,

Encl.

Notes(注释)

1. owe *vt.* 该把……归功于,认为是靠……的力量(后接介词 to);欠(债等),该向……支付

e. g. We owe your name and address to...承蒙……告知您公司的名称和地址。

owe sb. a large sum = owe a large sum to sb. 欠某人一大笔钱

vi. 欠款,欠钱

e. g. The company has paid up all that was owed. 该公司已全部付清欠款。

There is still a balance of $1000 owing(to) us. 仍欠我方余额 1000 美元。

2. inform *v.* 通知,告诉,报告

inform sb. of sth. 通知某人某事

e. g. Please inform us of the market situation on your side. 请告贵地市场情况。

We shall inform you of the date of shipment, name of steamer. 我们将把装运日期、船名通知贵方。

inform sb. that/what/which 通知某人……

e. g. You are requested to inform us which one of the three types is of interest to you. 请告知我方您对三种类型中的哪一种有兴趣。

We wish to inform you that business has been done at £200 per metric ton. 我们已以每公吨 200 英镑的价格成交,特此告知。

Please inform us what quantity you can purchase per year. 请告知每年可购买的数量。

please be inform that ...请通知……

e. g. Please be inform that we have already sent the samples required. 兹通知贵方,我方已将所索样品寄出。

keep sb. informed of/that... 随时告知……

keep sb. advised of/that...告知某人某事

keep sb. posted of/that...通知某人某事

e. g. We hope you will keep us informed of the market condition at your end. 希望随时报道贵地的市场情况。

3. avail oneself of...利用

e. g. We avail ourselves of this opportunity to express our thanks to you for your close cooperation. 我们借此机会对贵方的密切合作表示感谢。

4. approach *vt.* 同……接洽,同……联系;接近,近似,向……靠近

e. g. We shall approach the department concerned on this matter. 我们将同有关部门联系此事。

One of our clients approaches us with an order for 100 tons White Sugar. 我方一位客户向我方洽订 100 吨白糖。

As the manufacture of your order is approaching completion, you are requested to open your L/C without any further delay. 贵方订货即将制造完毕,请立即开证。

vi. 临近,靠近,接近

e. g. The date of delivery is approaching, but we have not yet received your covering L/C up to now. 交货日期日益临近,而有关信用证至今仍未收到。

5. corporation *n.* 公司

State-operated corporation 国营公司

State-owned corporation 国有公司

State-run enterprise 国营企业

Collective-owned enterprise 集体企业

Individual-owned enterprise 私营企业

Private-owned enterprise 私营企业

Merchandising enterprise 商业企业

Small and middle medium enterprises(SMEs) 中小企业

Township/Rural enterprise 乡镇企业

6. handle *v.* 经营,处理,装卸,搬运

e. g. We understand your corporation handles foodstuffs for export. 我们了解贵公司经营食品出口业务。

Fragile goods must be handled carefully. 易碎物品须小心装卸。

No complication will arise if the matter is handled properly. 此事如处理妥善不会引起麻烦。

7. adhere *v.* 忠于,坚持(后接介词 to)

e. g. We always adhere to our commitments. 我们一贯坚持履行我们的义务。

8. by joint efforts 共同努力

through (by) joint (mutual or collective) efforts 通过共同努力

9. look forward to ...期待(to 是介词,后接名词或动名词)

e. g. We are looking forward to your early reply. 盼早复。

We look forward to receiving your early reply. 盼收到你们的早日答复。

Letter 2:

Dear Sirs,

Through the courtesy of our Commercial Counselor's Office in London, we notice that you are interested in doing business with us.

Our lines are mainly textiles. We wish to establish business relations by the commencement of some practical transactions. To give you a general idea of the various kinds of textiles now available for export, we are enclosing herewith a catalogue and a price list for your examination. We would appreciate receiving your specific enquiries.

We look forward to receiving from you good news.

Yours faithfully,

Notes(注释)

1. courtesy *n.* 礼貌,谦恭,殷勤

2. catalogue *n.* (图书或商品等)目录,目录册

classified catalogue 分类目录

descriptive catalogue 带有说明的目录

illustrated catalogue 有插图的目录

catalogue of industrial products 工厂产品目录

3. price list 价目单

4. through the courtesy of 感谢某人(单位)的推荐(介绍)

by courtesy of 蒙……许可;由于……好意;经由……的途径

5. commencement *n.* 开始,开端

commence *vt.* 开始;着手;*vi.* 使……开始

e. g. The spring fair commence from May 1st. 春交会从 5 月 1 日开始。

辨析: begin, start 与 commence

begin 和 start 都是表示"开始"的最普通用字。从修辞角度看 begin 是中性词,口语、笔译都通用;而 start 的口语色彩较浓;commence 主要用于较为正式的场合。

begin 和 start 都能接名词、动名词或不定式。

begin 反义词 end 终止;start 反义词 stop;commence 反义词 conclude。

e. g. Now that you are all back, we'd better start the work right away. 你们既然都回来了,我们最好马上就开始工作。

Returning office, he began drawing up the contract. 回到办公室后,他开始草拟合同。

The opening ceremony of the fair will commence ai 10 a. m. tomorrow. 交易会的开幕典礼将于明日上午十时开始。

6. available *adj.* 可利用的,可供应的

e. g. We will ship by the first steamer available (the first available steamer) next month. 我方将通过下月首条可使用的船只进行装运。

This is the only stock available (the only available stock). 这是唯一可供之货。

Our terms are L/C available by draft at sight. 我们的条款是凭即期汇票支付的信用证。

7. appreciate *v.* 涨价;感谢(后接名词或动名词作宾语);理解

e. g. The price has appreciated. 价格已涨。

Your immediate attention will be appreciated. 我们将感谢贵方对此事的立即重视。

We shall appreciate it if you will make us a firm offer for 50 tons cotton goods. 如果报给我们一个 50 吨棉制品的实盘,我们将不胜感激。

We shall appreciate it if you will …是外贸书信中常见的句子，等于 please，但更客气一些。

We appreciate your difficulty in coping with competition. 我们理解你们应付竞争的困难。

We fully appreciate your anxiety that the shipment should be made as soon as possible. 我方完全理解贵方急切希望货物尽早装运。

appreciable *adj.* 可看见的，可感到的

appreciative *adj.* 感激的，感谢的

8. for your examination 供贵方参考，供贵方查阅

Letter 3:

Dear Sirs,

Your communication of the 28th May addressed to our sister corporation Shanghai has been passed on to us and reply as the export enamelware falls within the scope of our business activities.

However, we very much regret that we are not in a position to supply you with enamelware direct, as we are already represented by Messrs. Freemen and Brothers Co., 267 Broad Street…, for the sales of this commodity in your district. We would advise you to get in touch with them for your requirements.

In case you are interested in other items, kindly let us know and we shall be only too pleased to make you offers directly.

Yours faithfully,

Notes(注释)

1. enamelware *n.* 搪瓷器

2. represent *v.* 代表，代理

3. communication *n.* 通信，通讯，传达，函件

e.g. All communications are to be addressed to the Shipping Department. 所有的函件请寄交运输处。

communicate *v.* 通信

communicate with sb. 和某人联系

e.g. If you are interested, please communicate with us. 如有兴趣请和我们联系。

communicate…to…把某事告知某人

e.g. Please communicate this to your buyers. 请将此事通知你方买主。

4. scope *n.* 范围

e.g. Line within the scope of our business activities. 该产品属于我们的经营范围。

类似的表达方法有 be within (fall within, come under) the scope of our trade activities, be within (lie within, 或 fall within) our business scope (sphere)等。

5. We very much regret that…我们对……万分抱歉

regret 抱歉,惋惜,引为遗憾,其后可跟名词,动名词,也可跟从句。We regret 和 We regret to say (note, learn)用法不同。如果是为自己一方的不足或过失而表示遗憾,两个句子都可以用;如果对别人的不足或过失表示遗憾,则只能说 We regret to say (learn, note).

另外,当 regret 被状语 very much 修饰时常放在 regret 的前面。

e. g. We very much regret this mistake. 对这个错误我们深感遗憾。

We very much regret to learn that you are not in a position to entertain an fresh orders at present. 我们十分遗憾地获悉你们目前不能接受新订货。

6. position *n.* 情况,身份,(期货)交易,期货,(金融、银行用法)头寸

e. g. Please advise (telegraph) position of our No. 383. 请告知(电告)我方第 383 号订单的执行情况。

financial position 财务状况

cash position 现金头寸

easy position 头寸宽裕

to cover position 轧平头寸

long/bull position 多头交易,买空交易

short/bear position 空头交易,卖空交易

7. sale *n.* 出售,卖;销货,交易,销路;(存货的)减价出售,拍卖

e. g. We confirm the sale to you of 500 metric tons Yellow Soybeans. 兹确认向贵方出售 500 公吨黄大豆。

Bicycles command a ready sale in the US market. 自行车在美国市场得到畅销。

Large sales are reported to have been made. 据说大笔交易已经做成。

clearance sale 清仓拍卖

rummage sale/jumble sale 二手货大拍卖

summer sale 夏季大拍卖

white sale (床单、棉织物这些商品)降价出售

adj. 售货的,销货的,有关售货的

sales confirmation 销售确认书

sales contract 销售合同

sales department 营业部

sales account 销售账目

sales allowance 销货折让

sales promotion 推销活动

sales laws 销售法

sales tax 销售税

salesman(saleswoman) 营业员

sales manager 营业主任

8. in your district 在贵地区

in your place 在贵处

on your side 在贵地区或在贵处

at your end 在贵处

9. get in touch with 与……联系

e. g. When we are again in a position to supply, we shall not fail to get in touch with you. 当我们能再供应时,一定与贵方联系。

As this item is handled by our Shanghai Office, please get in touch with them directly. 由于此项商品是上海公司经营,请与他们直接联系。

10. item *n.* 项目,条款,(商品的)品种,款项

e. g. We are working on the other items and will cable you as soon as possible. 其他项目正在进行,将尽早电告。

There are several items of commission not yet paid. 有几笔佣金,尚未付清。

This is the best-selling item in this line. 这是这类商品中最畅销的品种。

Item two of the agency agreement should be altered as...代理协议的第二项应改为……

11. case

n. (实)例,事例;情况,状况;诉讼(事件),案件,判例;容器(箱,盒)

vt. 把……装入箱(或盒等)内;加盖于;包围,围住

in case 如果,假若;以备(万一),以防(万一)

e. g. Please tell us in case you are interested in this article. 贵方如对此商品感兴趣,请告知我方。

We would suggest you placing an order at present in case the new crop may fail. 建议你们现在订购,以防新货不足。

in any case 无论如何

e. g. In any case we are unable to effect shipment in this month. 这个月我们无论如何无法发运。

in case of 假若,如果,万一

e. g. In case of offer, please quote your best price. 如能报盘,请开最低价。

in no case 绝不

e. g. You may be assured that in no case will the L/C be delayed. 贵方可放心,信用证绝不会迟到。

in the case of 就……而言,至于

e. g. In the case of payment terms, we are unable to accept D/P at 60 days sight. 至于付款条件,我方无法接受远期 60 天的付款交单。

in this case 假使这样,既然这样

e. g. In this case, we will not fail to cable you an offer. 如果这样,定去电给您报盘。

such being the case 情况既然如此

e. g. Such being the case, we regret being unable to make you an offer at present. 情况

既然如此,抱歉我们目前无法报盘。

12. to be only too glad to …too 前若有 only,all,but,ready 修饰时,结构表示肯定,相当于 to be very glad to…,to be much glad to …,to be very much pleased to …,to be more than pleased to … 十分乐于做某事……

请注意:若“too”前面没有 only 时,就有反义的含义。

e. g. We would be only too glad to make offers on RMB basis. 我们十分乐意以人民币为基础向贵方报盘。

Your letter of credit arrives here too late for us to ship your order before the end of this month. 你们的信用证到得太迟我们不能在本月月底以前装运贵方订货。

Letter 4:

Dear Sirs,

Thank you for your enquiry of 5 June concerning silk blouses.

We regret to say that we do not manufacture clothing but only produce silk and supply textiles as a wholesaler and a manufacturer. However, we'd like to recommend you a local factory that makes high quality men's suits. And we are sure they can meet the highest European standards according to your own designs. That's Swan Textiles Corporation in the industrial zone, Zhuhai. We supply the factory with all their silk materials.

I enclose a swatch of our stock materials for you examination. Should you desire any of these samples made up into finished products, we can supply the swan factory with them.

We hope that this will be of help to you and wish you every success in your business dealings.

Yours faithfully,

Notes(注释)

1. wholesaler *n*. 批发商

agent *n*. 代理商

trader *n*. 零售商

2. enclose *v*. 随函寄附,把(文件等)放入信封内

e. g. We are enclosing (herewith) our commercial invoice in duplicate. 随函寄附商业发票一式两份。

Please refer to the price list enclosed in (herewith) our letter of August 5. 请查阅 8 月 5 日去信所附的价目表。

过去分词 enclosed 作宾语补足语时,亦常倒置于句首或置于谓语动词后。

Enclosed please find a copy of our price list. (或 please find enclosed a copy of our price list.)随函寄去我方价目表一份。

enclosed please find 可译为“随函寄去……请查收”

过去分词 enclosed 可作名词用,前面加定冠词。

enclosure *n*. 附件(信内有附件时,常用缩写 Encl. 或 Enc.)

e. g. We have received your letter of May 5 along with two enclosures. 贵方5月5日来信及随同两个附件均已收到。

3. made up 制成的，捏造的；预制的；化妆过的

Letter 5:

Dear Sirs,

Thank you for your letter of 7 June regarding your new desktop computers. I regret to say that we cannot agree to your request for an appointment.

We currently have the sole agency for another computer company. Under the terms of the contract, we are barred from stocking any other company's products. The sole agency comes under review in one year's time. Then please contact us and we may be able to consider your new products.

Yours faithfully,

Notes(注释)

1. desktop computers 台式电脑
2. appointment *n.* 会面；约会；任命；职务；职位
3. sole agency 独家代理
4. barred *adj.* 有木栅的，隔绝的，被禁止的
5. stock *n.* 股份，股票；库存；树干；家畜

adj. 常备的，存货的；陈旧的

vt. 提供货物；备有

Letter 6:

Dear Sirs,

We are pleased to announce that we intend to intensify our activities in your country. It is our serious and keen interest to realize such a development for our mutual benefit.

We are a trading company involved in import and export business throughout the world. We belong to a group of companies established during the turn of 20th century. The attached statement will give you some more information which will surely be helpful to open business relations between us.

Within the activities of the company, we have recently established a new department under the management of Mr. ××× Who has long experience in import of products from your country especially in:

Native produce and animal by-products

For the foodstuffs and chemical industry

Raw materials and semi-finished products

Chemicals/pharmaceutical raw materials

Minerals and essential oils

However, we will be also active in export of chemicals and we invite your inquiries.

We seriously hope that a voluminous and continuous business might be established and please rest assured that we are always doing our utmost to realize a good business relationship with you.

We would be very pleased to be of service to you and hope to submit to you our inquiries soon.

Yours faithfully,

Notes(注释)

1. intensify *vt.* 加强,加剧
2. statement *n.* 财务报告书
3. pharmaceutial *adj.* &*n.* 药学的,药物的,药用的成品,药品
4. essential *adj.* 提炼的,精化的
5. an essential oil (香)精油,香料油
6. voluminous *adj.* 广泛的,很多的
7. keen *adj.* 渴望的,热衷的,热心的(后接动词不定式或介词 on)低廉的,刺激的,刺人的

keen smell 刺鼻的气味

keen competition 激烈的竞争

e. g. Buyers are keen to have your firm offers. 买主渴望获得贵方实盘。

They are rather keen to purchase Chinese goods. 我们渴望购买中国货。

Please quote keen price. 请报低价。

Competition is very keen. 竞争激烈。

8. interest *n.* 兴趣,感兴趣的事物,利益(复数较普通),权利,所得的货物,利息(保险用语),股份,同业者,……界(以专有名词作定语,用复数),财团,财界

e. g. We have no interest in cotton piece goods. 我们对棉匹头不感兴趣。

This article is of special interest to us. 我们对这种商品特别有兴趣。

Some of our friends who profess interest for your porcelain ware have approached us for offers on the following. 我们有些朋友对贵方瓷器感兴趣的客户向我们联系下列各货的报盘。

We agree to 60 days time L/C provided you pay interest for the period intervening. 我们同意 60 天期的信用证,但此期间的利息须由贵方负担。

The interest insured is valued at £19500. 此货按 19500 英镑投保。

annual interest 年利息

compound interest 复利

credit interest 存息

interest bill 有息票据,计息票据

shipping interests 航运界,航运业者

equity interest 股权

banking interests 银行界

v. 引起兴趣

e. g. The offer (price, shipment, quality) does not interest us. 这个报盘(价格、船期、质量)引不起我们的兴趣。

Your price is too high to even interest buyers in counter-offer. 你的价格太高,买方连还盘都没有兴趣。

9. involve *v*. 牵涉,涉及,包含,使陷于,使卷入(复杂或困难情况)

e. g. Your delay in shipping the ordered goods has involved us in unnecessary expenses. 你方耽误发运所订货物使我们遭受不必要的花费。

To repack the goods would involve a delay of about two weeks in shipment. 改装此货使装运期延迟大约两星期。

10. turn of the century 世纪之交

e. g. The time at the end of one century and the beginning of the next century. 一世纪之末与另一世纪之初(世纪之交)。

Automobiles were strange things to see at the turn of the last century. 在上世纪之初,汽车是一件奇怪的东西。

11. industry *n*. (制造或生产的部门);工业,企业,行业,(行)业(提供服务的商业性部门)

small-scale industry 小型工业

cottage industry 家庭手工业

nationalized industries 国有化工业

tertiary industry 第三产业

tourist industry 旅游业

industrial *adj*. 工业的

industrious *adj*. 勤劳的,勤奋的

e. g. England became an industrial country in the 19th century. 英国在 19 世纪成为工业国。

The Chinese people are industrious. 中国人民是勤劳的。

An industrial worker is one who is engaged in industry. 产业工人是从事工业的工人。

12. by-或 bye *prep*. (与名词或动词连用)次要的,副,附带的

by-law 附则

by-product 副产品

by-work 业余工作

13. semi-同 demi-一样,都是拉丁语前缀,表示一半,hemi-是希腊语前缀,也表示一半

demi-tint 半浓半淡

semiannual 半年一次的,一年两回的

semicircle 半圆

hemisphere 半球

14. inquiry *n*. 调查,询问,询盘,要货

通常用 make inquiries 表示询问,很少用单数(指具体商品时,通常用介词 for,指一般情况通常用介词 about)。

在日常生活中 inquiry 和 enquiry 只是拼法不同,没有什么区别。

名词 enquiry 是动词 enquire 的派生词。

e. g. We will make inquiries about the business possibilities of this new product of yours. 我们将调查一下贵方这种新产品的销售可能性。

We will make inquiries at (of) the shipping company regarding the reason for the delay of the vessel. 我们将向轮船公司询问此轮迟误的原因。

We thank you for your enquiry for carpets. 我们谢谢您对地毯的询盘。

There are large enquiries for iron wire from the Mid-east countries. 中东国家拟购大量铁丝。

At the moment there are only small enquiries for this class of goods. 目前对这种货物仅有小数量的询盘。

v. 询问,询价,要货

e. g. We acknowledge receipt of your letter of May 30 enquiring for alarm clocks. 贵方5月30日询购闹钟的来信收到。

15. 公司的一些表述方式如下。

(1) line(s):(轮船、航空、航运等)公司

Atlantic Container Line 大西洋集装箱海运公司

Hawaiian Air Lines 夏威夷航空公司

(2) agency:公司,代理行

Austin Advertising Agency 奥斯汀广告公司

China Ocean Shipping Agency 中国外轮代理公司

(3) associates:(联合)公司

British Nuclear Associates 英国核子联合公司

Subsea Equipment Associates Ltd. 海底设备联合有限公司(英、法、美合办)

(4) office:公司,多与 head, home branch 等连用

3M China Limited Guangzhou Branch Office 3M 中国有限公司广州分公司

China Books Import and Export Corporation (Head Office)中国图书进出口总公司

(5) service(s):(服务)公司

Africa-New Zealand Service 非洲-新西兰服务公司

Tropic Air Services 特罗皮克航空公司

此外,exchange、center 等词在特定的上下文中也可转义表示"公司"。

American Manufacturers Foreign Credit Insurance Exchange 美国制造商品信用保险公司

Binks (Shanghai) engineering Exhibition Center, Ltd. 宾克斯(上海)涂装工程设备展示有限公司

3.5 Focal Words(焦点词汇及短语)

(1) commerce *n.* 商务,商业

Ministry of Commerce of the People's Republic of China 中国商务部

Chamber of Commerce at Home or abroad 国内外商会

Chinese Commercial Counselor's Office in foreign countries 中国驻外商务参赞处

commerce 与 business、trade、bargain、deal 均含"贸易、交易"之意,其区别如下。

commerce:多指大规模的买卖或易货关系。

business:指包括售货、购货、换货在内的综合商业活动,方式可以是批发或零售。

trade:普通用词,含义广。既可指某种具体的商业,又可指广泛的贸易。

bargain:多指买卖双方通过谈判、协商就商品质量、数量、价格等项达成协议所成的生意。

deal:口语用词,指买卖双方经过交涉达成协议成交。

(2) economy

① *n.* 节约;节省

They will have to practice strict economy if they are to survive the recession. 如果他们要想度过萧条时期,就必须厉行节约。

② *n.* 经济;经济情况;经济结构;经济体制

Our national economy is growing rapidly. 我们的国民经济发展迅速。

We have a healthy and vigorous economy. 我们的经济是健全的、欣欣向荣的。

planned economy 计划经济

collective economy 集体经济

market economy 市场经济

economies of scale 规模经济

national economy 国民经济

(3) trade

① *vi.* 经商;做买卖

trade with 与……做生意

We trade with other countries on the basis of equality and mutual benefit. 我们在平等互利的基础上与别国进行贸易。

trade in 经营(商品)

They trade mainly in light industrial products. 他们主要经营轻工业产品。

② *n.* 贸易;买卖

China Council for the Promoting of International Trade 中国贸促会

Our foreign trade is expanding day by day. 我们的对外贸易日益发展。

③ *n.* 手艺;行业

How long did it take you to learn your trade? 你学这门手艺用了多少时间?

有关 trade 的常见短语:

barter trade 易货贸易
barriers to trade 贸易壁垒
bilateral trade 双边贸易
compensation trade 补偿贸易
frontier trade 边境贸易
improvement trade 加工贸易
multilateral trade 多边贸易
transit trade 转口贸易,过境贸易
trade friction 贸易摩擦
trade gap 贸易失衡
trade practice 贸易惯例,贸易习惯
trade procurator 商务代理人
trade representative 商务代表
trade terms 贸易条件
(4) market
① *n.* 市场
The market determines what goods are made. 市场决定生产什么。
auction market 拍卖市场
bond market 证券市场
corner the market 囤积居奇
exchange market 外汇市场
financial market 金融市场
hit the market (口)投入市场
money market 金融市场
futures market 期货市场
niche market 利基市场,泥区市场
secondhand market 旧货市场
securities market 证券市场
service market 劳务市场
② *n.* 市价;行情
Your price is out of line with the market. 你方的价格与市价不符。
The market is strengthening. 市价行情上扬。
③ *n.* 销路
There is no market here for such goods. 这种商品在这儿没有销路。
④ be in the market for... 想要购买
They might be in the market for sophisticated equipments. 他们可能要购买尖端设备。
⑤ come to (into) the market 上市
We'll contact you as soon as the new crops come to the market. 一旦有收成上市,我们定将与您联系。

⑥ *v*. 销售;推销

This product is being marketed in all European countries. 这种产品行销所有欧洲国家。

marketing *n*. 营销;营销学

market (be) firm with an upward tendency 市场坚挺,有上涨趋势

market (be) weak with a downward tendency 市场疲软,有下跌趋势

market (be) brisk 市场活跃

market (be) dull 市场呆滞

market (be) uncertain 市场不稳定

(5) line

① *n*. 短函;行业;(一类)货色

As soon as you reach a decision, please drop us a line (a few lines). 一旦你们做出决定,请告知。

We have been for many years in the chemical line. 我们经营化工商品已有多年。

Their chief line is the import of oilseeds. 他们主要经营进口油籽。

a. along (on) these lines 关于这件事,用这种方式

We will write to you again along (on) these lines. 关于这件事我们将再给您写信。

b. fall in line with 同意,符合

We do not think we can fall in line with your views. 我们认为我们不能同意您的意见。

c. in line (out of line) 相符合(不相符合)

Your price is quite in line, but the time of shipment is too extended. 您的价格尚可,但船期太迟。

Your price is entirely out of line with the market. 您的价格与市价完全不符。

d. in line with 按照

In line with cables exchanged, we confirm having sold you the following. 按照往来电报,我们确认售给你们以下商品。

e. on sound line 用正确的方法

f. on the wrong lines 用错误的方法

We believe we are handling the matter on sound lines. 我们相信,我们是在用正确的方法处理此事。

It would seem that you are dealing with this problem on the wrong lines. 您似乎在用错误方法处理此问题。

② *v*. 安排(与副词 up 连用);衬里

We are trying to line up an offer for you and will cable you as soon as possible. 我们正努力为您准备报盘,并将尽快去电。

We may be able to line up 50 tons for you in the next few days. 几天后我们可能给您安排 50 吨货。

Please line the cases with wax paper. 箱内请用蜡纸衬里。

(6) export

① *n.* (单数)出口;(复数)出口货

We handle the export of metals. 我们经营五金出口。

What are the chief export of Canada? 加拿大的主要出口货是什么?

② *v.* 出口

We export a large quantity of textiles now. 我们目前出口大量纺织品。

③ exporter *n.* 出口商

They are leading exporters of electric goods. 他们是电器用品的主要出口商。

④ exportation 出口(一般可与名词 export 单数通用)

We are engaged in the exportation of chemicals. 我们经营化工产品出口。

有关 export 的常见短语:

amount of exports 输出额

export control 出口管制

export declaration 出口申报单,出口申请书

export drawback 出口退税

export dumping 出口倾销

export document 出口单据

export entry 出口报关

export license 出口许可证

export-oriented economy 出口导向型经济

export quote 出口限额

export volume 出口量

export subsidies 出口补贴

(7) import

① *n.* (单数)进口;(复数)进口货

We are interest in the import and export of foodstuffs. 我们对进出口食品有兴趣。

Their imports are both diversified and substantial. 他们进口不仅品种大,而且数量大。

② *v.* 进口

We used to import Silicon Sheets before; now we export to imports. 以前我们经常进口硅钢片,但我们现在出口这项商品了。

③ importer *n.* 进口商

For this traditional product no commission is allowed to importers. 这些传统商品对进口商是概不付佣金的。

④ importation *n.* 进口

They are regularly interested in the importation of arts and crafts goods. 他们经常对进口工艺品感兴趣。

(8) acquaint *v.* 使熟悉,使了解,使认识

① acquaint sb. with/of sth. …使某人了解……

acquaint sb. that…使某人了解……

You will have to acquaint us with the details. 你们必须让我们了解详情。

② be/get acquainted with... 使某人了解……

We are well acquainted with the market condition in Japan. 我们对日本市场行情很了解。

3.6 Useful Sentences(常用语句)

(1) A reliable friend recommends you to us. 我们的一位可信赖的朋友把贵公司介绍给我们。

(2) Our abundant resources and stable policy provide foreigners with the advantages they invest here. 我们的丰富资源和稳定政策为外商投资提供了有利条件。

(3) We always pay attention to improving our quality. 我们一贯注重提高我们的产品质量。

(4) We've been in this business for forty years. 我们从事这一行已经40年了。

(5) We sell/supply/provide a wide range of office automation devices. 我们销售/供应/提供/多种办公自动化设备。

(6) Our company mainly trades/deals in arts and crafts. 我们公司主要经营工艺品。

(7) We're developing software for computers. 我们正在开发计算机软件。

(8) I'd like to know some information about the current investment environment in your country. 我想了解一下你们国家目前的投资环境。

(9) For the past ten years, we have done a lot of trade with your country. 在过去的10年中,我们与贵国进行了大量的贸易。

(10) We have made a very good start in our business with in South Korea. 我们与韩国在业务上有了良好的开端。

(11) We mainly trade with European firms. 我们主要和欧洲商行进行贸易。

(12) If you're interested in leasing trade, please let us know. 如果你们有意做租赁贸易,请告诉我们。

(13) We wonder whether you are interested in counter trade. 我们不知道您是否对补偿贸易感兴趣。

(14) Our purpose is to explore possibilities of developing trade with you. 我们想与你们研究一下发展贸易的可能性。

(15) We are thinking of expanding business relations with China. 我们正在考虑扩大与中国的贸易关系。

(16) We are willing to enter into business relationship with your company on the basis of equality and mutual benefit. 我们愿意在平等互利的基础上与贵公司建立业务关系。

(17) We look forward to reactivating our business relationship. 我们盼望我们之间的业务关系重新活跃起来。

(18) Having been deeply interested in the quality of your products, we are desirous of

opening an account with you. 本公司对贵方的产品质量一直深感兴趣,意欲和您开启交易。

(19) We should like to discuss the possibility of expanding trade with you. 我方愿与贵方就扩大贸易的可能性进行讨论。

(20) We're very interested in the product you exhibited at the international exhibition. 我们对你们在国际展览会上展出的产品,很感兴趣。

(21) Your products are almost exactly what we're looking for. 贵公司的产品,简直就是我们所要的。

(22) We are willing to enter into business relationship with your firm. 我们愿与贵公司建立业务关系。

(23) We wish to establish relationship with you. 我们希望与你们建立贸易关系。

(24) Establishing business relationship between us will be to our mutual benefit. 我们之间建立贸易关系将对双方有利。

(25) Your desire to establish direct business relationship with us coincides with ours. 贵方渴望与我方建立贸易关系,正合我意。

(26) We assure you of our best attention to any inquiries from you. 对于贵公司的任何询盘,我们一定给予充分关注。

(27) We have heard from China Council for the Promotion of International Trade that you are in the market for Electric Appliances. 从中国国际贸易促进会获悉,你们有意采购电器用具。

(28) From... we have obtained your name and address and understand that you are experience importers of ...We have pleasure in offering you...of which we would appreciate your pushing the sale on your market. 从……获悉你们名称及地址并了解你们是……有经验的进口商。现很高兴地向你们报盘……,盼能在贵地市场推销。

(29) We learn from... that your firm specializes in..., and would like to establish business relationship with you. 从……获悉贵公司专门经营……,现愿与贵公司建立业务关系。

(30) Through the introduction of ..., we have learned that you are one of the representative importers of...承……的介绍,获悉你们是……有代表性的进口商之一。

(31) You name and address has been given to us by Smith Co. in New York, who has informed us that your firm has been recommended to us by the Chamber of Commerce in Tokyo, Japan. 据纽约的史密斯公司得悉贵公司的名称和地址,并得知你们日本东京商会已把贵公司介绍给了我们。

(32) The ...Bank in your city has been kind enough to inform us that you are one of the leading importers (exporters) ...and are interested in trade with China in these lines. 承贵地……银行通知,你们是……的主要进口商(出口商),并有意与中国进行这些方面的贸易。

(33) We are given to understand that you are potential buyers of Chinese ..., which

comers within the frame of our business activities. 据了解,你们是中国……有潜力的买主,而该商品正属于我们的业务经营范围。

(34) We are glad to send you this introductory letter, hoping that it will be the prelude to mutually beneficial relations between us. 我们欣然寄发这封自荐信,希望是我们之间互利关系的前奏。

(35) We have the pleasure to introduce ourselves to you with the hope that we may have an opportunity to cooperate with you. 我们有幸自荐,盼望能有机会与你们合作。

(36) We take the liberty of writing to you with a view to building up business relationship with your firm. 我们冒昧通信,以期盼与贵公司建立业务关系。

(37) We wish to introduce ourselves to you as a state operated corporation dealing exclusively in Light Industrial Goods. 现向贵公司做自我介绍,我们是国营公司,专门经营轻工业品。

(38) As you may be well aware, we are a state-operated corporation handling such items as...in both import and export business. 也许你们已有所知,我们是国营公司,经营……(商品)的进出口业务。

(39) As you are one of the leading importers in ..., we have pleasure in contacting you in the hope of establishing business relationship and rendering you assistance in a wide range of your requirements. 鉴于你们是……的主要进口商之一,特此很高兴的联系贵公司,盼望建立业务关系,以助于满足你们各项要求。

(40) We understand that you are interested in both the import and export of and it is on this subject that we wish to introduce ourselves in the hope of establishing mutually beneficial business relations between our two corporations. 了解到你们对……的进口和出口很感兴趣,故愿自荐,希望在我们俩公司间建立互利的业务关系。

(41) The high reputation, which you are enjoying as camera importers, has rendered us desirous of entering into business relations with you. Accordingly, we introduce ourselves to you by sending you our catalogs and price-list. 贵公司是信誉卓著的照相机进口商,我公司极愿与贵公司建立业务关系。为此,我们现在寄去商品目录和价目表,以向贵公司毛遂自荐。

(42) The commodities we are handling consist of the manufactures of the first-rate paper mills of this country, and so we are in a good position to serve your customers with the most reliable quality of the line you suggest. 我们经营的商品包括本国第一流造纸厂的产品,因此,我们有良好的条件就你们提出的商品,向你们的顾客提供质量最可靠的商品。

(43) Specializing in the export of Chinese Art & Craft Goods, we express our desire to trade with you in this line. 我们专门经营中国美术品和工艺品出口,愿与你们进行交易。

(44) We are willing to enter into business relationships with your firm on the basis of equality, mutual benefit and exchanging what one has for what one needs. 我们愿在平等互利,互通有无的基础上与贵公司建立业务关系。

(45) We wish to establish friendly business relationship with you to enjoy a share of mutually profitable business. 我们愿与你们建立友好业务关系,分享互利的交易。

(46) We wish to enter into direct negotiation with you with a view to introducing your special lines in our market. 盼直接洽谈,以便将贵公司特种经营商品引进我地市场。

(47) We are interested in the possibility of establishing sources of supply of crude oil from the People's Republic of China. 我们有意向中华人民共和国寻求原油供应来源的可能性。

(48) We trust that our experience in foreign trade and intimate knowledge of international market conditions will entitle us to your confidence. 相信我公司在对外贸易经验以及对国际市场情况的熟悉,可能使我们有资格得到你们的信任。

(49) Being closely connected with reliable wholesaler here, we shall be able to do considerable import business with you. 我公司与此地可靠的批发商有紧密的联系,能与贵公司开展可观的业务。

(50) We shall be glad to have your specific inquiry. 能得到对方特殊的询价,则甚为感激。

(51) We shall be pleased to receive your enquiries for the machineries. 如收到贵公司对机械产品的询价,我们将深表谢意。

(52) We are interested in your new product...and with the hope to have a catalog and price list. 我们对贵公司的新产品……甚感兴趣,希望能寄来贵公司的产品目录和价目表。

(53) We have seen your advertisement in The New Your Times and with the hope to have your price lists and details of your terms. 我们从纽约时报上看到贵公司的广告,但愿能收到产品的价目表和详细资料。

(54) We hear that you have put...on the market and with the hope to have full details. 获知贵公司有……上市,希望能赐寄完整的详细资料。

(55) We have duly received your letter of June 1, with samples and price-list of your wines. By testing, we find the qualities of the wines are satisfactory, but your prices are considerably above our usual figured. 贵公司6月1日的来信、葡萄酒样品和价目表均已收到。经试饮,我们发现酒的品质很好,不足的是价格比我们的惯常价格高出太多。

3.7 Exercise(练习)

1. Multiple choice.

(1) We are sending you the samples ________ requested.

A. be　　B. are　　C. as　　D. for

(2) We have been specializing ________ this line for many years.

A. in　　B. on　　C. at　　D. with

(3) We ________ of this opportunity to approach you for the establishment of trade

relations with you.

A. take　　B. avail　　C. avail ourselves　　D. take ourselves

(4) We owe your name and address ________ Italian Commercial Bank who has informed us that you are in the market ________ table-cloths.

A. from/for　　B. to/with　　C. from/with　　D. to/for

(5) We now have a good demand ________ the captioned item and therefore write to you in the hope of establishing trade relations.

A. for　　B. with　　C. on　　D. in

(6) As the item ________ the scope of our business activities, we shall be pleased to establish direct trade relations with you.

A. lies within　　B. fall within　　C. come under　　D. be within

(7) In order to obtain the needed information, the inquirer should simply, clearly and concisely write ________ he wants to know.

A. that　　B. so　　C. what　　D. because of

(8) Your letter of May 9th addressed to our Nanjing Branch Office has ________ to us for attention and reply.

A. been passed on　　B. passed

C. passed on　　D. been past through

(9) In case you need more information ________ our business status, we shall be glad to answer your inquiries at any time.

A. about　　B. in　　C. to　　D. with

(10) We take the liberty of writing to you ________ a view to establishing business relations with you.

A. in　　B. with　　C. to　　D. for

2. Put the following English phrases into Chinese or Chinese phrases into English.

(1) Chamber of Commerce

(2) enter into business relations

(3) on the basis of equality and mutual benefit

(4) under separate cover/by separate mail

(5) owing to/due to/because of

(6) 小册子

(7) 目录;目录册

(8) 推荐,介绍

(9) 财务状况

(10) 作为惯例

3. Translate the following Chinese sentences into English using the words or phrases in the brackets, and translate the following English Sentences into Chinese.

(1) 纽约史密斯有限公司向我们介绍,贵公司是家具业的主要进口商。(be kindly recommended)

(2) 我们有幸自荐,盼望能有机会与你们合作,扩大业务。(cooperate with)

(3) 我们是声誉卓著的出口商,长期经营下列商品的出口业务。(high reputation)

(4) This places our dealers in a highly competitive position and also enables them to enjoy a maximum profit.

(5) We now avail ourselves of this opportunity to write to you with a view to entering into business relations with you.

(6) We have obtained your name and address through the Commercial Counselor's Office of the Embassy of the People's Republic of China in your country and understood that you would like to establish business relations with us.

4. Translate the following letter into English.

(1)

敬启者:

我们从我国驻巴基斯坦使馆商务参赞处得悉贵公司的名称和地址,现借此机会与你方通信,意在建立友好的业务关系。

我们是一家国有公司,专门经营台布出口业务,我们能接受顾客的来样订货,来样中可具体要求产品的花样图案、规格及包装装潢的要求。

为使贵方对我公司各类台布有大致的了解,我们另航寄最新的目录供参考。如果贵方对产品感兴趣,请尽快通知我方。一收到贵方具体询盘,即寄送报价单和样本。

盼早复。

谨上

(2)

敬启者:

我们从瑞士驻北京大使馆商务参赞处得知贵公司的名字和地址,并且很高兴地给您寄去我公司 2008 年的山地自行车的说明书,希望您会感兴趣。

我们是一家国有公司,经营自行车在亚洲的进出口业务。有关本公司的新产品——鹿牌山地车自从去年上市以来,亚洲各地已经涌来许多询价。使用者的报告更加确定了我们的信心——这是目前市场上最好的山地自行车。仅此随函附上产品说明书——列出了我们目前经营的自行车的种类。

如果您要了解某种或更多型号的产品,请告知我们。我们会非常高兴地给您寄去更多的资料。

我公司在这一行业有 20 多年的经营经验,因此我们完全有信心令客户满意。

期待您的回复。

谨上

Unit 4

Status Enquiries

资信调查

4.1 Study Aim(学习目标)

(1) 掌握从何种渠道开展资信调查。

(2) 掌握资信调查函写作的基本要点。

(3) 了解回复资信调查函的几种情况,掌握相应信函的写作技巧。

4.2 Introduction(专业背景知识介绍)

从事国际商务活动的企业由于距离相隔甚远,彼此了解对方的难度增大。一旦遭遇商业欺诈,或是由于贸易过程中对方信用不佳,将会导致巨大的损失。古语有云:"知己知彼,百战不殆。"敏锐的感悟洞察能力,强烈的防范意识,是商人在商战中必须具备的素养。开展国际商务资信调查,善抓信息,是选择客户的必要过程。

资信调查(Status Enquiries),就是在同客户正式开展商务交往前,除了应对其政治态度、社会地位进行了解之外,还须对潜在商务伙伴的财务状况、信用、声誉以及业务做法等有一个比较全面的了解,获得即将与之建立业务关系的有关商行的一切可能获得的信息。

国际商务工作者可以通过以下的渠道获得相关资信。

(1) 银行(bank)

(2) 有过业务往来的企业(trade reference)

(3) 商会(chamber of commerce)

(4) 咨询机构(enquiry agencies)

(5) 中国的驻外商务机构(Chinese commerce agencies in foreign countries)

(6) 外国的驻外商务机构(foreign countries' commerce agencies in China)

(7) 国内外咨询公司(enquiry companies at home and abroad)

在所有获得资信情况的渠道中,银行和有过业务往来的企业这两个渠道运用最为广泛。原因在于银行作为没有偏向性的中立方,所给予的资信回复是最为可靠的,而通常与该企业有过业务往来的客户企业所给出的信息和评价来自与被调查企业的实际交易经验,其资信回复是较为可靠的。我们通常将作为资信证明人的银行称为银行资信证明人

(Bank Reference),将作为资信证明人的商户称为客户资信证明人(Trade Reference)。有的银行不会直接向素不相识的商人提供信息,除非信用咨询来自他们的同行。因此,商人如要获得银行给予的信息,需要通过与之有密切业务往来的银行协助完成资信调查。

资信调查通常包括以下的调查内容。

(1) 财务状况(financial position)

(2) 信用(credit)

(3) 声誉(reputation)

(4) 业务做法(business methods)

(5) 管理能力(management capacities)

资信调查函的行文,应以平实坦诚的文风和得体精当的文字为特点。所谓平实坦诚,是对希望了解的对象提出具体明确的咨询内容,就是对你所介绍的对象做出中肯的评价。同时,应在资信调查函中表明对对方提供信息支持的感激之情。

写资信调查的复函,应以实事求是的态度真实地提供情况,表明态度,并要求对方严守秘密,说明自身对提供的情况不负有任何责任。拟就一封充满肯定性评语的资信证明,并不费力。然而,为一个资信不太好的调查对象写证明材料时,就要注意用词得体,即避免使用彻底否定的语言或轻率地做出无根据的结论,还要尽可能少说,但也应该让了解者明白那位潜在的客户应引起注意。

通常,在资信调查函的信头上标有“机密(Confidential)”或“机密并亲启(Confidential & Private)”的字样。同时,这些字也同样应出现在信封的 Remarks 部分。

4.3 Writing Skills (写作技巧)

建立业务关系的信函的写作步骤及常见表达方式如表 4-1 所示。

表 4-1 建立业务关系的信函的写作步骤及常见表达方式

写作步骤	表达方式
1. 直截了当地说明写信的意图	Our prospective customers SONY Company have given us your name as a banking reference. (我们的潜在客户索尼公司把您定为他们的银行证明人。)
	They state that they have done business with you for the past two years and have given us the name of your company as a reference. (他们向我们表示,他们在过去的两年中与您有过生意来往,并且指定贵公司作为他们的证明人。)
2. 说明想要调查的细节和原因	We could be very grateful if you could let us have some information about the financial and business standing of the above firm. (如能提供上述商行的财务和经营情况,我们将十分感谢。)

续表

写作步骤	表达方式
2. 说明想要调查的细节和原因	We shall appreciate it if you will inform us of your own experiences with the firm by filling in the blanks of the attached sheet and returning it to us in the enclosed envelop.（如贵公司能告知我们贵公司与该公司业务往来情况，并填妥附表寄还我方，我方将不胜感激。）
3. 保证保守秘密	Any information that you may give could be treated in strict confidence.（贵银行所提供的任何信息我们都将严格保密。）
	Any information you may give us will be treated as strictly confidential and expenses concerned from this inquiry will be gladly paid by us upon receipt of your bill.（你公司提供的信息，我们将予以保密，与此次调查有关的费用在我方接到贵公司的账单后支付。）
4. 提前感谢对方或期待对方早日答复	Thank you in advance.（提前感谢您。）
	We await your early reply.（期待早日回复。）

回复建立业务关系的信函的写作步骤及常见表达方式如表 4-2 所示。

表 4-2　回复建立业务关系的信函的写作步骤及常见表达方式

写作步骤	表达方式
1. 感谢对方的信任，表达愿意提供信息的意愿	We welcome the opportunity to report favorably on the ABC company.（我们很高兴有这次机会来报告有关 ABC 公司的实际情况。）
	Thank you for your inquiry about the business standing of the Pacific Trading Company, we are pleased to supply you with the following information.（感谢你查询有关太平洋贸易公司的资信情况，我们愿意向您提供以下信息。）
2. 有利的答复	In reply to your inquiry of March 16th, the firm you inquired about enjoys the fullest respect and unquestionable confidence in the business world.（兹复您 3 月 16 日的咨询，您咨询的这家公司在业界颇受尊敬，信誉很高。）
	After some difficulty during the first year, the firm has met its liabilities regularly and punctually.（度过开头一年的困境之后，此公司运行正常，而且按时履行义务。）
3. 不利的答复	We are sorry to say that our experiences with the company which you inquired about in your letter of April 2 has been unsatisfactory.（我们很遗憾地告知您，我们与您在 4 月 2 日来函中提到的那家公司的业务交往经历是不令人满意的。）
	In the past three years, the company has experienced a serious difficulty in finance and delayed in executing their normal payment.（在过去的 3 年里，该公司经历了严重的财务困难，并且延迟支付正常款项。）

续表

写作步骤	表达方式
4. 希望对方对所提供的报告保密	We hope that we have been of assistance to you, and that you will recognize the importance of keeping this communication strictly private.(我方希望这些帮助对你方有用,也望你方理解保守此秘密的重要性。)
	The above information is passed on to you for your personal reference only and without any responsibility on our part.(以上向您提供的信息仅供您私人参考,我方不负任何责任。)

4.4 Specimen Letters(样函)

Letter 1:

Dear Sirs,

We are very pleased to receive your order for our goods to the values of $25000.

Since it is the first time we contact, we could be highly appreciated if you could provide us your bank name and address. As soon as the enquiry is satisfactorily settled, we shall be happy to send you the goods you ordered.

We sincerely hope this will be the beginning of a long and pleasant business association. We shall do our best to make it so.

Yours faithfully,

Notes(注释)

1. contact *n.* 接触;触点;[医](传染病)接触人;门路

vt. 使接触;与……联系;与……通信(或通话)

vi. 联系,接触

e. g. I don't have much contact with my uncle. 我和叔父甚少联系。

I'll contact them soon. Meantime don't tell them I'm back. 我会尽快和他们联系。在此期间,不要告诉他们我回来了。

contactable *adj.* 可感染的(疾病)

2. appreciate *vt.* 欣赏,赏识;感谢,感激;体会,领会、察知;正确地评价,鉴别

e. g. Her talent for music was not appreciated. 她的音乐才能无人赏识。

They deeply appreciated his kindness. 他们对他的好意深表感谢。

I am afraid you have not appreciated the urgency of the matter. 恐怕你还没有意识到这件事的紧迫性。

vi. (土地、货币等)增值

e. g. Land will continue to appreciate. 土地将继续增值。

3. settle *vt.* 解决;安排;使定居;使沉淀;付清(欠款);结算(账单);结(账)

vi. 下沉;定居

n. 高背长靠椅

e. g. They agreed to try to settle their dispute by negotiation. 他们同意通过谈判来努力解决纠纷。

Both sides are looking for ways to settle their differences. 双方都在寻求消除分歧的方法。

I settled the bill for my coffee and his two glasses of wine. 我为我的咖啡和他的两杯葡萄酒付了账。

As far as we're concerned, the matter is settled. 我们这边已经安排妥当了。

That's settled then. We'll exchange addresses tonight. 那就定下来了,我们今晚交换联系地址。

Refugees settling in Britain suffer from a number of problems. 在英国定居的难民面临很多问题。

This was one of the first areas to be settled by Europeans. 这是欧洲人最早的定居地之一。

Once its impurities had settled, the oil could be graded. 一旦杂质沉淀下去,油就可以分级了。

4. association *n*. 协会,社团;联合,关联,交往,联系;联想

The British Olympic Association 英国奥林匹克协会

e. g. Research associations are often linked to a particular industry. 研究协会常与某个特定的行业挂钩。

The company has six-year association with retailer J. C. Penney Co. 该公司与零售商 J. C. 彭尼公司 6 年的业务往来。

The association between the two companies stretches back thirty years. 这两家公司的往来可以追溯到 30 年前。

Black was considered inappropriate because of its associations with death. 不宜用黑色,因为它让人联想到死亡。

Published in association with the Council for the Protection of Rural England, the book provides refreshing solutions to the long-term problem of water conservation. 这本书与英格兰乡村保护委员会合作出版,就节约水资源这个长期问题提供了全新的解决方法。

5. order *n*. 订单,订购,所订的货;汇票

e. g. We accept the order subject to payment in advance. 如果预付货款我们就可以接受订货。

We expect to ship your order sometime next week. 我们预计在下周内装运你方所订的货。

表示所订的商品时,名词 order 一般后接 for 或 of。

e. g. If the first shipment turns out satisfactory, we shall be able to place substiantial orders with you. 假如第一批货物令人满意,我方将能继续向你方大量订货。

有关 order 的常见短语:

accept an order 接受订单
article made to order 定制品
bank money order 银行汇票
be in order 已订购(尚未发货)
banker's order 银行汇票
block order 整批预订
cancel an order 取消订单
carry out an order 执行订单
confirm an order 接受订单
cut an order 取消订单
decline an order/turn down an order 谢绝订单
execute an order 执行订单
fill/fulfill an order 供应订货
first order 首批订单
goods an order 订购货品
hold up an order 暂停执行订单
initial order 首批订单
job order 分批订货
mail order 邮购
pending order 未完成的订单
repeat order 重复订单
rescind an order/revoke an order/withdraw an order 取消订单
refuse an order 拒绝订单
suspend an order 暂停执行订单
trial order 试购订单

v. 订购,订(货)

e. g. If you order immediately, we can probably arrange 5000 cases. 如贵方立即订货,我方可能安排 5000 箱。

We note that you contemplate ordering 2000 Footballs at the same price as last. 我们注意到贵方打算照上次价格订购足球 2000 个。

6. do one's best 尽全力;勉尽力量;尽心竭力;卖

e. g. Do one's best solve the main problem of existence? 力求解决存在的主要问题。

Improving one's last effort instead of comparing with others does one's best. 使他们在尽全力之后得到提高,而不是把他们和别人作比较来达到目的。

Letter 2:

Dear Sirs,

Thank you for the catalogue and price-list received earlier this month. We now have pleasure in sending you a first order.

For the information concerning our credit and business operation, please refer to the following firms:

Shanghai Hexagon Trading Company

No. 7, Lane 51, Xi Xiang Road Shanghai

Shanghai Electronics Import and Export Corporation

8-17/F, Aerospace Building, 525 Si Chuan Bei Road Shanghai

Yours faithfully,

Notes(注释)

1. pleasure *n.* 愉快,快乐,高兴,满意

to have/take pleasure in doing (to do) sth. 乐于做某事

to have/take pleasure of doing (to do) sth. 乐于做某事

e. g. We take the pleasure of making you a firm offer as follows: 兹(乐于)报实盘如下:

with pleasure 愉快地接受、同意

"May I borrow your car?" "Yes, with pleasure." "可以借您的车么?" "行,乐意之至。"

2. operation *n.* 操作,经营;手术;[数]运算;作用;公司,企业

e. g. The two parent groups now run their business as a single combined operation. 这两个母公司现在合并为一家企业经营业务。

Charles was at the clinic recovering from an operation on his arm. 查尔斯的胳膊动了手术,正在这家诊所进行康复治疗。

Until the rail links are in operation, passengers can only travel through the tunnel by coach. 在铁路连线开通之前,乘客只能乘坐长途客车穿越隧道。

Cheaper energy conservation techniques have been put into operation in the developed world. 更经济的节能技术在发达国家已经投入使用。

3. refer *vi.* 提到;针对;关系到;请教

vt. 归因于……;使求助于;送交;认为……起源于

vt. & *vi.* 参考,查阅

e. g. In his speech, he referred to a recent trip to Canada. 他在讲演中提到了前不久的加拿大之行。

Our economy is referred to as a free market. 我们的经济被称作自由市场经济。

He referred briefly to his notebook. 他简单地看了看自己的笔记。

Letter 3:

Dear Sirs,

The under-mentioned firm in New York has recently asked if they could represent us in the marketing of our products in the United States as our sole agent, the firm and its address is:

Friendship International Trade Co. ,Ltd.

250 Royal Road

New York, NY. 30786

We could be very grateful if you could let us have some information about the financial and business standing of the above firm.

Any information that you may give could be treated in strict confidence and we await your early reply.

Yours faithfully,

Notes(注释)

1. under-mentioned 下述的

e. g. I am sending you by m. s. "Suwa Maru" the under mentioned goods, and herewith I enclose a bill of lading for same. 下列货物现正装上货轮"诹访号"付运,并在本件函内附上该货的提单。

Please feel maker and advise if compromise possible under terms mentioned 请试探厂家并劝导他们,如能调停,请按我方原先所述之条件。

Extraction rate for raffinose reached 95% under conditions mentioned above, and the content of free gossypol was lowered from 0.085% to 0.029% , lower than 0.04% as FAO stated for edible product standard. 在棉子糖的提取率达到95%以上的条件下,游离棉酚含量由原来的0.085%降低到0.029% ,低于FAO所规定的0.04%的食用标准。

2. represent *vt.* 表现,象征;代表,代理;扮演;作为示范

e. g. The offer has yet to be accepted by the lawyers representing the victims. 受害者的代理律师还没有接受这个提议。

The general secretary may represent the president at official ceremonies. 总书记可以在一些官方仪式上代表主席。

The pieces on view are not grouped around any one theme, but rather represent superb examples from various periods. 展出的作品并非围绕着一个主题,而是不同时期的经典之作。

These developments represented a major change in the established order. 这些发展代表了现有秩序的重大转变。

3. market *n.* 交易;市集;需求;交易情况,行情

vt. 在市场上出售某物;推销

e. g. The two big companies control 72% of the market. 两大公司控制了72%的市场份额。

Every year, 250000 people enter the job market. 每年有25万人进入就业市场。

The market collapsed last October. 去年10月股市崩盘。

in the market of = interested in buying sth. 有意买某物

4. sole agent 包销人,独家代理,独家经销商

e. g. Should he open his own office, or employ a sole agent, or many different agents? 他是设立自己的办事处,还是雇用独家代理商,还是雇用多家不同的代理商?

I may even consider appointing you as our sole agent in China. 我会考虑任命您为我们在中国境内的独家代理。

He is the sole agent for the airline. 他是这家航空公司的独家代理商。

5. treat *n*. 款待;招待;乐事;乐趣

vt. 处理;探讨;对待;请(客)

vt. & *vi*. 请客,款待 *vi*. 论述;探讨(与 of 连用);交涉;商议

e. g. Do not treat this serious matter as a joke. 不要把这件严肃的事情当作笑料。

She treated me all right. 她对我还不错。

This substance must be treated with acid. 这材料得用酸来处理。

The book treats some political problems. 该书论述某些政治问题。

The doctors were not able to treat this disease. 医生治不了这种病。

We'll treat you to dinner. 我们请您吃饭。

This book treats of economic problems. 这本书探讨经济问题。

I'll treat today. 今天我做东请客。

It's my treat. 我请客。

It's a great treat for them to go to the theater. 他们去看戏真是乐事。

For dessert we had fresh strawberries—a real treat. 饭后甜点我们吃鲜草莓——真是难得的享受。

6. confidence *n*. 信心;信任;秘密

adj. 骗得信任的;欺诈的

e. g. This has contributed to the lack of confidence in the police. 这导致了大家对警方缺乏信任。

His record on ceasefires inspires no confidence. 他以往在停火方面的表现让人对他毫无信心。

I always thought the worst of myself and had no confidence whatsoever. 我老是妄自菲薄,没有一点儿信心。

We told you all these things in confidence. 我们告诉您的这些事都需要保密。

Letter 4:

Dear Sirs,

We have received a sudden bid from the American Trading Co. , Ltd, 600 Mission Street Francisco, with which you are now doing business and firm gives us your name as a reference.

We shall appreciate it if you will inform us of your own experiences with the firm by filling in the blanks of the attached sheet and returning it to us in the enclosed envelop.

Any information you may give us will be treated as strictly confidential and expenses concerned from this inquiry will be gladly paid by us upon receipt of your bill.

Yours faithfully,

(Attached Sheet)

1. whether they are in the wholesale trade
2. if their financial position is considered strong
3. if they are among leading wholesale firms in your city
4. whether they have the reputation of paying promptly
5. what credit it could be safe to allow them
6. whether they appear to have suffered very much from the strike in your district

Notes(注释)

1. bid *vt.* (买方)出价,递盘;(卖方)要价,索价;(拍卖时货商品交易所中叫价,喊价)

vi. (买方)出价,递盘;(卖方)要价,索价;(拍卖时货商品交易所中)喊价,叫价;投标(以求承包一项工程或供应货物)

e. g. Last week we bid ¥ × × per ton for Green Tea. Now we can do a little better. 上星期我们对绿茶递价每吨人民币××元。现在我们可以出得稍多一些。

One minute before the auctioneer struck his hammer, a Chinese firm bid $35 for your product. 拍卖人击槌前一分钟,一家中国公司对贵方产品出价35美元。

We hope you will bid for this article if you have interested it. 贵方若对此货有兴趣,望出盘。

2. receipt *v.* 收到,接到

e. g. We acknowledge with thanks receipt of your letter of June 5. 贵方6月5日来函收到,谢谢。

The goods will be sent upon receipt of your remittance. 收到贵方汇款后即发货。

We are in receipt of your letter of August 22 offering us 50 metric tons of the captioned goods at ¥2360 per metric ton on the usual terms. 我们收悉拟8月22日函,向我方供应50公吨标题货物,惯常条款,每公吨2360元人民币。

n. 收据,收条

cargo receipt 货运收据

freight receipt 运费收据

mate's receipt 大副收据、收货单

parcel post receipt 邮包收据

deposit receipt 存款凭证

n. (复数)收入、收进的款项或物

e. g. This month's receipts are estimated to be in the region of £30000. 本月进款估计在3万英镑上下。

3. enclose *vt.* (用墙、篱笆等)把……围起来;把……装入信封;附入

e. g. The rules state that samples must be enclosed in two watertight containers... 规则要求样本必须装在两个水密容器中。

Enclose the pot in a clear polythene bag... 将罐子装在透明的塑胶袋中。

The surrounding land was enclosed by an eight foot wire fence. 周围的土地围有8英尺高的铁丝栅栏。

I have enclosed a cheque for £10. 我已随信附上10英镑的支票。

He tore open the creamy envelope that had been enclosed in the letter. 他撕开了随信寄来的奶油色信封。

The enclosed leaflet shows how Service Care can ease all your worries. 随信寄上的宣传页将说明"服保"如何能为您解除所有烦忧。

I enclose here with a draft for the sum of 100 dollars. 兹附上100美元汇票一张。

Before posting a letter, you should enclose it in an envelope. 在把信寄出之前您必须把它装入信封内。

4. expense *n.* 费用;花费的钱;消耗;花钱的东西

vt. 向……收取费用;把……作为开支勾销

e. g. To avoid extra expense and mess later on, try to decide on fittings before the plastering finished... 为避免将来出现额外的开支和不必要的麻烦,尽量在抹灰完工之前把固定设施确定下来。

It was not a fortune but would help to cover household expenses. 这笔钱不算多,但是能帮助支付家庭开支。

As a member of the International Olympic Committee her fares and hotel expenses were paid by the IOC. 作为国际奥林匹克委员会的成员,她的交通费用和酒店住宿费用都由国际奥委会支付。

Can you claim this back on expenses? 这个您能报销吗?

5. wholesale *n.* 批发;趸售,大规模买卖

adj. 批发的,整批卖的;大规模的

adv. 大量地,大批地;广泛地,大规模地

vt. 批发

vi. 经营批发业;批发售出

e. g. Warehouse clubs allow members to buy goods at wholesale prices. 仓储式会员店允许会员以批发价购买商品。

The fabrics are sold wholesale to retailers, fashion houses, and other manufacturers. 这些纺织品被批发给零售商、时装店和其他制造商。

They are only doing what is necessary to prevent wholesale destruction of vegetation. 他们只是在采取必要措施避免大规模的植被破坏。

6. reputation *n.* 名气,名声;好名声;信誉,声望;荣誉,名望

e. g. This college has a good academic reputation. 这所大学有良好的学术声誉。

Barcelona's reputation is as a design-conscious, artistic city. 巴塞罗那作为一个具有设计意识的艺术城市的声誉。

7. suffer *vi*. 受痛苦;受损害;变糟;变差

vt. 忍受;容忍;容许;遭受

e. g. Within a few days she had become seriously ill, suffering great pain and discomfort... 几天的时间,她就病得很严重了,疼痛难忍,周身不舒服。

I realized he was suffering from shock. 我意识到他休克了。

Romania suffered another setback in its efforts to obtain financial support for its reforms. 在为改革努力寻求经济援助时,罗马尼亚再次受挫。

It is obvious that Syria will suffer most from this change of heart. 很明显,这一态度的转变对叙利亚的影响最大。

Without a major boost in tourism, the economy will suffer even further. 旅游业如果没有大的起色,经济状况会每况愈下。

Letter 5:

Private & Confidential

Dear Sirs,

In reply to your letter of August 18, we want to inform that we have now received from Barclays Bank of London the information you require.

St. Polo & Co., Ltd. was established in 1948 with a capital of 300000 pounds. Their chief line is in the import and export of all kinds of foods, trading principally with China, Japan, Germany, Britain and America. Their supplier's business with them is report to have been satisfactory. The bankers have a high regard for their operating ability and financial standing. Its reputation here is very good.

We believe that you can deal with them freely. Of course, this is our personal opinion and we assume no responsibility in your proposed business negotiations.

This information should be supplied in the strictest confidence.

Yours faithfully,

Notes(注释)

1. in reply to 答复,……答复

e. g. A response may only be sent in reply to a request. 一个响应只能回复一个请求。

2. established *adj*. 既定的,已被证实的

e. g. The said company is a long established firm in this country. 该公司是在本国已创立多年的企业。

It is our established policy to trade with the people of all countries in the world on the basis of equality and mutual benefit. 在平等互利的基础上与世界各国人民进行贸易是我们的既定政策。

established fact 既成事实

3. line *n.* 排;线路;线条;方法

vt. 排队;用线标出;[棒球](击球手)击出(平直球);给……安衬里

vi. (在某物的内部)形成一层;排队,排列成行,排齐(常与 up 连用);[棒球](击球手)击出平直球;(击球手因击出的平直球被对方接住而)出局

e. g. Draw a line down that page's center. 沿那一页的中心画一条竖线。

The ball had clearly crossed the line. 球明显出界了。

The sparse line of spectators noticed nothing unusual. 那一排稀稀落落的观众没留意到任何不寻常之处。

The next line should read: Five days, 23.5 hours. 下一行应该是: 5 天,23.5 小时。

a dotted line 虚线

4. deal with 惠顾; 与……交易;应付; 对待

e. g. In dealing with suicidal youngsters, our aims should be clear. 在对待有自杀倾向的青少年时,我们的目标应当很明确。

The President said the agreement would allow other vital problems to be dealt with. 总统说这项协议将能使其他关键问题得到解决。

When I worked in Florida I dealt with British people all the time. 在佛罗里达工作时,我总与英国人有生意往来。

He's a hard man to deal with. 要跟他这个人做生意很难。

Letter 6:

Private & Confidential

Dear Sirs,

We regret our inability to let you know any positive information concerning the firm in question in your letter of the June 6.

It is true that we had business with them during the past few years, but the amount of business was not so large that we can not supply any responsible opinion on the business capability and credit standing.

We suggest you make further enquiries from other enquiry agencies.

Yours faithfully,

Notes(注释)

1. in question 考虑之中的,被谈论着的

e. g. That is not the point in question. 那不是要考虑的要点。

The lady in question is not in office now. 所谈的那位女士现在没在办公室。

That is not the point in question. 那不是要考虑的要点。

Did the matter in question occur on or about ten o'clock on the fifteenth of June? 那事是在 6 月 15 日 10 点或 10 点左右发生的吗?

2. responsible *adj.* 尽责的;承担责任;负有责任的;懂道理的

e. g. The government will be responsible to the President alone. 政府只对总统一人

负责。

He feels that the media should be more responsible in what they report. 他觉得媒体应该对报道的内容更负责任些。

The government is responsible for the provision of health care. 政府负责提供医疗服务。

3. business capability 业务能力

e. g. The enlargement of the company's overseas business activities. 公司海外业务的扩展。

4.5 Focal Words(焦点词汇及短语)

(1) pay *vi*. 付款,值得,合算

pay in advance 预付

pay in cash 付现金

pay by check 支票付款

pay in installments 分期付款

pay on delivery 货到付款

vt. 付(款项,费用等);给予(注意等);进行等

e. g. We trust you will pay our draft on presentation. 我们相信你方在见到我们的汇票时即付款。

payment *n*. 支付、支付的款

e. g. We enclose a cheque for US $3665 in payment of all commissions due to you up to date. 兹附去3665美元汇票一张,付截至目前所欠贵方的全部佣金。

(2) standing *adj*. 持续的,长期有效的,永久的,固定的

standing charges 固定的费用

standing order 常年订单

standing permit 长期准许证

n. 地位,身份,名望;期间,持续

credit (financial, credit and financial) standing 资信情况

e. g. You may refer to our banker, the Bank of China in London for our financial and credit standing. 贵方可向我往来行伦敦中国银行查询有关我方资信情况。

(3) account *n*. 账目,账款,账户

for account of 为……,代……,受……委托

e. g. We hereby issue an irrevocable L/C in your favour for account of China Trading Co., Shanghai. 我们受上海的中国贸易公司委托,在此开立以您为受益人的不可撤销信用证。

for account of 由于,因为

to take... into account 考虑,重视

on one's own account 为自己的利益,自行负责

not on any account 无论如何不

e. g. Not on any account shall the safe be opened without my express orders. 没有我的明确指示,无论如何不能打开保险箱。

It is impossible for us to account for the delay. 我们无法解释耽误的原因。

Oil exports account for 30% of the total export bill. 石油出口额占出口总账单的30%。

(4) in agreement with 与……一致

e. g. The stipulations in the L/C are not in agreement with the contract. 信用证的规定与合同不一致。

agreement *n.* 协议书;协议

come to an agreement 达成协议

reach an agreement 达成协议

agree *v.* 同意

e. g. We regret cannot agree to your terms. 我们抱歉不能接受贵方的条款。

agree on *v.* 双方同意或商定

agree in *v.* 对某事有相同看法或取得一致意见

agreeable *adj.* 同意的,合意的

agreed *adj.* 双方商定的,互相同意的

e. g. The goods are not up to the agreed specifications and quality. 这批货未能达到双方商定的规格和质量。

(5) examine *vt.* 检查,调查;审查,审核考试;诊察;审问

vi. 检查;调查

e. g. The goods were carefully examined before shipment. 货物在装运前经过仔细检查。

The issuing bank shall have a reasonable time to examine the documents. 开证行应有一个合理的时间来审核单据。

I have given the matter much thought, examining all the possible alternatives... 这个问题我已经考虑了很多,分析了各种可能的选择。

The plans will be examined by EU environment ministers. 欧盟各国环境部部长将仔细研究这些计划。

examination *n.* 检查,审核

e. g. The proposal requires careful examination and consideration. 那项提议需要经过仔细研究和考虑。

4.6 Useful Sentences(常用语句)

(1) We'd like to see your annual report for the last three years. 我们想看看贵公司过去3年来的年度报告。

(2) As soon as these inquires have been satisfactorily settled, we shall be pleased to ship your order. 一旦这些资信调查获得令人满意的答复之后,兹乐意运送贵方订购的货品。

(3) Here's the financial report of our company. 这里是本公司的财务报告。

(4) These are the profit and loss figures. 这些是损益数目。

(5) For any information as to our credit standing, please refer to Bank of China, Beijing Branch. 有关我方信誉的任何资料,请向中国银行北京分行查询。

(6) Please be kind enough to obtain for us all information possible concerning the standing of the credit of Toyoda & Co. of Yokohama city? 恳请贵方尽量收集有关横滨市丰田公司的信用状况方面的材料。

(7) As we on the point of transaction some important business with them, we should like to know exactly how their credit stands. 因为本公司正要和该公司达成某项重要交易,所以希望准确地了解该公司的信用状况。

(8) I shall feel under great obligation if you will tell us something about the appraisement of the company among its neighbors and customers. 恳请惠予告之该公司的近邻与顾客对其的评价,本人将深表谢意。

(9) Any information you may give me will, of course, be treated as strictly confidential. 对于贵公司所提供的情报,无论内容如何,一定会严守秘密。

(10) It could give us great pleasure to be able to render you a similar service should opportunity occur. 以后如有机会,我们乐于为贵公司提供同样的服务。

(11) You would greatly oblige me by obtaining for me information as to the present financial position of the firm named on the attached slip. 如有幸由贵处得知附件中所提及的公司目前的财政状况,本公司将不胜感激。

(12) Smith & Co. of your city, desire to open an account with us, and have given us your name as a reference. 贵市史密斯公司希望与本公司开展交易,指定贵处为资信证明人。

(13) Toyota & Co. of Yokohama city, is desirous of entering into business relationship with us and has given us your esteemed address as reference. 本公司接到横滨市丰田公司来函,表示愿意与本公司建立贸易关系,并指定贵方为该公司信用证明人。

(14) Calcutta bankers advise that the company was originally established in 1947 by Mr. Charles E. Smith, to conduct a business in chemicals, cement, paper, milk-products, etc., as importers. 根据加尔各答银行通知,该公司是由查尔斯·E. 史密斯先生在 1947 年创立的,其主要业务为进口药品、水泥、纸张及乳制品等货物。

(15) In reply to your letter of April 3 we give you the following information you have asked for. 兹对贵方 4 月 3 日来信所问之事给予如下答复。

(16) They may be rated as an A-level company. 他们可以被评为一等公司。

(17) The company was established in 1948, and has supplied our firm with qualified goods for over 20 years. 该公司成立于 1948 年,供应我方品质优良的货物已经逾 20 年了。

(18) They have always provided complete satisfaction with in-time delivery, moderate prices and superior quality. 他们交货及时，所提供的货物价格适中，品质优良，始终令人满意。

(19) This is a strictly confidential response to a request made by the firm. 这是对该公司的要求严格保密的回函。

(20) We inform you that we can give nothing but favorable information about the firm in question. 我们只能告知您，该公司在各方面均博得好评。

(21) They command considerable funds and an unlimited credit, and the executives are thorough businessmen. 该公司资金雄厚，其信用可以说是“无限”，而其高级职员可谓精明强干。

(22) We learned that though they had not been long established, stood pretty well, but were not supposed to be rich. 该公司自创办至今虽然时间很短，但在商业界已有相当信用，然而仍不能算是富有的公司。

(23) We are informed, “The company is a newly-formed corporation, having been chartered in September of 1946 with an authorized capital of $50000 with only $500 recorded as having been paid in.” 据我们所得到的情报，“该公司为创立的新公司，1946 年 9 月创立时，其登记资本额为 5 万美元，但实际上缴纳金额总计仅为 500 美元而已。”

(24) We shall be pleased to render you any further services, and we ask you to consider this information as given in strict confidence. 今后如有吩咐，我们将乐于为您效劳，但请务必对本报告严守秘密。

(25) In reply to your inquiry of the June 1, we inform you that our business relationship with the firm have hitherto been most satisfactory. 贵方于 6 月 1 日发来的查询函收悉，本公司与该公司的交易关系到目前为止颇为满意。特此函复。

(26) The firm enjoys the fullest respect and unquestionable credit in the business world. 该公司在商业界颇受尊敬，信誉极高。

(27) Replying to your letter of July 10, we inform that we have no personal knowledge as to the standing of Yada & Co. of our city. 7 月 10 日您来函询问本市矢田公司的信用状况，对此我们也不太明了。

(28) We consider them good for business engagement up to an amount of 300000 pounds. 本行认为与他们进行金额 30 万英镑内的交易是稳妥的。

(29) For large transaction we suggest payment by sight L/C. 如果交易额更大，本行建议您以信用证付款方式与之成交。

(30) Of late, payment has been quite irregularly made, and more than one occasion we have had to press for them, but in vain. 最近，该公司付款相当不规律，我们不止一次进行催告，然而毫无结果。

4.7 Exercise(练习)

1. Multiple choice.

(1) We understand that you will treat this information as ________.

A. confidence B. confident C. confidential D. confidently

(2) Will you please inform us, ________, of the extent of their resources and also as to their reputation?

A. with confidence B. in confidence

C. as confidential D. of confidentially

(3) We ________ consider the said firm quite reliable for ________ engagement as you mention.

A. should/such an B. with/such as

C. shall/such a D. would/such like

(4) We should be grateful if you would say ________ they are likely ________ a credit up to US $10000.

A. what/to be reliable for B. if/to be reliable at

C. whether/to be reliable for D. that/to be reliable of

(5) Will you please let us know ________ your experience ________ in your dealing with him?

A. how/are B. what/has been C. which/is D. that/have had

(6) This firm is a ________ private company of import and export merchants, ________ in 1981.

A. high/registered B. height of/to register

C. highly/registered D. highest/to register

(7) We shall appreciate ________ us ________ an opinion as to the credit standing, respectability and responsibility of the following firm.

A. your providing/with B. provided/by

C. to provide/with D. your provision to/by

(8) Any information you kindly give us will be treated in strict confidence and ________ on your part.

A. without any responsibility B. hasn't any responsibility

C. is no responsibility D. is not to have responsibility

(9) For information ________ our ________ we refer you to Bank of China, Shanghai Branch.

A. regards/credit standing B. as to/standing credit

C. involving/credit standard D. concerning/credit standing

(10) We inform you that we can give nothing ________ favorable information about the firm in question.

A. at B. but C. from D. in

2. Put the following English phrases into Chinese or Chinese phrases into English.

(1) financial standing
(2) be in strict confidence
(3) delay payment
(4) trade reference
(5) small business engagement
(6) 经营方式
(7) 开立账户
(8) 私营公司
(9) 告知
(10) 追讨到期货款

3. Translate the following Chinese sentences into English using the words or phrases in the brackets, and translate the following English sentences into Chinese.

(1) 由于交易额不大,本公司无法提供有关其商务能力及信用状况的可靠意见。(credit standing)

(2) 该公司在本地极可信赖,信誉良好。(reliable)

(3) 大量订购可能将是一项严重的错误。(order)

(4) They have now a sound business standing with an excellent business turnover.

(5) We should be much obliged if you could give us some information on their financial standing and their way of doing business.

(6) However, this is our personal opinion and we assume no responsibility for your proposed business with them.

4. Translate the following letter into English.

(1)

敬启者:

如贵公司能告知我们有关贵市的华尔森琼斯纽约加索国际贸易有限公司的资信情况我们将不胜感激。据我所知,贵公司与该公司已有稳定的生意往来,故冒昧地寻求贵方对该公司资信情况的意见,以避免今后的麻烦。

对贵方所提供的一切情况,我方将不胜感激并严格保密,今后如需我方服务,我们将乐意回报类似服务。

期待回复。

谨上

(2)

敬启者:

我们刚刚完成您在4月4日信中所提到的公司的资信情况调查。

我们的调查未显示出这家公司是不诚实的。一年前这家公司受到了供货商偿还到期欠款的起诉,尽管欠款最终全额偿还。

在我们看来这家公司的困难是由于管理不善,尤其是超额贸易造成的。该公司大多供货商或者只给予有限数目的短期信用,或者通过付现形式交货。

以上信息需严加保密,本行对所提供信息不负任何责任。

谨上

Unit 5

Enquiries and Offers

询盘与发盘

5.1 Study Aim(学习目标)

(1) 掌握询盘与发盘函电中常用的词汇及表达方式。

(2) 掌握各类型询盘的写作技巧。

(3) 掌握各类发盘的写作技巧。

5.2 Introduction(专业背景知识介绍)

1. 询盘 (Enquiry)

(1) 询盘的含义

当业务关系建立后,交易一方往往会向另一方询问一些关于预订货物的细节问题,包括价格、样品、付款方式,运输条件等其他条款,通常我们把这种询问行为称作询盘(enquiry),又称为询价。

(2) 询盘的分类

按询问内容的不同,询盘可分为一般询盘(general enquiry)和具体询盘(specific enquiry)。一般询盘的内容包括要求报价,索取产品目录与样品。通常,一般询盘也是首次询盘(first enquiry)。具体询盘的内容则包括特定商品的各种交易条件的具体细节。一般性询盘属于了解摸底性质,而具体询盘则意味着询盘方已准备买卖,请另一方就特定商品报价。询盘不是每次交易的必需环节,如果交易双方彼此了解情况,则不必使用询盘。

(3) 询盘的发出方

在实际业务中,询盘一般由买方向卖方发出,但也有由卖方发出的询盘。买方询盘会向不同的国家、地区厂商发出,目的在于了解国际市场行情,以争取最佳贸易条件。卖方询盘一般在某商品市场处于动荡变化或市场上供求关系反常情况下出现,主要目的在于打探市场的虚实、主动寻找有利的交易条件、选择最佳交易时机。

(4) 询盘函电写作时应注意的问题

写作询盘函电时,应注意它的目的是询问了解。首先,在写作之前写作者必须明确到底想要了解什么信息。写作时把所需阐述得越具体越详细,越能够确保对方清楚明了地回复所有问题。其次,在写作询盘函电时,应尽量避免问及对方公司机密的信息。如果确有需要,也应在函电内说明询问的缘由。此外,也应注意防止在询盘函电中过早透露采购的数量、价格、折扣等信息,以防止被对方摸清底细,从而丧失在交易磋商中的有利地位。最后,如果是首次询盘,询盘方还应该在函电中作一个简略的自我介绍。这部分的内容已在第 3 章建立业务关系函中介绍过,在实际业务中,有把二者合而为一的做法。

另一方在收到询盘后,根据实际情况进行回复。对于询盘的回复分为肯定回复(favorable reply)和否定回复(unfavorable reply)。肯定回复称为发盘,如果由于货物紧缺、货物脱销等原因无法报盘,也应函电告之。

2. 发盘(Offer)

(1) 发盘的含义

发盘是指交易一方欲按一定交易条件(如价格、数量、规格型号、付款条件、交货期等)购买或出售某商品,而向另一方表示成交意愿的行为。非向一个或一个以上特定的人提出的建议,仅应视为邀请作出发盘,除非提出建议的人明确地表示相反的意向。这里请注意区分发盘与发盘邀请(invitation to offer),发盘邀请指一个建议不是向一个以上的特定的人提出,没有或内容不十分确定,或没有表明承诺将按发盘条件与对方订立合同,并受约束的意思。因此,发盘不仅是一种商业行为,而且是一种法律行为。构成发盘的条件一般有以下四个:①向一个以上的特定的人提出;②发盘的内容必须十分的确定;③表明按发盘条件与对方订立合同,并受约束的意思;④必须送达受盘人。

此外在实务中,quotation 也有"报价"的含义,应注意区分它与发盘的不同。报价(quotation)通常仅仅给出品名、规格以及价格三项信息,其他交易信息或条件没有发盘完整。

(2) 发盘的撤回与撤销

发盘的撤回(withdrawal of offer)指在发盘尚未生效前,发盘人采取某种行动阻止发盘生效。而发盘的撤销(revocation of offer)指在发盘已经生效后,发盘人采取某种方式解除发盘的效力。

此外,在贸易实务中还有以下三种情况造成发盘的失效或终止(termination of an offer):①发盘人在受盘人接受之前撤销该发盘。②发盘中规定的有效期届满。③其他方面的问题造成发盘失效,包括政府发布禁令或限制措施造成发盘失效。另外还包括发盘人死亡、法人破产等特殊情况。

(3) 发盘的分类

发盘既可以在对方询盘的要求下发出也可以在没有询盘的情况下发出,通常在贸易实务中,发盘多由卖方发出,由卖方发出的也被称为售货发盘(selling offer) 但买方亦可发出,由买方发出的叫购货发盘(buying offer)或者递盘(bid)。

发盘分为实盘(firm offer)和虚盘(non-firm offer)两种。实盘是发盘人(offerer)承诺在一定期限内受发盘内容的约束,非经接盘人(offeree)或受盘人同意不得撤回或对盘中任何条款进行修改变更。

一个完整的实盘应包括明确完整的交易条件,如:产品名称(product name)、数量

(quantity)、质量(quality)、支付方式(payment)、装运(shipment)、有效期(validity)等。实盘中不应有保留条款,如以货物的未售出为准(subject to goods being unsold)或以我方最后确认为准(subject to our final confirmation)。此外,写作实盘函时也应尽量避免使用模棱两可的表达。

虚盘是发盘人虽愿意按一定交易条件达成交易,但不作任何承诺,亦不受发盘内容的约束,它是一种有保留的意愿的表达。虚盘不需要像实盘那样有明确完整的交易条件,也不必标明有效期限。不像实盘内容会成为贸易合同的组成部分,并具有法律效力,虚盘仅仅是一种交易意愿的表达,不具有法律效力。

(4) 发盘函电写作时应注意的问题

写作发盘函电时,写作者应注意:第一,首先感谢对方的来信。第二,对询盘函电中的问题进行简洁准确的回答;如果所涉及的问题确实无法回复,应告之对方原因。第三,回复涉及货价、规格等具体内容应确保准确、清晰、完整。最后可在结尾处陈述市场现状,表明产品价格、质量等方面具有竞争力,敦请对方早日下订单。

5.3 Writing Skills(写作技巧)

一般询盘函电的写作步骤及常见表达方式如表 5-1 所示。

表 5-1 一般询盘函电的写作步骤及常见表达方式

写作步骤	表达方式
1. 说明信息来源(告知对方你从何种渠道得知对方公司的情况)	Your company has been kindly introduced/recommended/given to us by...贵公司由……介绍给我们。
	From...,we know/understand that your company specializes in...通过……(渠道)获悉贵公司专营……
	We learn from/We have heard from... that you are a leading ...in your country/...我们从……处了解到您是在贵国的……(行业)……主要的……
2. 对本公司作简单的介绍(首次询盘)	Our company is a...我们是……公司。
	We are a company dealing in...我公司主要经营……
	We are producers/importers/exporters... of... 我们是……(某领域/某类产品/……)的制造商/进口商/出口商。
3. 询盘:说明自己的需求,要求对方提供什么信息、服务	Would you please send us your...? 贵方能否惠寄……给我们?
	We have great interest in your...if you could send...we will appreciate it very much. 我们对贵公司的……很感兴趣,如能惠寄……将不胜感激。
	When replying, please state...回复时请说明……
	Please inform us...请告知我们……
	Kindly let us have...请回复我们……
4. 表达与对方合作及早日收到回复的愿望	Your immediate reply will be highly/greatly appreciated. 对您的回复我们不胜感激。
	We are looking forward to doing business with you. 期盼与您能建立贸易关系。

具体询盘的写作步骤就结构而言与一般询盘组成结构大体相同,但由于具体询盘涉

及询问具体信息或具体说明要对方做什么因此在函电的主体部分会进行更加具体的展开，如表 5-2 所示。

表 5-2 具体询盘函电的写作步骤及常见表达方式

写作步骤	表达方式
1. 说明信息来源（告知对方你从何种渠道得知对方公司的情况）	Your company has been kindly introduced/recommended/given to us by...贵公司由……介绍给我们。
	From...,we know/understand that your company specializes in...通过……（渠道）获悉贵公司专营……
	We learn from/We have heard from... that you are a leading ...in your country/...我们从……处了解到您是在贵国的……（行业）……主要的……
2. 对本公司作简单的介绍（首次询盘）	Our company is a...我们是……公司。
	We are a company dealing in...我公司主要经营……
	We are producers/importers/exporters... of... 我们是……（某领域/某类产品/……）的制造商/进口商/出口商。
3. 具体询盘：写作时尽可能详细清楚	Would you please send us your latest price-list/catalogue illustrate/... ? 能否将贵公司最新的价格表/带插图的目录单寄给我们？
	We would like to receive/have your samples? 我们希望能收到贵公司的样品。
	We request you to inform us of the detailed specifications, earliest date of delivery and terms of payment. 我们请求贵方告知具体规格、交货日期以及付款方式。
	If you can assure us of competitive/workable prices, we will send you an order. 如果贵方能保证一个有竞争力/可行的价格，我们将向贵方订货。
	Please inform us whether we can receive the goods before June. 请告知六月初前能否收到货物。
	If you have sufficient inventory and can deliver promptly, we are pleased to place a large order with you. 如有充足的存货且能及时交货，我们将大额订购此货物。
4. 表达与对方合作及早日收到回复的愿望	Your immediate reply will be highly/greatly appreciated. 对您的回复我们不胜感激。
	We are looking forward to doing business with you. 期盼能与您建立贸易关系。
	We appreciate your cooperation and look forward hearing from you as soon as possible. 对您的合作，我们不胜感激，期盼您的及时回复。
	We look forward to hearing from you by return. 望你方尽快回复。

在实务中对于询盘函电的回复是关系到公司业务的最关键环节，对每一项询盘函电的回复都应做到及时、专业、耐心且细致，这样能够为一笔成功的交易打下良好的基础，如表 5-3 所示。

表 5-3 询盘函电的回复的写作步骤及常见表达方式

写作步骤	表达方式
1. 感谢对方的询盘	Thank you/Many thanks for your letter of April 24th enquiring about our...感谢贵方 4 月 24 日关于我方……的询盘函。
	In reply to your enquiry of April 24th, we have great pleasure of offering you silk skirts as follows. 感谢贵方 4 月 24 日询盘，现报真丝裙盘如下。

续表

写作步骤	表达方式
1. 感谢对方的询盘	It is a pleasure for us to have/receive your letter of April 24th enquiring about.... 感谢贵方4月24日关于……的询盘函。
	We are pleased to note from your enquiry letter dated April 24th that you are interested in the Model. HQ5965 textile machinery. 收到贵方4月24日的询盘信函,得知贵方有意购买型号HQ5965纺织机械,我方十分高兴。
2. 购货发盘	We would like to purchase/buy... at ...US dollars per case CIF Wuhan. 我们想购买……,每箱CIF(到岸价)武汉……美元。
	We want to order/book 2000 silk skirts at the price reached last time for immediate shipment. 我们想按上次谈成的价格订购2000件真丝裙,立即装运。
3. 售货发盘	We can supply 1000 tons of copper at HK $67200 per ton FOB Hong Kong. 本公司可提供1000吨铜,每吨67200港元,FOB(离岸价)香港。
	This is our offer for 300 units of DVD player at the market price, to be shipped at the end of may. 这是本公司300台DVD播放器的发盘,5月底前交货。
4. 表明发盘的有效期限	This offer is open for ... days. 此发盘有效期为……天。
	The offer is valid/remains firm until...(date). 该发盘有效期至……(某月某日)。
	The offer holds good till ...(date) our time. 该报盘有效期至我地时间……(某月某日)。
5. 实盘	The offer is firm, subject to your reply/acceptance reaches us before ...(date)/reaching us by...(date). 我们发实盘,以……(某月某日)前答复到达我方为有效。
	We would like to make you a firm offer at this price. 我方愿意以此价格向贵方发实盘。
6. 虚盘	Without engagement. 不负任何责任。
	It is an offer without obligation. 此盘不负任何责任。
	Subject to goods being free. 以有货可供为条件。
	Subject to goods being unsold. 以货物未售为条件。
	Subject to prior sale. 以先售为条件。
	Subject to change without noticing. 如有变更,不另行通知。
	Our offer is subject to approval of ...(documents). 我方报价以……(某单证)有效为条件。
	Subject to our final confirmation. 以我方最终确认有效。
	This offer is good/valid/open 15 days. 此报盘15日内有效。
7. 希望对方满意回复或报价并希望尽快下订单	We look forward to receiving your order. If you have any queries, please do not hesitate to let us know. 我方期待收到你方的订单。如还有疑问,请随时与我方联系。
	As the orders and the cost of raw materials rise sharply, we hope you can take advantage of this attractive offer. 鉴于订单数量和原材料价格猛涨,我们希望贵方勿错失良机。

5.4 Specimen Letters(样函)

Letter 1:

Dear Sirs,

Your company has been kindly recommended to us by Messrs. Dawson & Sons. We understand that your company specializes in exporting home textile in your country. Since there seems to be a growing demand for high-quality bedding, we believe there is a promising market in our area for your goods.

We are large dealers of home textile in the United State, including bedding sets, duvet sets, pillows, cushion, mattresses, other d cor & sundry.

We would like you to send us your latest illustrated catalogues, price-lists, terms and conditions of sales, quote your lowest possible CIF Sacramento prices and state earliest shipping time. We can supply you with business and bank references.

We look forward to hearing from you.

Sincerely yours,

Notes(注释)

1. Messrs. *abbr.* 各位先生,用作 Mr. 的复数(源自法文 messieurs)

e. g. Messrs. Johnson, Wills and Hardy 约翰逊、威尔斯、哈代诸位先生

Messrs. Anderson & Bros. 安德逊兄弟公司各位先生

2. bedding *n.* 寝具;床上用品

e. g. two full sets of bedding 两整套床上用品

3. market *n.* 市场;行销地区;行情;需求

a ready market 畅销

a rising market 上涨的行情

e. g. Our country has a poor market for your goods. 我国对贵公司产品需求不大。

v. 出售;推销

短语:

in the market for 有意购买某物

on the market 待售;出售

a good/poor market 畅销/滞销

market price 市场价格;市值;时价

market share 市场占有率

4. dealer *n.* 商人;经销商

短语:

authorized dealer 授权经销商;认可交易商

franchised dealer 特许零售商;特约经销商

retail dealer 零售商

5. set *n.* 一组;一套;一副
bedding set 床上用品套件
短语:
a set of 一套;一组;一副
complete set 整套
6. duvet *n.* 羽绒被
cushion *n.* 垫子
mattress *n.* 床垫
décor *n.* 装饰;装饰物
sundry *n.* 杂货;杂项
短语:
sundry goods [贸易]杂货
daily-use sundry goods 日用杂货
7. illustrated *adj.* 有插图的 *n.* 画报,画刊,有插图的报刊
8. terms and conditions of sales 销售条款和规定
业务中常见的短语还有:
usual terms 惯常条款
price terms 价格条款;价格术语
trade Terms 贸易术语
credit terms 信用证条款
implied terms 默认条款

Letter 2:

Dear Sirs,

Thank you for your enquiry and we are pleased to send off our latest sales catalogues for the complete range of home textile products as per your request.

We are sending you separately a copy of our latest price list giving CIF Sacramento prices. The immediate shipment could be made upon receipt of a firm order.

We look forward to receiving your order. If you have any questions please let us know.

Sincerely yours,

Notes(注释)

1. send off (短语) 寄出或发出某物
e. g. We have sent the samples off. 样品已寄出。
2. range *n.* 成套或成系列的东西;种类;限度;范围
a range of 一系列;一套
a full range of sales literature 全套促销资料
3. as per [书面语、商业用语] 按照,根据
as per = as according to

e. g. We will arrange the delivery time as per your instruction. 我们将按你方指示安排交货时间。

4. separately *adv.* 分别地;个别地

e. g. You can keep one copy of the contract separately as a backup. 您可以单独留存一份合同副本作为备份。

under separate cover = by separate letter 另邮

5. receipt *n.* 收到;收据;收入

upon/on receipt of 一收到……, 收到……后

e. g. Upon receipt of your letter, we have send you the samples by airmail. 收到贵方来函后,我们马上将样品以航空邮件形式寄出。

receipt (of sth.) (正式)收到

acknowledge receipt of an order 签收订单

receipt (for sth.) 收据

e. g. sign a receipt for your expense 在你的开销收据上签字

(be) in receipt of sth. [商业用语] 已收到某物

e. g. We are in receipt of your letter of the May 11. 我们已收到您 5 月 11 日的来函。

短语:

bank receipt 银行水单;银行收据

warehouse receipt 仓单

cargo receipt 承运货运收据

return receipt 回执

trust receipt 信托收据

place of receipt 收货地;收货地点

6. firm *adj.* 坚定的;结实的;牢固的;

firm quotation 实价

firm market 行情坚挺的市场

n. 公司;商行

e. g. This firm need a manager assistant. 这家公司需要一名经理助理。

Letter 3:

Dear Sir or Madam,

When we attended the 113th Canton Fair last month, we visited your stand and deeply impressed by the novel design and excellently tailored woolen garments. We want to introduce your products into our market; therefore, we would like to know the styles that are now available for both men and women.

We are important dealers in ready-to-wear clothes and have been in this business for more than 20 years.

If you could send us your latest catalogues, your terms and conditions of sales and your lowest quotation, we think it would be helpful for to place the order.

For any information as to our credit standing, please refer to Bank of China, Guangzhou Branch. Your immediate reply will be highly appreciated.

Sincerely yours,

Notes(注释)

1. Canton Fair 广交会;广州交易会

2. stand *n*. (用于陈列、展览、宣传等目的的)摊位;展位;(置物的)架、坐台

a stand at the book fair 书展中的一个展位

v. 站立;位于;忍受;抵抗

3. novel *adj*. 新的;新奇、新颖的

a novel fashion 新的风尚

n. 小说

4. garment *n*. 衣服;覆盖

短语:

garment industry 成衣业;制衣业

garment factory 制衣厂

fur garment 毛皮服装

5. available *adj*. 便于利用的;可获得的,可得到的

e.g. We will inform you as soon as the goods are available. 一有货物我们会马上通知您。

available funds 可用基金;可动用的资金

6. ready-to-wear *adj*. 做好的;立即可穿的;现成的 *n*. 成衣

Letter 4:

Dear Sir or Madam,

Thank you for your letter of July 30th enquiring for our woolen garments for both men and women. Attached are the latest illustrated catalogues and price-lists. All the quotations are on the term of CIF Guangzhou in RMB.

Payment : by 100% irrevocable L/C at sight. Shipment will be effected within 15 days after receipt of the relevant L/C.

We are looking forward to receiving your first order.

Sincerely yours,

Notes(注释)

1. attach *v*. 某物系在、缚在或附在(另一物)上

Attached are the latest... 一句中 Attached... = Attached to this letter, ……随信附上……

e.g. a document attached to a letter 随函附寄一份文件

attached please find[书信英语] 随信附上……请查收

e.g. Attached please find information. 请查收附件资料。

2. irrevocable *adj.* 不能改变的;不能撤回的;不能取消的;最后确定性的

L/C = letter of credit 信用证

3. effect *n.* 效应;结果;后果 *v.* 产生效果;达到目的

e. g. Insurance is to be effected by the buyer. 由买方投保

The contract will take effect beginning from December 12th. 本合同从 12 月 12 日起生效。

The main idea of our client's E-mail is to the effect that they want to place further and larger order with you. 我方客户的电子邮件的主要意思是加大订货量。

短语:

come into effect (尤指法律、规则等)实行,实施

take effect 实施;实行;起作用

to the effect 大意是;带有那个意思

in effect 实际上;生效

put into effect 执行

have effect on 生效;对……有作用;对……有效果;见效

Letter 5:

Dear Sir or Madam,

Thank you for your reply of March 20. After reading through your catalogues, the practical design and the superb workmanship impressed us. Before placing the order with you we would like to enquire further information for the trading.

If you could send us the detailed specifications and your lowest quotations for the items, we will greatly appreciate your cooperation. If the quality of the goods can meet our expectation and the prices are acceptable, we can place an order with you immediately.

As to our credit standing, please refer to Citibank, Toronto Downtown Branch. We are looking forward to receiving your immediate reply.

Sincerely yours,

Notes(注释)

1. practical *adj.* 实用的,务实的

2. superb *adj.* 极好的;卓越的;杰出的

e. g. The quality is superb. 品质一流。

3. workmanship *n.* 手艺;技艺;工作质量;工艺

superior/poor workmanship 精湛的/拙劣的工艺

4. specification *n.* [尤作复数]规格;规格说明;详述

product specification 产品规格

specification sheet 规格单

performance specification 性能说明

5. item *n.* 条款;项目;一则;(在外贸函电中常用来指价格单或商品目录中的)商品

item number 产品编号;品目号

6. Citibank *n.* 花旗银行

Letter 6:

Dear Sirs,

We are glad to acknowledge the receipt of your letter for various types of mountain bicycles dated March 29 with thanks. In response, we offer firm, subject to your reply reaching us by or before April 30. We are pleased to quote as follows:

Felt Speed 1 2010 Mountain Bike	at US $640 per unit
Passion 9.8 Mountain Bike	at US $700 per unit
Megafly 74-7 Elite	at US $510 per unit
Remedy 9.9	at US $890 per unit

All prices FOB Vancouver.

T/T Payment before shipment.

If you order the goods in a large scale, we can offer you 5% discount off net price. Would you place your order at your earliest convenience?

Sincerely yours,

Notes(注释)

1. acknowledge *v.* 告知已收到(某物);承认(某事物)属实;供认;为(某事物)表示感谢

acknowledge (receipt of) a letter 告知已收到一封信

acknowledge inform 对告知表示感谢

短语:

acknowledge receipt 证实收到……

acknowledge receipt of 收到……

acknowledge orders 接受订单

2. unit *n.* (量词)台;架

3. T/T = Telegraphic Transfer 电汇

4. scale *n.* 规模;比例

e.g. If the quality of your goods can meet our requirements and the price is reasonable we would place the order on a large scale. 若贵方货物质量符合我方要求且价格合理,我方会大规模订购。

5. net price 净价,指不包括折扣,不包含任何方面的佣金或回佣的价格,在实务中也指剔除附加费用后的实际价格

e.g. This is the net price without commission. 这是净价,不含佣金。

6. convenience *n.* 方便;便利

短语:

at one's convenience 在某人方便时

for convenience 为方便起见

Letter 7:

Dear Sir or Madam,

Your enquiry about our men's jacket of January 29 has received our immediate attention. In response, we would like to offer 700 pieces men's Jacket style No. d617s694 at US $25 per piece CIF New York. Delivery will be within two weeks of receipt of your order. This offer is given without engagement. We believe its design will appeal to your market.

This is the best offer we can make. As you may aware that we are receiving a lots of orders, the large demand for above commodity will result in price increasing. Therefore, we would recommend you place the order immediately.

Sincerely yours,

Notes(注释)

1. response *v*. 回复

response to sb./sth. =as an answer to 回答;答复

e.g. In response to your enquiry, we send you this form 兹复您的询盘,我们向您发送此表格。

2. delivery *n*. 交付(货物、信件等);递送,投递

e.g. Please pay on delivery. 请交货时付款。

短语:

delivery address 交货地址

delivery date 交货日期

delivery time 交货时间

delivery of goods 商品的交付

delivery order, D/O 提货单

delivery term 交货条款

prompt delivery 即期交货

express delivery 快递,限时专送

3. engagement *n*. 约定;诺言

e.g. We remind you that the above offer is without engagement. 我们想提醒您,以上报价无约束力。

The offer is made without engagement and all orders will be subject to our written acceptance. 此报盘为虚盘,所有订单需以我方书面接受为准。

短语:

be under an engagement (to) 有约

break an engagement 违约

enter into an engagement with 同……订约

make an engagement with 同……订约

meet one's engagements 履行(契约等)义务；偿还债务

4. appeal to (词组)对……有吸引力;恳请呼吁

e. g. We think the excellent quality and reasonable price will appeal very much to your clients. 我们相信优良的品质和公道的价格会对您的客户有很大的吸引力。

5. best offer 最低报价,最优惠报价

6. aware *adj.* 意识到的;知道的;有……方面知识的;懂世故的

aware that…; aware of sb./sth. 对某人/某事物知道、明白;察觉到、意识到

e. g. We are well aware that on-time delivery will be pressed for time. 我们都很清楚按时交货时间紧迫。

7. demand *n. & v.* 要求;请求;需要

demand (for sth./sb.)需求,需要

e. g. We blames poor overseas demand for the car's failure. 我们将汽车滞销归咎于海外需求量太低。

短语:

market demand 市场需求

supply and demand 供应与需求

meet the demand 满足需要,满足要求;符合要求

in demand 受欢迎的;非常需要的;销路好;有需要

in great demand 需要量很大

strong demand 强烈要求;殷切需求

on demand 见票即付;即期

Letter 8:

Dear Sir or Madam,

Thank you for your order for 4000 units Model NST-395 microwave oven dated June 14. We regret to inform you that our present stock for this commodity is not sufficient.

In view of our longstanding cooperation we want to recommend an excellent substitute Model CXY-484. Its quality is as good as Model NST-395, but 10% lower in price. Besides, it has already found a market in your area.

We would appreciate your prompt reply.

Sincerely yours,

Notes(注释)

1. sufficient *adj.* 充足的;充分的

e. g. We would like to know if you have sufficient stocks to meet our demand? 我方想知道贵方有足够的存货满足我方的需求吗?

2. in view of (词组)鉴于;由于;考虑到

e. g. In view of the earthquake, we regret being unable to deliver the goods on time. 由于地震,很遗憾我们无法按时交货。

3. longstanding *adj*. 长时间的;长期存在的

e. g. I sincerely hope that this will mark the beginning of longstanding business cooperation between us. 我真诚地希望这标志着我们之间长期稳定的商业合作的开始。

4. substitute *n*. 代替者;代用品

e. g. We think this model of computer is a poor substitute for that one. 我们认为用这款电脑来代替那款十分勉强。

v. 用……代替;取代

take/accept A as a substitute for B 用 A 来替代 B

e. g. In this recipe, some people accept honey as a substitute for sugar. 一些人用蜂蜜来替代这个菜谱里的糖。

substitute A for B; substitute B by/with A 以 A 替代 B

e. g. Without our approval, you cannot substitute margarine for cream. 除非我方许可,你方不可以用人造黄油替代奶油。

Enclosed please find an amended order substitute for the previous one. 随附一份已修改的订单以替代之前那一份。

Letter 9:

Dear Mr. Cleveland,

We acknowledge the receipt of your letter of the 11th inst. with thanks. We are sorry to say that we are unable to offer you the concerning the security system of our security doors. In fact, such information is kept by most of our competitors as highly confidential.

We sincerely hope that this will not bring you inconvenience anyway. If there is any other way to help you please let us know. Again, sorry for the inconvenience we may cause.

Sincerely yours,

Notes(注释)

1. inst. (abbr.) = instant (商) 本月

e. g. your letter of the 11th inst 您本月 11 日的信

在商务函电里,还有其他一些缩写也能够表示时间,例如:

ult. = ultimo 上个月

e. g. We beg to acknowledge receipt of your letter dated 21st ult. 兹确认收到贵方上月 21 日来函。

prox. = proximo 下个月

e. g. The goods will be dispatched on 17th prox. 货物下月 17 日发出。

2. concerning *prep*. = about; regarding 关于; 就……而言

e. g. For more information concerning this product please consult our sales manager Mr. Henry Douglas. 关于此款产品的更多信息请咨询我们的销售经理亨利·道格拉斯先生。

3. security *n*. 安全;防护;抵押品;(常以复数形式)证券

give sth. as a security 以某物作抵押

e. g. National banks can package their own mortgages and underwrite them as securities. 国家银行能够合并自己的抵押贷款并以证券形式包销。

4. competitor *n*. 竞争者;对手;敌手

e. g. Our firm has better products than its competitors. 我们公司的产品比其对手的好。

competitive *adj*. 竞争的,有竞争力的

e. g. We believe our quotations are competitive. 我们相信我们的报价是有竞争力的。

compete *v*. 竞争

e. g. Several companies are competing to gain the contract. 几家公司正为争取一份合约而竞争。

competition *n*. 竞争

e. g. Competition should beat the price down. 竞争一定会使价格下跌。

intense/fierce competition 激烈的竞争

5. confidential *adj*. 秘密的,机密的

e. g. All the detailed information in your offer will be strictly confidential. 您发盘函中的所有信息细节都会被严格保密。

短语:

private and confidential 机密并亲启

6. anyway *adv*. 无论如何;即使如此

any way (词组) 任何方法,任何方式

Letter 10:

Dear Sir or Madam,

We are Naughty Island, a trading company and wholesaler of children's wear in China. We want to establish business relation with you and import your BB Cat Series Boy's T-shirt urgently.

Please send us your rock bottom prices CIF Shanghai for the whole collection. We shall appreciate your prompt reply.

Sincerely yours,

Notes(注释)

1. wholesaler *n*. 批发商

e. g. We are the largest wholesaler of auto diagnostic tools in Louisiana. 我们是路易斯安那州最大的汽车检测工具批发商。

wholesale *n*. & *adj*. & *v*. 批发;成批卖出

2. children's wear 童装

wear *n*. 穿戴的衣物

ladies' wear/menswear/underwear/sportswear/casual wear 女装/男装/内衣/运动服装/便装

3. import *v*. 进口;输入;引进

e. g. We would like to import raw silk from this Chinese company. 我们希望能从这家中国公司进口生丝。

n. 进口;输入;引进

e. g. The British Government has imposed strict reins on the import of meat products. 英国政府对肉类制品设置了严格的控制手段。

短语:

import agent 进口代理商

import duty 进口税

import declaration 进口报单;进口声明书

import license 进口许可证;进口执照

import permit 进口护照;进口准许证

import substitution 进口替代

import tax 进口税

4. series *n*. (单复数同形)一系列的事物

a series of movies 一系列电影

5. urgently *adv*. 紧急地

短语:

be urgently in need of 是迫切需要的

be needed urgently 被迫切需要的

be urgently required 急需

urgent *adj*. 紧急的

6. rock bottom price (or rock-bottom price) 最低的价格

rock-bottom *adj*. 最低的

Letter 11:

Dear Sirs,

We received your letter dated March 15th and thank you for your enquiry for our BB Cat Series of Boy's Wear.

As inner land of China is one of our most important potential markets, and in order to open the market there, we prefer to give you a special offer. CIF Shanghai US $12 per piece, and we give 5 percent discount for cash.

At the most competitive price we offer, we hope to receive your order soon. If you have any question, please feel free to contact us.

Sincerely yours,

Notes(注释)

1. potential *adj*. 潜在的,有潜力的;可能的

e. g. We believe this product will help us to find many potential clients. 我们坚信这款产品会使我们获得许多潜在的客户。

n. 可能性;潜力

2. open the market 打开市场;打开销路

open *v*. 开张,营业

e. g. We want to open the new company overseas. 我们想在海外开新公司。

3. a special offer 特别优惠价

4. cash *n*. 现金,现款

e. g. Which payment do you prefer by cash or by check? 您愿意哪种付款方式,现金还是支票?

5. contact *v*. 联系;接触

e. g. We contacted with our manufacturer as soon as we received your order. 一接到贵方订单,我们马上就与制造厂商取得了联系。

短语:

contact with 接触

in contact with 与……有联系

contact information 联系方式

contact person 联系人

5.5 Focal Words(焦点词汇及短语)

(1) offer

① *n*. 发盘,报盘

Would you please make/give/send us an offer for Harry Potter Series Boy's T-shirts? 请您就哈利波特系列男童T恤给我方作报价?

I am writing for confirming if you have got our offer for stainless knife dated inst 4th. 此次来函我想确认我方于本月4日关于不锈钢道具的发盘贵方是否收到。

Please make us a cable/fax offer. 请来电报/传真报盘。

The official offer will reach you before next Friday. 正式报盘将会在下周五前到达贵方。

You will enjoy the preference of our offer. 我们会优先向您报盘的。

The lump offer means you have to accept all or none. 综合发盘意味着要不全部接受,要不全部不接受。

相关衍生词汇:

offeror 发盘人;报价人;要约人

offeree 被发盘人;受盘人;受要约人

实际业务中常用的短语:

combined offer 搭配发盘

firm offer 实盘

lump offer 综合报盘(针对两种以上的商品)

non-firm offer 虚盘
an official offer 正式报价(发盘)
the package offer 一揽子发盘
offer letter 报价书
offer list/book 报价单
offer sheet 出售货物单
to accept an offer 接受发盘
to alter an offer 变更发盘
to cable an offer 电报(进行)报价
to confirm an offer 确认发盘
to decline/turn down an offer 拒绝发盘
to entertain an offer 考虑发盘
to extent offer 延长发盘
to fax an offer 传真(进行)报价
to forward an offer 向……提出发盘
to get an offer(or to obtain an offer) 获得……发盘
to give an offer 给……发盘
to improve an offer 更改发盘
to make/send an offer by post 通过邮寄形式发盘
to renew an offer 重新报盘
to repeat an offer 重复报盘
to send an offer 给……寄送发盘
to submit an offer 提交发盘
to withdraw/cancel offer 撤回发盘

② *n.* 提议,建议

e. g. In the light of the community remarks, the officer turned down my offer. 有鉴于社区的评价,那位警官回绝了我的提议。

③ *v.* 发盘,报价

e. g. We offer you firm FOB Genoa for 40 sets of 980mm × 466mm Book Packing Machine Types SI-6. 我方向贵方报 40 台 980mm × 466mm 规格书本装订机型号 SI-6 实盘,FOB 热那亚价。

Please offer us 500 cases of Maotai Wine FOB Copenhagen. 请报 500 箱茅台酒 FOB 哥本哈根价。

④ *v.* 提供机会;给予

e. g. The cooperation with Agilent Technology will offer us an opportunity to open the oversea market. 与安捷伦科技公司的合作将为我们提供一个开拓海外市场的机会。

实际业务中常用的短语:

offer to buy 认购,要约买入

offer to sell 销货要约

(2) quote

① *v*. 报(价),开(价)

e. g. The first class Chinese Tea is currently being quoted at US $3.5 per can. 一等品中国茶叶现在报价每罐 3.5 美元。

That's the best price we can quote you. 这是我们能给您报的最优惠的价格了。

In early trading in Hong Kong yesterday, gold was quoted at US $1320.21 an ounce. 在香港昨天早些时候的交易中,黄金的牌价为每盎司 1320.21 美元。

We can quote you a price lower than the international market price. 我方能够向您报比国际市场价更低的价格。

We have great interests in your product for summer promotion. Would you please quote us as soon as possible? 我们对您的夏季促销产品十分感兴趣。贵方能否尽快向我们报价?

Your enquiry is vague and it is difficult to quote without full details. 您的询盘太模糊,没有关于细节的说明,我方很难报价。

② *v*. 提到

e. g. Please quote this reference number when reordering stock. 再次订货的时候请贵方提供这个编号。

③ *v*. 引用

e. g. She is quoted as saying she disagrees with the decision. 用她的话说,她不同意这一决定。

(3) quotation

① *n*. 估价,报价

e. g. What was today's market quotation on wheat? 今天小麦的市场报价如何?

The insurance company requires three quotations for repairs to the car. 保险公司要三份修理这辆汽车的报价单。

We would like to have you lowest quotation CFR Dar-es-salaam. 我们想请您报贵方 CFR 呃斯萨拉姆价。

② *n*. 行情,牌价

e. g. I advise you should better not enter the market hastily seeks the counter potential quotation. 我建议你最好不要仓促入市博取逆势行情。

(4) enquiry

① *n*. 询问;询盘

e. g. If you have any further requirements please do not hesitate to send us your specific enquiry. 如果贵方还有进一步的要求请给我寄送您的具体询盘。

In answer your recent enquiry, the goods you mention are not available. 您近日询问的货物现在暂时无货,谨此奉复。

Nowadays, more and more companies use a printed enquiry form instead of a letter. 现

在,越来越多的公司用打印好的询盘表来替代询盘信函。

② *n.* 调查

e. g. After the death of a small child the public called for a major enquiry. 在一名幼童死亡后公众要求进行大范围的调查。

实际业务中常用的短语:

to make an enquiry 发出询盘;向……询价

enquiry sheet 询价单

specific enquiry 具体询盘

an occasional enquiry 偶尔询盘

enquirer *n.* 询价者

v. 询盘;询价;询购

e. g. A representative of the Finland company enquired about our mohair sweaters. 那家芬兰公司的一名代表前来询问我们的马海毛毛衣。

If you have any enquire about our product, please feel free to contact with us. 如果您想咨询购买我公司的产品,敬请随时与我们联系。

We would like you to enquire into Smith & Nolting Associates financial standing on our behalf. 我们想请贵方代表我们对史密斯与诺尔汀联合公司的财政状况进行查询。

v. 询问;打听

e. g. We would like to enquire about your company's detailed address. 我们想询问贵公司的具体地址。

实际业务中常用的短语:

to enquire about 对……询价

to enquire into 对……询问

(5) stock

① *n.* 存货;现货

e. g. We are sorry to inform you that this type of personal computer is out of stock. 我们很遗憾地通知您,此款个人电脑没有存货。

We want to sell out our summer stock at price lower than the market price, please do not miss this opportunity. 我们会以低于市场价的价格处理夏令存货,请勿失良机。

② *n.* 股票,证券;股份

e. g. The Hills family holds more than 50% of the stock in this company. 在这家公司里希尔斯家族持有超过 50% 的股份。

Changes in the stock market is highly unpredictable. 股市的变化难以预计。

实际业务中常用的短语:

supply ... from stock 供……现货

e. g. Your order can be supplied from stock. 您的订单可以从仓库中提取。

have ... in stock 有……现货

e. g. The store has many patterns of children's shoes in stock. 这家商店有多款童鞋

现货。

out of stock 脱销

e. g. This item is out of stock, we are waiting for replacement. 此款产品已脱销,我们正在等待新货。

(6) subject to...

① *adj.* 易受……的,使遭……的

e. g. Public transportations are subject to delays after the heavy storms. 大暴雨后公共交通往往会延迟。

② *adj.* 以某事物为条件;取决于某事物

e. g. The final delivery date is subject to contract signed by both sides. 最终的装运日期取决于双方所签订的合同。

All technical parameter are for reference only and subject to changes without prior notice. 以上所有技术参数仅供参考,并按需要时更改,恕不作任何形式的通知。

③ *adv.* 在……条件下,以……为条件,只要(和介词 to 连用引导状语短语)

e. g. We offer 5000 pieces Cotton pillowcases at EUR 3 per piece CIF Rotterdam, this offer subjects to first available steamer. 兹报盘 5000 件棉枕套, 每件 3 欧元 CIF 鹿特丹价, 以装第一艘轮船为准。

We take great pleasure in offering the under-mentioned goods, subject to import license. 我们很乐意就下列商品进行报价,以获得出进口许可证为准。

(7) subject *n.* 主题;对象

e. g. While on the subject of agency, we would ask you to give us an approximate estimate of the volume of business you expect to do annually. 在谈代理问题时,请告知你们预期每年可成的交易额的大概数额。

5.6 Exercise(练习)

1. Multiple choice.

(1) Which of the following shows the most responsibility of the seller? ________

A. EXW　B. FOB　C. CIF　D. CFR

(2) ________, we have sent our latest illustrated catalogues and price-lists.

A. For you requested　B. As your request

C. At your request　D. As requested

(3) We are now ________ receipt of your enquiry for our Chinese Black Tea dated January 17th .

A. in　B. in the　C. on　D. on the

(4) Which of the following offer is a firm offer? ________

A. This offer is to be firm for two weeks.

B. This offer will remain effective for 3 days.

C. We offer GBP 110 per set for your air conditioner Model UHI367. As you are our regular customer, other conditions are same as usual.

D. Subject to goods being unsold we will make you our offer as follow.

(5) We make ________ to your letter of August 13th.

A. thanks B. acknowledge

C. acknowledgement D. confirmation

(6) Through the courtesy of Mr. Jonathon, we have known that your company is one of the ________ importers of agricultural goods in your area.

A. leaden B. lead C. leading D. chief

(7) Under some circumstances, the lapsed offer is no longer binding on the offeror. Which of the following is not mentioned in the Convention? ________

A. The time validity stipulated in the offer becomes due.

B. Special events occur such as legal person's bankruptcy.

C. An offer terminates owing to force majeure.

D. The offeror revokes the offer at random.

(8) Your great help in this respect will be highly ________.

A. thanked B. grateful C. appreciated D. appreciating

(9) According to different criteria, offers can be classified in to various kind. If an offer is made by a buyer, we should call it as a ________.

A. firm offer B. non-firm offer C. selling offer D. buying offer

(10) Which of the following statement is a false one? ________

A. An offer may be revoked if the revocation reaches the offeree before he has dispatched an acceptance.

B. If an offer does not stipulate the validity time, the offeree can make acceptance at any time, and the acceptance is effective.

C. It is reasonable for the offeree to conceive the offer irrevocable the offeree has taken actions in reliance on the offer.

D. According to the Convention, an offer can be withdrawn if the withdrawal reaches the offeree before or at the same time with the offer, even if it is irrevocable.

2. Put the following English phrases into Chinese or Chinese phrases into English.

(1) 贸易及银行资信材料

(2) 发盘的撤销

(3) 本月 15 日

(4) 广州交易会

(5) 销售条款

(6) CIF

(7) give sb. a quotation for sth.

(8) credit standing

(9) rock-bottom price

(10) termination of an offer

3. Translate the following Chinese sentences into English using the words or phrases in the brackets, and translate the following English sentences into Chinese.

(1) 按照贵方要求,我们报 50 台空调的实盘如下,以自本日起 15 日内贵方复到为准。(as …request)

(2) 随函寄去我们最新的带插图目录表和报价,此报价的有效期仅为 7 天。(subject to…)

(3) 一收到贵方的具体询盘,我们将立即向您报出低于国际市场价的亚洲主要港口到岸价。(on/upon receipt of…)

(4) We received your enquiry letter of the April 6th for our oranges, and we take pleasure in sending you the following offer for your consideration.

(5) In reply to your letter of September 2nd, we are now sending off the samples by airmail.

(6) This offer is firm, subject to your immediate reply reaching us before the end of this month and that there is little likelihood of the goods remaining unsold once this particular offer has lapsed.

4. Translate the following letter into English.

信函一:

敬启者:

当参加 2012 年度莫斯科国际汽车配件、售后服务及设备展览会(Automechanika Moscow & MIMS 2012)时我们参观了您的展台。贵方的汽车真空吸尘器给我们留下了深刻的印象。贵方专业的真空吸尘器能够轻松地清除车垫(carpet)的深层(deep-down)污垢,我们相信这一产品会在中国畅销。

我们是一家专营洗车的公司,在过去的 13 年里我们在全国主要城市里创立了超过 300 家的洗车连锁店。目前我们已经建立起大量牢固的业务关系,并且在行业内享有盛名。

请惠寄贵方汽车吸尘器的最新产品目录表、出口价目表以及销售条款。我方的信用状况请咨询中国银行北京分行。

希望此信能给双方带来长期有益的业务关系并盼答复。

谨上

信函二：

尊敬的亨利·沃特斯先生：

我们已经收到了贵方7月4日的来函，对您的询盘我方深表感谢。7月4日来函中您询问我方能否提供5000台SGR-95型号洗衣机。十分遗憾地告知您此型号洗衣机已脱销。

鉴于我们双方长期的合作关系，我们特向您推荐另一款型号TU-28洗衣机。这款洗衣机性能更佳且价格更优惠。此外，这款洗衣机在贵方市场受到热捧，享有一定市场。如果您的订单数额超过十万欧元我们还能给您提供九折的优惠。

此款洗衣机我们的存货充足，一旦订货能够按你方要求立即交货。我们希望能收到您的订单。

谨上

Unit 6

Counter-offers and Acceptance

还盘与接受

6.1 Study Aim(学习目标)

(1) 掌握还盘的技巧。

(2) 掌握还盘函、接收函及其回复的写作技巧。

(3) 掌握还盘与接收函电中常用的词汇及表达方式。

6.2 Introduction(专业背景知识介绍)

1. 还盘(counter-offer)

(1) 还盘的含义

受盘人或受盘人(offeree)在接到发盘后并不会随便地接受发盘内容,如果受盘人不满意发盘中的某一或某些交易条件,或是认为其中某些条款与他所预期的有出入,他就可能拒绝原发盘进而提出修改或变更意见,这种表示被称为还盘(counter-offer),也称为还价。还盘既可以用书面形式,也可以用口头形式表达。在贸易磋商过程中,贸易一方在发盘中提出的条件很少出现一发盘,就被对方无条件全部接受的情况。虽然从理论上来说还盘不像询盘,是交易磋商的必经环节,但在贸易实务中,还盘的情况是经常出现的。

涵盖商品的价格、结算方式、包装、交货日期、运输方式、保险等方面。还盘时一般只需针对原发盘中的不同意或需要修改的部分,同意的部分在还盘时可以省略不提。接到还盘后原发盘方应该与原发盘进行认真核对,找出还盘中的新内容,结合市场行情和本公司的销售意图认真对待和考虑。

(2) 还盘的法律效力

还盘在法律上被称为反要约,它被视为由受盘人向发盘人提出的一个新的发盘。原发盘人成为新盘的受盘人,因为受盘人对原发盘拒绝,原发盘因为受盘人还盘而失效,原发盘人也不再受到原发盘的约束。

(3) 反还盘(counter-counter-offer)

当原发盘人收到还盘后,不接受部分或全部新发盘的贸易条件、要求,提出自己的新意见,即是对还盘的还盘,被称为反还盘(counter-counter-offer)。国际贸易中一项交易在成交前可能会经过多次的还盘与反还盘。

2. 接受（acceptance）

（1）接受的含义

在发盘的有效期内，受盘人无条件同意发盘中所列的所有贸易条件，并愿意按这些条件与对方达成交易、订立合同的一种表示。接受与发盘一样，它既是一种商业行为，也是一种法律行为。接受在法律上称为“承诺”，接受一经送达发盘人合同便宣告成立。发盘人与受盘人应该履行合同所规定的义务并享受相应的权利。接受是交易磋商过程中的最后一个环节，也是磋商必经的一个环节。此外还应注意，在接受的函电中，如果双方的交易条件比较简单，则不必复述全部；相反，则应在接受时复述全部交易条件，避免造成疏漏或误解。

（2）构成有效接受的条件

① 接受必须由受盘人发出，如果第三方通过某种途径了解到发盘的内容，向发盘人做出的接受不能被视为接受，而只能算是一项新的发盘。

② 必须以声明或其他行为来表示，缄默或不行动不等于接受。比较常见的习惯做法有：卖方开始生产货物、卖方开始备货、卖方发运货物、买方支付货款等。

③ 接受必须在发盘规定的有效期内送达发盘人。

④ 接受的内容必须与发盘相符。

（3）逾期接受（late acceptance）

接受的通知若超过发盘规定的有效期，或发盘为规定有效期而超过了合理期限才送达发盘人，就构成逾期接受。在一般情况下逾期接受被视为一项新的发盘。但有时为了有利于双方合同的处理，“联合国国际货物销售合同公约”做出一些特殊情况规定，使得逾期接受在符合这些特殊情况时，也具有接受效力。

（4）接受的撤回（withdrawal of acceptance）

在接受送达发盘人之前，如果受盘人撤回接受，则撤回的通知必须在该项接受送达发盘人之前或与它同时送达到发盘人，该项接受才可以撤回。

按照英美法系国家的“投邮原则”，接受一经投邮立即生效且合同成立，因此，在英美法系法律条款中不存在接受的撤回问题。

6.3 Writing Skills（写作技巧）

接到还盘函电后收信方应该迅速地做出回复，一方面应该把想要达成的交易条件准确表达，另一方面也要注意措辞上的礼貌与客气。还盘函电的写作步骤及常见表达方式如表 6-1 所示。

表 6-1　还盘函电的写作步骤及常见表达方式

写 作 步 骤	表 达 方 式
1. 确认收到对方的报盘并表示感谢	Thank you for your letter of June 1 for Men's leather jackets. 感谢贵方 6 月 1 日关于男式皮夹克的发盘。
	We acknowledge with thanks the receipt of your quotation of April 3 and the samples you enclosed. 很荣幸收到你方 4 月 3 日发来的报价以及随信附寄的样品。
	In reply to your detailed quotation dated November 13,…回复你方 11 月 13 日的详细报价,……
2. 对不能接受报盘表示歉意	We regret to say that we could not accept the price you quoted. 很遗憾我们无法接受贵方的报价。
	Regretfully, we find out that your price is too high. 很遗憾,我方觉得贵方价格太高。
	However, we are sorry to note you that at this price we cannot place the order. 然而我们很遗憾地告知您此价格我方无法下订单。
3. 说明无法接受的原因并提出希望达成的交易条件	The old mode of packing you offer could not meet our clients' need. 贵方提供的旧的包装方式无法满足我方客户的要求。
	May we request you to shift the delivery time from "in March" to "in February" because of something unexpected? 由于意外情况的发生,我们可否要求装运期由 3 月份提前到 2 月份?
	We would like to ask for a 5% reduction in price because our order is an exceptional one. 由于我们的订购量特别大,因此我们想争取一个 5% 的折扣。
	We have considered your proposal to pay by confirmed, irrevocable letter of credit. It will cost us large amounts of money, could you offer us an easier payment terms. 我方已经考虑你方提议以保兑的、不可撤销的信用证来支付。这种支付方式会使我们花费巨大,可否报更宽松的付款方式?
4. 希望对方能够接受还盘所提出的交易条件,希望有机会促成交易	In light of our long and mutual relationship, we wish you will put our suggestion into serious consideration. 鉴于我们长久互惠的合作关系,希望贵方能够认真考虑我方的建议。
	We look forward to receiving your prompt reply. 期待你方能尽快回复。

接受函电的写作步骤及常见表达方式如表 6-2 所示。

表 6-2　接受函电的写作步骤及常见表达方式

写 作 步 骤	表 达 方 式
1. 确认收到对方的报盘并表示感谢	Thank you for your counter-offer of March 12 for Women's leather shoes. 感谢贵方 3 月 12 日关于女式皮鞋的还盘。
	We acknowledge with thanks the receipt of your counter-offer of July 17. 很荣幸收到你方 7 月 17 日发来的还盘。
	We are in receipt of your letter of August 21 for 5000 pieces cotton pillowcase. 我们已经收到贵方 8 月 21 日关于 5000 件纯棉枕套的还盘函。

续表

写作步骤	表达方式
2. 表示接受还盘,可以对还盘中的具体内容复述避免误解或疏漏	We are pleased to inform you that we accept your counter-offer. 我们很高兴地告知贵方我们接受贵方的还盘。
	Many thanks for your prompt reply of April 12. We accept your request to shift the delivery time from "in September" to "in August". 感谢贵方4月12日的回复。我们接受贵方的关于从"9月"提前到"8月"的交运时间要求。
	We confirm that, as requested in your letter, the goods will be packed in one bag of 5 kilograms net each, two bags to a carton. 我方确认贵方来函中的要求:所有商品每5千克装一袋,每两袋装一箱。
3. 表达希望能够早日收到订单或订立合同	We take pleasure in concluding this contract with you. We hope we can have many future orders from you. 我们很高兴与贵方订立本次合同。希望以后能够有更多生意上的合作。
	We look forward to receiving your formal order by return. 期待贵方能尽快以正式订单回复。

6.4 Specimen Letters(样函)

Letter 1:

Dear Sir or Madam,

We acknowledge your letter concerning the offer for 10000 square meters latex coated glass cloth. We regret to inform you that the price you quoted gives a big pressure on our company.

Goods of similar quality which are sold at the prevailing market level are cheaper than yours. Accepting your present quotation means to lose the market shares, let alone makes profits. We would like to place an order with you if you can make a 10% reduction in price.

Please kindly inform us of your decision as soon as possible.

Yours faithfully,

Notes(注释)

1. latex *n*. 乳胶

2. coat *v*. 为……加上、覆盖上一层东西

e. g. The table coated with dust. 桌子上覆盖了一层灰。

3. regret *n*. 遗憾、痛惜;失望

e. g. We feel regret about a missed opportunity to establish business relationship with you. 对于错失了与你方建立业务关系的良机,我们深表遗憾。

Please accept our regrets that we must refuse. 有拂雅意,深以为憾。

v. 感到后悔、抱歉

e. g. We regret that we cannot accept your request. 很遗憾我们不能接受你方的要求。

regretful *adj*. 抱歉的，遗憾的

e. g. It is regretful that we can not reach consensus in dealing conditions and dates. 很遗憾我们双方在交易条件和时间上不能达成一致。

regrettable *adj*. 令人痛惜的，令人遗憾的

regrettably *adv*. 十分遗憾，遗憾的是

e. g. Regrettably, the negotiation ended in failure. 很遗憾，谈判以失败告终。

4. prevailing market level 当前市场行情、价格水平

prevailing *adj*. 盛行很广的，普遍的，流行的

prevailing rate 先行汇率

prevailing price 现价

5. share *n*. 股份，份额

e. g. Mr. Alex Stuartholds 50000 shares in a shipping company. 亚历克斯·斯图尔特先生持有某航运公司 50000 股股份。

share index 股票指数

6. let alone 不必考虑；更不用说

e. g. We have not decided on the item, let alone placed the order. 我们还没有选定商品，更不要说下订单了。

7. reduction *n*. 减缩之量，(尤指)减去的价格

e. g. Can you make reductions on the following articles? 贵方能否对下列商品减价？

Letter 2:

Dear Sirs or Madams,

Thank you for your letter of March 29. We are sorry to know that you find our price too high and out of line with the prevailing market level. However, we do our best to keep the price as low as possible without sacrificing quality. As the price of the raw material is higher than before; we feel sorry that it is impossible for us to grant your request.

We believe that our cordial relationship will continue in spite of this loss of business. Hope that we will have other opportunities to cooperate in the near future.

Yours faithfully,

Notes(注释)

1. out of line 不协调，不一致

e. g. Our quotations are out of line with those of our competitors. 我方的价格与竞争对手的相差悬殊。

line *n*. 商品(项目)；行业；(一类)货色

e. g. We have been engaged in the banking line for over a hundred years. 我们从事银行类业务已经超过百年了。

2. sacrifice *v*. 牺牲；亏本卖出

e. g. It is wrong to sacrifice quality to low price. 牺牲质量去追求低价是错误的。

n. 牺牲

e. g. He will sell his shares at a sacrifice because his fund is tight now. 因为他最近资金紧张,他将亏本出售他的股票。

3. raw *adj*. 生的,未加工的

chemical raw material 化工原料

raw product 初级产品

4. grant *v*. 同意给予,允许(所求)

e. g. The bank refused to grant them long-term credits. 银行拒绝给他们长期信贷。

5. request *n*. 要求

e. g. Catalogues are available on request. 备有商品目录以供索取。

v. 请求

e. g. We just request compliance with the rules. 我方仅要求遵守规则。

短语:

transportation request 运输申请

pending request 等待请求

capital appropriation request 资本划拨请求

special request 特别要求

6. cordial *adj*. 诚恳的,热诚的,友好的,衷心的

e. g. They gave a cordial welcome to their business partners. 他们给商业伙伴一个热诚的欢迎。

7. loss *n*. 损失;丧失;失败

e. g. The loss of this contract would be very serious. 未能签成这一合同关系重大。

His company made a loss on the deal. 他的公司这笔交易赔了钱。

We suffer losses in the export market. 我公司在出口市场中亏损。

loss-leader [商](为招揽顾客)亏本出售的商品

短语:

gross loss 亏损总额

exchange loss 汇兑损失

capital loss 资本亏损

profit and loss (财年)盈亏账面

Letter 3:

Dear Sir or Madam,

Thank you for your letter of March 15 asking for the confirmation of payment terms. In view of the harsher economic climate and the prevailing high interest rates, we prefer to ask for an easier payment terms. What's more, as our funds being tied up in numerous commitments, we propose cash against documents on arrival of goods at destination.

We hope this suggestion will meet your approval and look forward to receive your earliest reply.

Yours faithfully,

Notes(注释)

1. confirmation *n.* 证实;批准;肯定;加强巩固;确认书

e. g. We are waiting for confirmation of our proposal. 我们在等待建议是否被确认。

短语:

bank confirmation 银行询证函

booking confirmation 订舱确认

delivery confirmation 发货确认,妥投确认

sales confirmation 售货确认书

purchase confirmation 购买确认书

order confirmation 订单确认,订货确认

confirmation letter 确认信函,询证信函

written confirmation 书面证明

confirmation in writing 以书面形式确认

2. harsh *adj.* 严酷的;严厉的;苛刻的

e. g. We could not accept these harsh terms. 我们无法接受这些苛刻的条件。

3. interest *n.* 利息;兴趣;利益;[商] 股权

e. g. You have to pay interest on the capital sum. 您必须支付此笔资金的利息。

These influential interest groups influence the government's actions. 有影响力的共同利益集团影响着政府采取的措施。

His family has many business interests in Singapore. 他的家族在新加坡有许多公司股权。

短语:

accrued interest [会] 应计利息

beneficial interest 收益权

controlling interest 控股(多数)股权,控股权益

compound interest 复利

interest income 利息收益

interest expense 利息支出

4. rate *n.* 率,比率

类似表达:

exchange rate 汇率

discount rate 贴现率

tax rate 税率

5. fund *n.* (复数形式 funds) 资金;基金;现款

e. g. He is short of funds, he could afford such luxurious car. 他手头缺钱,他不可能负担得起这么豪华的汽车。

短语:

accumulation fund 公积金

capital fund 资本基金
exchange fund 外汇基金
bond fund 债券基金
open-end fund 开放型基金
housing fund 住房公积金
investment fund [经]投资基金
trust fund 信托基金
International Monetary Fund (IMF) 国际货币基金组织

6. be tied up 被占用,将(资金)用于投资致使难以动用

e.g. Most of his money was tied up in property. 他的大部分钱都投资在房地产上无法动用。

The buyer's capital will be tied up from the time of remitting it until the goods arrive and are sold. 从汇款时起直到货物到达并销售完毕,买方资金一直会被占用。

7. commitment *n.* 承担;保证;投身的事

e.g. Owing to heavy commitments, we are not in a position to accept new orders. 由于承约太多,我方现在无法在接受新的订单。

短语:

commitment fee 承担费,承诺费
firm commitment 包销
loan commitment 贷款承诺
commitment letter 承诺函

8. propose *v.* 建议,提议

e.g. We propose issuing a time draft for EUR €350000. 我方建议开具价值35万欧元的远期汇票。

9. approval *n.* 批准;认可;赞成

e.g. The deal had the tacit approval of the General Manager. 这笔交易得到了总经理的默许。

The new business proposals have won the approval of a famous adventure capitalist. 这些新的商业企划书得到了一位有名的分析投资家的认可。

短语:

examination and approval 审查准许
final approval 最后核准
official approval 正式批准;官方批准
on approval 试销
unanimous approval 一致通过
approval procedure 审核手续;批准程序
approval documents 批准文件

Letter 4:

Dear Sir or Madam,

We have received your letter of January 30. We feel regretful that our price for 5000 sets of Iris color TV is too high for you to work on. In your letter you mentioned that some of your clients "feel worried" that accepting the quotation would only leave them with "a small margin" of profit on their sales.

We accept what you say, but we do our best to keep the price as low as possible without sacrificing quality. We regret that we could not accept your counter-offer.

The best we can do is to give you a 3% discount if you can place order of more than 8000 sets.

It is our sincere hope that this deal will be successful.

Yours faithfully,

Notes(注释)

1. client *n*. 客户;委托人;顾客

e. g. Heavy reliance on one client is risky when you are building up a business. 在创业时期,过分依赖某一个客户是有风险的。

2. margin *n*. 余地;保证金;[商]盈利,利润

e. g. This is a business operating on small/tight margins. 这项生意的利润不大。

The lower the costs required generating a dollar of revenue, the higher the profit margin. 产生一美元收入所需要的成本越低,利润边际就越高。

短语:

margin of profit/profit-margin 利润率

margin trading 保证金交易(交存一定金额的保证金不支付全部货款的交易)

margin requirement 法定保证金

gross margin 毛利

interest margin 利息差幅

3. profit *n*. 利益;利润;好处

e. g. We will make a profit of one pound on every set we sell. 我们每卖出一台获利一英镑。

The company gained a fat profit in the property market. 这家公司在房地产市场里获利丰厚。

短语:

average profit 平均利润

net profit 净利润

gross profit 毛利;总利润

profit and loss 损益

profit sharing 分红制

profit from... 得益于……

profit by... 得益于; 从……中吸取教训

4. discount *n.* 折扣;[商]折息贴现

v. 打折;将(票据)贴现

e. g. Usually, we only discount acceptance trade and commercial bills. 通常,我们只贴现已承兑的商业票据。

As you place an initial order, we can extend to you a special discount of 4%. 鉴于您是首次订购,我方可以给您一个 4% 的折扣。

All the bills that are paid promptly will be discounted at 3%. 对所有即付的账单都将给予 3% 的折扣。

The rate was discounted at 3% a year. 利率以每年 3% 进行贴现。

短语:

discount house 贴现公司;贴现银行

discount shop 折扣店

Letter 5:

Dear Sir or Madam,

Thank you for your letter of July 4 for discussing the shipment of 10000 porcelain tea sets.

You suggested that the goods are simply packed as your usual practice in the 5-layer corrugated cartons. In view of the fragile of the goods, taking good care of well packing is of great importance for reducing the losses in transporting. We insist that all the goods should first be packed in bubble bags separately, and then packed them in strong wooden cases bedded with foamed plastic for protection for being broken.

We hope our request will meet with your arrangement and look forward to your early reply.

Yours faithfully,

Notes(注释)

1. shipment *n.* 装船,装运;装载的货物

e. g. When the goods are ready for shipment, please fax us as soon as possible. 当货物已备好准备装船时,请及早以传真方式告知我方。

We are sorry to inform you that this shipment was not up to our standard. 很遗憾地通知您这批货物达不到我方的标准。

短语:

advance shipment 提前装船

advice of shipment 装船通知;装运通知

date of shipment 装船日期

immediate shipment 立即装船

partial shipment 分批装运
prompt shipment 即期装船
shipment date 装船日期;装运期
2. porcelain *n.* 瓷,瓷器
3. practice *n.* 惯例,常规
e. g. It is accepted practice to pay a deposit with one's order. 在预订时交付订金是一般遵守的惯例。
It is the international practice for a bank to confirm an irrevocable L/C. 国际惯例是银行可以保兑不可撤销的信用证。
4. corrugated *adj.* 有瓦楞的,波纹的
e. g. corrugated board 瓦楞纸板
corrugated paper 瓦楞纸
5. carton *n.* 纸板箱
e. g. We asked for a carton of 200 cigarettes, with 10 packets of 20. 我方要求一条香烟共 10 包,每包 20 支,200 支为一纸箱。
6. fragile *adj.* 易碎的;不强健的
a fragile economy 疲软的经济
e. g. The fragile goods could not survive from the bumpy journey. 易碎商品无法经受这种颠簸的行程。
7. separately *adv.* 分别地;分开地
e. g. Can the engine and the gearbox be supplied separately? 发动机和变速箱能够分开供应吗?
Corporation's earnings are accumulated separately from its paid-in equity capital. 股份有限公司的盈利是在其缴入的业主权资本之外单独累积的。
8. bed *v.* 使某物固定或安置稳固;嵌入某物中
e. g. The bricks are bedded in the concrete. 用混凝土砌砖。

Letter 6:

Dear Mr. Cedric Smith,

We acknowledge receipt of your letter dated August 10 and have pleasure in informing you that we accept all the terms but shipment.

It was stipulated the shipment is to be made in October. October is the busiest season for us; the earlier shipment can help us to catch it. Such being the case, may we suggest that you shift the shipment from "in October" to "in September".

We shall appreciate it very much if you will make a concession and telex us your acceptance as soon as possible.

Yours faithfully,

Notes(注释)

1. stipulate *v.* 规定,讲明
e. g. It was stipulated that the goods should be delivered within 50 days after the

confirmation of the contract by both sides. 按照规定货物须在合同经双方确认后 50 日内送交。

stipulation *n.* 契约;合同;规定

e. g. On the stipulation that all the goods should be packed in strict accordance with our instruction. 按规定,所有货物必须严格按照我方的指示包装。

2. season *n.* (一年中有某事物或有关活动的)时期、时候;旺季;季,季节

e. g. In the off season, it is irrational to raise the price. 在淡季,涨价行为是不理智的。

短语:

busy season/peak season 旺季

low season/off season 淡季

regular season 赛季

in season 应时的,在旺季;当令

out of season 不当令;不在旺季

3. such being the case(词组)在这种情况下;情况既然如此

e. g. Such being the case, we have no reason to continue the negotiation. 情况既然如此,我们没有必要再继续谈判下去了。

4. shift *v.* =(from...to...)移动;改变;转变

e. g. The wind shifted from east to north. 风向由东风转变为北风。

5. concession *n.* 让步,妥协;(对某类人的)减价;特许权

e. g. We have already made a great concession to the matter. 我方在这个问题上已经做出了很大的让步。

Concession means a grant by a public authority to a person of authority to do something. 特许权是指由政府机构授予个人从事某种事务的权利。

Free trade and the tariff concession become the trend of international trade. 自由贸易和关税减让已经成为国际贸易的发展趋势。

短语:

tax concession 赋税减免

make concession 让步

concession term 特许期

concession bill 特许权法案

6. telex *v.* &*n.* 电传

e. g. We used to dispatch telex to shipper and consignee to inform them the change of shipment date. 我们通常是以电传形式通知寄货人或取货人装运日期的更改。

tested telex 加押电传

Letter 7:

Dear Madame Anne Cecilienhof,

Thank you for your letter of August 13 asking for a change in shipment.

It is our usual practice to ship the goods as per the stipulation, no matter the order is large-sized or small-sized. As direct steamers to your port are few and far between, we have been informed that there is no available space on ships sailing from here to your port before September 20. If you insist in an earlier shipment, we can only make a partial shipment of 100 long tons polished rice in September and the balance of 100 long tons in October.

Our accommodation in this respect should not set a precedent for future transaction. Please fax us your decision as soon as possible.

Yours faithfully,

Notes(注释)

1. steamer *n.* 轮船

e. g. When does your steamer sail? 贵方的轮船什么时候起航?

vessel、liner、ship、steamer、tramper 都有“船”的意思,下面我们进行同义词区分。

vessel 一般是指运送旅客和货物的远洋大船,或在海上充当工作基地的船。

liner 是指定期定航线的货船也被称作“班轮”,在国际贸易中比较常见。

e. g. Freight forwarders are mainly concerned with liner freight rates. 货运代理人关注的主要是班轮的运价。

ship 是指航海的大船,通常是以机器为动力的。在国际贸易中一般习惯与 steamer 连用。

e. g. The cargo ex S. S. (steamer ship) “Victoria” have been inspected. 由“维多利亚”号货轮卸下的货物已经验收。

steamer 早期是指由蒸汽驱动的船只,现在指一般的船只,在国际贸易里多指货轮。

tramper 是指不定期货船,即海运经营者根据海运需求的时间、地点和内容等所发生的变化,而不断变更航线和货种的一种不规则运输方式。

2. few and far between (词组) 稀少的,不多;不经常发生

e. g. Good jobs are few and far between on the market these days. 近来提供的好工作实在是太少了。

3. partial *adj.* 部分的,不完全的;

partial loss 部分损失

partial payment 分批付款

4. long ton 英吨,长吨 1 long ton =1.016 ton

short ton 美吨,短吨 1 sh. ton =0.907 ton

5. polish *v.* 磨光;擦亮

polished *adj.* 磨光的,擦亮的

6. accommodation *n.* 调解;和解;通融,调整

e. g. The two sides failed to agree on every point but came to an accommodation. 双方并非在每一点上意见都一致,但已经达成和解。

7. precedent *n.* 先例、事件等

e. g. There is no precedent for such an action. 这种行为没有先例可循。

短语：

have no precedent to go by 无先例可循

set/create a precedent for... 为……开先例

8. transaction *n*. 交易；业务

e. g. Payments by check easily outnumber cash transaction. 用支票付款在数量上大大超过现金交易。

In view of our longstanding business relationship, we can conclude the transaction. 鉴于你我双方的长期贸易关系，我们可以达成这笔交易。

短语：

credit transaction 信贷交易

exchange transaction 外汇交易

spot transaction 现货交易

futures transaction 期货交易

transaction tax 交易税

Letter 8：

Dear Sir or Madam,

We acknowledge with thanks the receipt of your offer, of ladies knitting clothes, dated October 17. We agree all the proposals except the minimum quantity we have to take.

For a trial order, 10000 suits are too much. In case you can reduce the minimum quantity to 7000 suits, there is a possibility of placing order with you.

We are looking forward to receiving you earliest reply.

Yours faithfully,

Notes（注释）

1. knitting *n*. 编织，针织

knitting machine 编织机

knitting needles 编织针

2. proposal *n*. 建议，提议

e. g. Various proposals were put forward for increasing sales. 为提高销售额而提出了各种建议。

In the meeting, the proposal to give a discount to regular customers was disapproved strongly by the chairman. 在会上，对老主顾予以折扣优惠的建议遭到主席强烈的反对。

短语：

proposal for something/doing something 提案，建议

proposal to do something 计划；方案

3. minimum *adj*. 最小的，最少的　*n*. 最小量，最低限度

e. g. Your CPF savings earn a minimum risk-free interest of 2% guaranteed by the government. 您公积金储蓄的2%最低风险收入是由政府进行担保的。

This price is our minimum, we could not lower it any further. 这已经是我们的最低价格了,我们无法再做任何降价。

短语:

minimum lending rate (央行某时期贷款的)最低利率

minimum wage (法定) 最低工资

minimum requirements 最低要求

minimum rate 起码运费

Letter 9:

Dear Sir or Madam,

We are in receipt of your counter-offer of January 17, which we herewith acknowledge with best thanks. We are pleased to inform you that we accept your counter-offer for 1000 metric tons northeast China soybean. We have specially accepted your counter-offer simply because we wish to make this as the forerunner of many future orders from you.

We hope we can conclude a prolonged contract before long and await your prompt reply.

Yours faithfully,

Notes(注释)

1. herewith *adv.* 随同此信(书、文件)

e. g. Thank you for your application we have received today. Please fill the form enclosed herewith. 我们已收到您的申请函,十分感谢。请填写随函附上的表格。

We enclose herewith our latest illustrated catalogues. 我们随信附上最新的带插图的目录表。

2. metric ton 公吨

metric *adj.* 公制的

metric system 公制;十进制

metric unit 公制单位

3. forerunner *n.* 先驱;先兆

4. conclude *v.* 达成;决定;缔结(条约等)

e. g. Once the price had been agreed, a deal was quickly concluded. 一旦价格商定了,交易很快就达成了。

conclude a contract 订立合同

conclusion *n.* 商定

e. g. All of us look forward to the conclusion of this business. 我们所有人都盼望这笔生意能最终商定。

在国际贸易中表示"达成交易"的表达还有:

close a deal/transaction

put through the business/transaction

Business is done.

finalize a deal/transaction

materialize business

5. prolonged *adj*. 持续长久的

prolong *v*. 延长;使……持续久

e. g. The two companies prolonged signing an contract until all details could be agreed on. 两家公司推迟了合同的签约,直到就所有细节达成协议。

6. contract *n*. 合同;契约

e. g. You should not enter into a contract until you have studied its provisions carefully. 在您签合同之前,您应该先仔细研究合同的条款。

We have a contract with the ABC Company for the supply of 5000 pieces cotton bed-sheets. 我们已经与 ABC 公司订有一份提供 5000 件棉质床单的合同。

He has agreed all the terms and conditions of sale and is ready to sign a contract. 他同意了所有的销售条款和规定,准备签订合同。

contract *v*. 与某人签订合同或契约;缩减

e. g. Having contracted with them to supply vehicles, we cannot withdraw now. 我们与他们订有提供车辆的合同,现在不能撤销。

Our business has contracted a lot recently. 我们的生意近来大幅减少。

contractor *n*. 订约者;(尤指建筑工程的)承包商

短语:

sales contract 销售合同

purchase contract 购货合同

contract note 成交单据

contract price 合约价格;发包价格

contract terms 合同条款

7. before long (词组)不久以后;很快

e. g. He prepares to close out his business affairs before long. 他准备不久之后结束自己的业务。

8. await *v*. 期待;等待;等候

e. g. We shall await your answer to our enquiry with eagerness. 我们急盼贵方对我方询盘的回复。

Letter 10:

Dear Mr. Gordon Marshall,

We write to confirm your prompt reply of November 21 to our enquiry for Hero pens. We find that the quality of the products is satisfactory. We are impressed with their excellent workmanship.

We enclosed our official order for 150 cases Hero pens. And we know you can supply them from your stock. Our order is placed on the following terms and conditions:

As you request, we pay by confirmed, irrevocable L/C. The goods should be shipped within one month after receipt of the L/C. Pens should be packed 12 pieces to a box and 100 boxes to a wooden case.

We take pleasure in concluding this contract with you. We hope we can have many future orders from you.

Yours faithfully,

Notes(注释)

1. satisfactory *adj*. 符合要求的,满意的

e. g. The arrangements, if mot ideal, are fairly satisfactory. 安排虽不算理想,但也相当令人满意。

2. impress *v*. 给予某人深刻印象

e. g. It is vital to impress the consumer with fashionable design. 至关重要的是要以时尚的设计给消费者留下深刻的印象。

短语:

impress something on 留下印记、印象

impress upon sb. 使某人铭记某事物

3. official *adj*. 正式的,官方的

e. g. an official receipt 正式收据

an official statement 正式声明

Letter 11:

Dear Sir or Madam,

We confirm having received your order of May 11 for 2000 metric tons corn protein powder. In compliance with your kindly request, we are making a final confirmation as follows:

We accept your quotation for 2000 metric tons corn protein powder of 2013, EUR 650 per metric ton, CFRC5 Rotterdam. The article will be packed in single gunny bags, 100 kilograms per bag, gross for net. The payment is to be made by T/T. 60% before delivery, 40% after we fax the copy of B/L. The shipment will be effected by the end of May.

As this is the first deal we have, your cooperation would be highly appreciated.

Yours faithfully,

Notes(注释)

1. compliance *n*. 遵从;听从;服从;顺从

in compliance with *phr*. 按照

e. g. In compliance with your request, we have withdrawn our order. 遵照您的要求,我方已经撤销了订单。

2. article *n*. 商品、货物,是商业领域的常用语,多用单数形式,尤指某种具体商品

e. g. When you are in a position to supply this article, please let us know. 当贵方能够提供此项商品时,请及时告知我们。

3. gunny *n.* 粗麻布;黄麻布

4. gross for net(词组) 以毛作净,指在国际贸易中按照毛重计算重量来作为计价的基础,货物的包装重量和价值不再另计。

gross *adj.* 总共的,毛的,全体的

gross amount 总额;总量

gross expenses 总开支

gross loss 总损失;毛损

net *adj.* 净的,纯的

net profit 净利润

net sale 经销售额(指扣除销货折扣和退货后的净额)

net value 净值

net weight 净重

5. B/L = Bill of Loading 提单

6. effect *n.* 效应,结果

v. 使产生,使发生,引起

e. g. The contract will come into effect upon signature. 此项合同在签字后生效。

We usually effect insurance for 110% of the invoice value. 我们通常按照发票金额的110%来投保。

短语:

bring/put something into effect 使某物开始使用

in effect 事实上,实际上;实行,起作用

take effect 生效;产生预期的结果

to the effect that 意思是,大意是说

Letter 12:

Dear Sir or Madam,

We wish to refer to the telegrams exchanged between us in recent three weeks. We hereby confirm having placed with you an order for 2000 pieces blue raincoat for schoolboy, Model RU4964.

Commodity: blue raincoat

Price: US $5.5 per piece CIF New York

Quantity: 2000 pieces

Packing: in cartons

Insurance: to be covered by the seller for 110% of the invoice value against All Risk

Shipment: sailing direct to port of destination

Payment: payable by confirmed irrevocable Letter of Credit.

We hope that from now on we shall enjoy a business relationship profitable to both of us.

Enclosed you can find our official order No. 9865.

Sincerely yours,

Notes(注释)

1. refer to (词组)谈及,接洽
2. hereby *adv*. 以此方式;据此;特此
3. invoice *n*. 发票

6.5 Focal Words(焦点词汇及短语)

(1) acceptance *n*. 接受,答应,同意,认可;(商)承兑,认付(票据)

e.g. Please confirm your acceptance of this offer in writing. 请您以书面的形式确认贵方接受此项报盘。

Their acceptance of the contract is still in doubt. 他们是否接受这项合同还说不准。

The offer is subject to your acceptance reaching us before September 3rd. 此项报盘以贵公司的接受于9月3日之前到达本公司为准。

Our acceptance will hinge upon the terms. 我方是否接受还需依照条件而定。

An acceptance once given cannot be revoked unless the offeror consents. 除非要约人同意,否则承诺一经做出即不得撤回。

All credits must stipulate an expiry date for presentation of documents for payment, acceptance or negotiation. 一切信用证均需要规定一个交单付款、承兑或议付的到期日。

The receipt shall specify the date of presentment for acceptance and shall be signed. 回单上应该记明汇票提示承兑的日期,并签字盖章。

Bankers' acceptance is a bank's commitment to pay a stipulated amount of money on a specific future date under specified conditions. 银行承兑汇票是由承兑行保证按规定在指定未来某日期无条件支付一定金额给收款人或持票人的票据。

v. 接受, 同意,认可;承兑(票据)

e.g. I am sorry to inform you that we cannot accept your quotations. 很遗憾地通知您,贵方的报价我们无法接受。

If you do not accept the above terms and conditions of sale, please do not bid. 如果不能接受以上的销售条款,请勿竞价。

Much to our regret, we cannot accept payment by D/A. 非常遗憾,我方无法接受承兑交单的付款方式。

Our bank will accept the bill of exchange. 我方银行将会承兑汇票。

acceptable *adj*. 可接受的,可容忍的

e.g. We find that the terms of this contract are acceptable. 我们认为这个合同的条款都是可以接受的。

In the negotiation, they agreed to water down their original stiff demand to one acceptable to both sides. 在谈判中,他们同意把原来的强硬要求降低到双方都可以接受的范围。

(2) deal *n*. 协议,(尤指)交易(等同于 transaction)

e. g. The deal had the tacit approval of the General Manager. 这笔交易得到了总经理的默许。

Suppose this is an export deal and we have bought ex-works and sold CIF. 假设这是一笔出口贸易,我们按工厂交货价买进再以到岸价格卖出。

Before we left Shanghai, we closed a deal and realized a large profit on it. 在我们离开上海前,我们做出了一笔生意并且大赚了一笔。

The deal fell through. 交易告吹。

v. 交易;经营

常用的搭配:

deal in 经营(一般指具体的商品)

e. g. We deal in light industrial goods. 我们主要经营轻工业产品。

deal with 处理,与某人有商业、社交等关系

e. g. I do not like to deal with large impersonal companies. 我不喜欢与那些没有人情味的大公司打交道。

dealing *n*. (与某人)有关系(尤指在商业上)

e. g. We have had no previous dealings with this company. 我们以前和这家公司没有商业往来。

dealer *n*. 商人

dealer、trader、merchant 这三个词都有“商人”的意思,在国际贸易中 trader 一般指从事国际贸易的公司。

e. g. This company is an international trader in ore. 这家公司是从事国际矿石贸易的公司。

merchant 一词指大批量出售某种进口商品的商人。

e. g. He traded as a timber merchant. 他是做木材生意的商人。

dealer 一般指专门出售某类商品,并对之有专业知识的商人。

e. g. He is a dealer in second-hand cars. 他以经营二手汽车为业。

(3) discount *n*. 折扣,从某物的价格中扣去的数目

e. g. We can extend to you a special first order discount 3%. 鉴于您是第一次订货,我们可以给您一个特别优惠——给您 3% 的折扣。

The rate of discount in London now is 4%. 现在伦敦的贴现率是 4%。

If you can meet our minimum quantity requirement—to place an order of 1000 metric tons, we will give you trade discount. 如果贵方能够达到我方最小起订量 1000 吨,我们就同意给您折扣。

Please put us on your very best shipping terms as regard discount. 请告知我们最好的装船条件,作为折让。

v. 打折;贴现

e. g. We do not discount at all. 我们的商品一概不打折。

You can either hold it to maturity or discount it with the negotiation bank. 您可以保留它直到到期，也可以向议付行进行贴现。

试比较下列一组近义词。

discount 作名词时有折扣的含义，指卖方在原有价格基础上给买方的一定比例的优惠、减让。给商品打折的做法既可以保持商品的价位，又可以通过提供给买家一定的优惠来进行促销。在国际贸易实务中折扣的表达见下面的例子。

CNY ¥5300 per Metric ton FOB3.5% Guangzhou FOB 广州价每公吨人民币5300 元，折扣 3.5% 。

rebate 作名词时也有"折扣"的含义，但具体指回扣。回扣也是一种促销手段。与折扣不同的是，回扣这是在卖方收到全部的货款后，再按照事先约定比例，将一部分款项退还买方。

e. g. In the meeting, the sales manager came up with a floating rebate plan. 在会上，销售经理提出了一个浮动回扣的方案。

allowance 折让或销售折让，指由于品种、质量等不符合事先约定，卖方在不退货的前提下给予一定比例的让价。表达该含义时，与 discount、rebate 是近义词，但在国际贸易中的索赔环节中 allowance 则指赔偿费。

e. g. As the mistake is ours, we agree to make an allowance of 3%. 由于这是我方的过错所造成的，我们同意支付 3% 的赔偿费用。

The carrier made an allowance of 6% for later delivery. 托运公司由于延迟交货需要付出 6% 的折让费。

短语：

cash discount 现金折扣(为促使买方尽快付清货款而提供的折扣)

functional discount 功能折扣(一般是制造商向履行了某种功能的特定者，如推销员提供的折扣)

special discount 特别折扣(为实现某种特殊目的所给予买方的折扣)

quantity discount 数量折扣(一般给予大批量购买者的一种折扣)

seasonal discount 季节性折扣(一般在销售淡季给购买者的一种折扣)

trade discount 商业折扣(一般根据市场的供需情况或目标顾客的不同给予的一种折扣)

(4) commission *n.* 佣金，指卖方或买方提供给中间人或代理的服务酬金

e. g. The indent agent takes a commission on the value of his purchase. 这种订货代理商按所订购的货物价值收取佣金。

As a rule, we will give 4% commission to our agent. 通常情况下，我们会给我们的代理 4% 的佣金。

They will deduct 10% from our payment commission for the tax. 他们会在给我方的回款佣金中扣除 10% 的税费。

Our partners hope you can grant them a 2% commission to cover the additional risk. 我们的贸易伙伴希望贵方能给予 2% 的佣金用于补偿所受到的额外风险。

短语:

accumulative commission 累计佣金

sales commission 销售佣金

buying commission 购货佣金;代买佣金

overriding commission 追加佣金

commission agent 佣金代理人

commission system 佣金制

(5) delivery *n.* 交付,递送

e. g. Please pay on delivery. 请交货时付款。

We hope you may agree upon the extension of the delivery period. 我们希望贵方能够同意将交付期延长。

After we have received your remittance, we will make the delivery within 2 days. 当我们收到汇款后,我们将在两日内发货。

You have to take delivery as soon as the goods are unloaded at the seaport. 货物一旦到达海港并卸货,贵方应尽快提货。

We are sorry to inform to inform you that because of the hurricane we have to postpone the delivery date. 非常遗憾地通知贵方:由于飓风,我们不得不推迟交货日期。

This afternoon you go to take delivery of the goods from the carrier and, if necessary, pay the freight costs. 今天下午您去承运人处取货,且如有需要,支付运费。

deliver *v.* 递送;交付

e. g. If your order is less than 10000 sets, we can deliver them with two weeks. 如果您的订单量少于 10000 台,我们可以在两周之内交付。

Would you please inform us by return of the time when you can deliver the goods? 请回函告知我们贵方能够交货的时间。

We can deliver 1000 yards from stock. 我们能够现货交付 1000 码。

短语:

delivery receipt 送货单;交货回单

delivery term 交货运输方式

delivery inspection 交船检验

delivery release 发货通知

delivery expense 送货费用

(6) pay *v.* 付款

e. g. You are under no compulsion to pay immediately. 您不必马上付款。

One has the right to demand payment from the endorser of a commercial paper when the first party liable fails to pay. 追索权是当有支付义务的一方不能支付时,权利人可以向商业票据的背书人要求支付。

Under the terms of this agreement, you have to pay by check. 根据这份协议中的条款,您需以支票支付。

payment *n*. 支付;付款;缴纳

e. g. Payment must be made by cash. 必须以现金履行支付。

Here is the receipt for half payment on goods. 这是支付一半货款的收据。

As our usual practice, for the large order, we insist on payment by Letter of Credit. 我们的惯例,对于金额大的订单,我们坚持用信用证来支付。

We cannot accept payment terms this time. 这次的支付方式我们无法接受。

Do you accept the payment by D/A? 您接受以承兑交单形式来付款吗?

短语:

down payment 定金;头期款

deferred payment 延期付款

immediate payment 立即付款

full payment 全额付款

payment agreement 支付协定

payment terms 支付条款

payment procedure 支付手续

6.6 Exercise(练习)

1. Multiple choice.

(1) We ________ to report that your letter of credit has not yet reached us up to the time of writing.

A. regrettable B. regrettably C. regret D. regretful

(2) Which of the following would not be considered to alter the terms of the offer materially? ________

A. Extent of one party's liability to the other.

B. Differences on the settlement of disputes.

C. Additional or different terms relating to the place and time of delivery.

D. Proposals about different packing way.

(3) The negotiation process of a sales contract must go through all the four steps ________.

A. enquiry, quotation, packing and insurance

B. enquiry, offer, counter-offer and counter-counter-offer

C. enquiry, reply, acceptance and shipment

D. enquiry, offer, counter-offer and acceptance

(4) An acceptance of an offer becomes effective at the moment of ________.

A. the indication of assent reaches the offeror

B. the indication of assent sends off

C. the indication of assent is delivered by the postman

D. the indication of assent is handed in for dispatch

(5) In a letter you may see the following words: "While the quality of your bicycles are good, we find your price is on rather high side. However, in order to develop our market in your place, we have decide to accept your counter-offer as an exceptional." This letter is a(n) ________.

A. offer B. acceptance

C. counter-offer D. counter-counter-offer

(6) We have ________ a transaction with Shenzhen Huaxin Tech. Company on a large variety of digital cameras.

A. declined B. accepted C. established D. concluded

(7) The two essential steps of business negotiation are ________.

A. enquiry and acceptance

B. offer and contract

C. acceptance and establish business relationship

D. counter-offer and acceptance

(8) A late acceptance is effective or not depends on the indication of assent given by ________.

A. receiver B. offeree C. consignee D. offeror

(9) An acceptance of an offer becomes effective should include the following elements EXCEPT ________.

A. It should be made by the offeree

B. An acceptance should exactly match the terms of an offer

C. An acceptance shall reach the offeror within the period prescribed in the offer

D. The indication of assent can be delivered by all means of communication

(10) Which of the following statement is True? ________

A. According to United Nations Convention on Contracts for the International Sale of Goods, silence and inactivity can not be regarded as acceptance in any case.

B. Late acceptance is not effective in any case.

C. Counter-offer can be interpreted as a new offer and a rejection to the original offer as well.

D. An acceptance is binding upon its maker and can only be made by the buyer.

2. Put the following English phrases into Chinese or Chinese phrases into English.

(1) 付款交单

(2) 有条件地接受

（3）不可撤销信用证
（4）承兑交单
（5）接受的撤回
（6）be tied up
（7）gross for net
（8）accumulative commission
（9）special discount
（10）minimum quantity

3. Translate the following Chinese sentences into English using the words or phrases in the brackets, and translate the following English sentences into Chinese.

（1）必须明确地理解，我们这样的做法是下不为例的。（precedent）

（2）按照贵方 8 月 15 日的来函要求，我们随函寄去贵方所需要的电气设备、变速箱以及其他物料的估价单。（in compliance with, herewith）

（3）对由于 QGD858 型号电脑缺货而无法供应给您所带来的不便，我们十分抱歉。我们承诺一旦有货并备妥将马上通知贵方。（regret）

（4）We suggest that you should reconsider your quotations, and bring them into line with the international market price.

（5）Considering the above-mentioned reasons we do not feel that the prices we quoted are extortionate and unreasonable, but bearing in mind the long-standing relationships between our firms in the future, we quote again as bellows.

（6）Although your price is below our level, we have finally decided to accept your counter offer of EUR €12.5 per can FOB Singapore with a view to initiating our business with you at an early date.

4. Translate the following letter into English.

信函一：

敬启者：

关于我们双方之间在过去的两个月间往来的传真和电子邮件，现在我方很高兴地确认与贵方达成如下交易。我方接受贵方关于货号 107 印花棉布五万码的还盘。请告知我们颜色搭配，并请按照合同规定开立以我方为受益人的有关信用证。贵方同意对货物分批装运，这使得我方能够在两周内发货。

这笔交易的达成肯定不是一个结束，它仅仅是一个开端，一个我们之间良好的、长久友好的贸易关系的开端。

谨上

信函二：

敬启者：

我方已收到贵方 1 月 17 日关于两万罐中国绿茶的信件，谢谢。由于春节长假，延误了我们的回复。

在贵方的来函中提到我方绿茶质量令人满意但价格偏高，并且在信中还提到有其他一些供应商的每类商品报价比我们的低 3%。我们想说价格不是唯一的要素，贵方还应该考虑质量因素。我们一级绿茶的存货正在减少。我们给贵方报了最低的价格，按照这个价格我们已经与其他英国客户做成了许多笔交易。由于国际价格的上涨，我们坚信，在未来的几个月中，您很难按此价格购买到同品质的商品。

所报的价格都是经过精确计算的，价格合理适中，建议按照此价格成交。我们希望在不久的将来能够收到贵方的订单。

谨上

Unit 7

Order and Their Fulfillment

订单及履行

7.1 Study Aim(学习目标)

(1) 掌握下订单、接受订单函电的写作技巧。

(2) 掌握拒绝订单并建议订购替代品、取消订单的函电写作技巧。

(3) 掌握订单及其履行函电中常用的词汇及表达方式。

7.2 Introduction(专业背景知识介绍)

在经过交易磋商的四个环节:询盘、发盘、还盘以及接受后,买方就可以向卖方或供货方下订单了。

1. 订单(order)简介

订单是订购货物的合同或单据,它是为了要求卖方或供货方供应某一特定数量、型号、款式等货物而提出的一种要求。在进出口业务中,卖方在收到订单后会将销售合同(sales contract)或者是销售确认书(sales confirmation, S/C)缮制一式两份,签署后会寄给对方,要求其签署后将其中一份寄回,存档以备日后有需要时查询。也有交易一方将自己的订单寄给对方,以确保对方能够据此履行交货以及交单等义务。寄来一式两份要求对方签署后退回一份的行为被称为"会签"(counter-signing)。订单实际上起到的作用相当于销售合同或销售确认书。根据商法的规定,买方订单只是一种购买意愿的表现,其在信函中所做出的购货安排是不具有法律约束力的,只有等到卖方表示接受后才具有法律约束力。

卖方接到订单后,如果接受就应该立即表示确认(acknowledgement),如由于对方所要求的货物库存不足或价格、规格已发生改变不能接受,也应该在拒绝接受订单的函电里仔细说明原因,并明确表达今后如有机会希望继续与对方保持贸易往来。最好能够介绍一些适合的替代商品,劝说买方接受。

传统订单可以用信函、传真、电子邮件等形式发送,此外有些公司有已经印制好的订单表格(order form)可以直接寄送给对方。

订单的主要特点就是准确和清楚。一份订单或订购函电应该包含以下内容。

第一,表明向对方订购货物。

第二,对订单内涉及的主要内容重复确认,一般订单的主要内容包括商品名称(name of commodity)、货号(item number)、规格(specification),如型号、尺码、颜色等、数量(quantity)或重量(weight)、价格(一般需要包括单价和总价)、包装(package)、装运期和装运方法、支付条款(terms of payment)。

第三,表达继续合作的愿望。

2. 订单的写作特点

订单函电写作时,首先应该在函电一开始写清楚订单的内容和订单号、订购内容等。订单函电的主体部分应该对所订购货物的相关信息重复,以确保贸易双方清楚了解,不会产生误解。货物的相关信息可以包括颜色、尺寸、数量、折扣等,如果订购信函随函附寄了订购表格,则信函主体部分只需重复确认商品名称和订单号即可。此外信函主体部分还应该提及支付方式等其他相关重要的条款,提醒收件方对这些条款进行确认;还可以在信中督促收件方尽早装运货物。

如果因缺货、订货数量过小等原因而需要对订货要求表示回绝时,拒绝订购函中应把拒绝的原因陈述清楚,同时有三种方法可以选择:①建议类似的替代品进而促成交易;②进行还盘,达成双方都能够接受的条件,促成交易完成;③拒绝接受。

写订购函电时应尽可能简洁、全面、具体地说明信息,应该让收信人了解你是在订货而不是在询价。

7.3 Writing Skills(写作技巧)

订单函电的写作步骤及常见表达方式如表 7-1 所示。

表 7-1 订单函电的写作步骤及常见表达方式

写作步骤	表达方式
1. 表明向对方订购货物(如随信附有订单表格,应在信中明确指出)	We have received your letter of September 10th and are very pleased to place an order with you for the following goods. 我们已经收到贵方9月10日的来函,并非常高兴地向贵方订购以下货物。
	We acknowledge with thanks the receipt of your letter of April 3th. And we have pleasure in confirming the revised order as follows. 很荣幸收到贵方4月3日发来的信函。我们十分高兴地向贵方确认修改后的订货如下。
	We would like to place an order with your corporation for 10000 pieces cotton bed-sheets. 我们想向贵公司订购 10000 条纯棉床单。
	We find both quality and prices of your Men's leather shoes are satisfactory and enclose our order form NO. S/C4843 for prompt supply. 我们对贵方男式皮鞋的报价和质量都很满意,随信附寄我们的订单,订单号 S/C4843,请即期交货。

续表

写作步骤	表达方式
2. 确认双方达成的交易条件(包括商品名称、价格、支付方式、包装、装运期和装运方法等);告知具体订货安排	We would like to confirm that this order has to be delivered on or before October 1. 我们想和贵方确认这个订单需要在10月1日或之前发货。
	We would like to thank you for the 5% special discount you allowed us. 我们十分感谢贵方向我们所提供的5%的特别折扣。
	Our usual practice for payment is cash against documents and we hope it will be acceptable to you. 我们支付通常是付现交单,希望贵方能够接受此种方式。
	It is necessary that the specification conform to the requirements. (货物)规格必须与订单要求的一致。
	We are arranging for the establishment of the relative L/C with the Citibank, New York. 我们正在安排通过花旗银行纽约分行开立。
3. 敦促对方尽快发货	Since our customers are in urgent need of the goods, we will appreciate your prompt delivery. 由于我们的客户急需这批货物,如果贵方能即期发货,我们将不胜感激。
	We look forward to learning soon when the goods are due to arrive here. 我方希望尽快得知什么时候货物能够到达我处。
	Looking forward to your early reply. 期待您的早日回复。

回复确认订货函电的写作步骤及常见表达方式如表7-2所示。

表7-2 回复确认订货函电的写作步骤及常见表达方式

写作步骤	表达方式
1. 表示感谢对方的订单	We thank you very much for your order of August 14th. 很高兴收到贵方8月14日的订单。
	Your order of September 1 has been received with thanks. 感谢收到贵方9月1日的订单。
	We are glad to receive your order for 1200 pieces men's skirts. 我们非常高兴收到贵方订购1200件男式衬衫的订单。
2. 对所订的货物进行好的评价、赞美	The structure of our coffee table is made of thicker stainless steel pipes and the high quality will promise it can be used well within ten years. 我们的咖啡桌的框架是用加厚的不锈钢管做的,良好的品质保证在十年内使用无后顾之忧。
	High quality, new style, reasonable price has earned a favorable market response in the North America. (该产品的)优良的品质、全新的设计风格以及合理的价位,使得它刚投入北美市场就受到好评。
	You will be happy you bought our goods. 您会感到购买我们的产品是物有所值的。
	We appreciate your interest in our products which are of good quality and best price. 我们的产品品质优良、价格公道,能吸引您的注意我们十分荣幸。

续表

写 作 步 骤	表 达 方 式
3. 表示会迅速认真执行订单里的安排	We will give our due attention to your order. 我们会十分重视贵方的订单。
	Your order has been given our great attention. 贵方的订货已经引起我方的高度重视。
	We are now arranging the shipment of your ordered goods. 我们正在安排装运您所订购的货物。
	We promise to effect shipment of your order as promptly as possible. 我们承诺将尽快安排贵方的订单装船发货。
4. 向对方推荐其他可能感兴趣的产品;宣传、推销	For your information, we have produced several new products. 告知贵方,我们又生产了一些新的产品。
	We enclose our latest catalogues. If you are interest in our new products or have any decision, please contact us. 随寄上我们的最新产品目录表。如果对我们的新产品感兴趣并决定购买,请与我们联系。
	Our company recently introduced a new style racing car toy to the market. This new style is both excellent workmanship and fashionable design. We believe it will satisfy your clients. 最近我们公司向市场上投放了一款新的玩具赛车。新款玩具赛车做工精良,设计时尚,相信会使您的客户感到满意。
	We think you may be interested in the new formula hair shampoo we have just introduced to the market. 我们认为贵方可能会对我们刚刚投放市场的新配方洗发香波感兴趣。
5. 希望对方能够再次订购	Thank you for your cooperation, and we hope this transaction will be a good beginning for our further business. 感谢贵方此次的合作,并且我们希望这次交易能够成为我们以后合作的良好的开始。
	Please confirm upon receipt of this letter. Look forward to working with you. 收到此函请确认,希望能够完成此次交易。
	We are sure this is just a beginning of our business. 我们相信这次(交易)只是我们之间生意的开始。

如果客户对订购的货物满意,可能会继续订购,由于有了之前的沟通与合作,因此在写续购函电的时候会比较简洁,有时在信函中说明按照上次订货的某条款即可,无须详细展开,如表 7-3 所示。

表 7-3 续购函电的写作步骤及常见表达方式

写 作 步 骤	表 达 方 式
1. 表示对上一次订购的货物表示满意	We are glad to inform you that we find the goods are quite satisfactory. 我们很高兴地通知您:贵方的货物我们很满意。
	Thank you for the goods sent by ex S. S. Star. We are satisfied with quality of the goods. 感谢经由“星辰”号轮船运来的货物。对于货物的质量我们十分满意。
2. 写明按照上次所约定的条款再续订若干该类产品	We are very glad to place a repeat order as follows: 我们十分高兴向你方续订以下商品:
	We wish to place with you a repeat order for 5000 dozens of the same style and size 6. 我们希望能向贵方续订 5000 打相同款式的尺码为 6 号的商品。

续表

写作步骤	表达方式
3. 盼望对方及早接受并答复	We shall appreciate it if you can ship the goods as soon as possible. 如果能早日装运货物我们将不胜感激。
	Please kindly let us have your confirmation. 请及早回复确认。
	Looking forward to the arrival of our order in time. 希望能够早日收到我们订购的货物。

拒绝订购的函电应该写得委婉而礼貌,为的是给对方留下良好的印象希望将来双方能够继续保持商业往来。当写作拒绝订购的函电时应把拒绝的原因写清楚,同时有三种方法可以选择:第一,建议类似的替代品进而促成交易;第二,进行还盘,最终达成双方都能够接受的条件,促成交易完成;第三,直接拒绝接受。如表7-4所示。

表7-4 拒绝订购函电的写作步骤及常见表达方式

写作步骤	表达方式
1. 表示感谢对方的订单	We acknowledge receipt of your order No. 6970 with thanks. 我们已经收到贵方编号6970订单,谢谢。
	We are glad to receive your order of June 23th. 我们很高兴收到贵方于6月23日发来的订单。
2. 说明拒绝订货的原因	We are very sorry to inform you that we have to decline your order because we do not have sufficient goods to supply. 我们十分遗憾地通知您,我们不能接受贵方的订单,因为我们没有足够的货物可提供。
	Much to our regret, we cannot at present entertain the new order owing to heavy commitment. 十分遗憾地告知贵方,由于有大量订单,我方目前无法接受新订单。
	We regret to say we have to decline your order because we do not produce this product any more. 我们十分遗憾,不得不拒绝您的订单,因为此款产品我们已经不再生产了。
3. 建议类似的替代品供选择;或还盘	We enclose our latest catalogue for your reference. 我们随函附寄了最新的商品目录表供贵方参考。
	We would like to recommend an excellent substitute. 我们想向贵方推荐一款非常好的替代产品。
	In order to meet your requirement, we recommend you a new model which enjoys the superior quality. 为了满足贵方的要求,我们推荐一款质量更好的新型号。
4. 表示希望能与对方完成交易;或能够保持生意上的往来	As soon as we are in a position to supply it ,we will contact you. 一旦我方能够供应,我们将会与您联系。
	We hope to receive your order again in the near future. 我们希望在不久的将来能再次收到贵方的订单。
	We are looking forward to your order. 期盼能够收到贵方的订单。
	However, we wish to do business with you in the near future. 但是我方依然希望在不久的将来能与贵方做生意。

7.4 Specimen Letters(样函)

Letter 1:

Dear Sir or Madam,

Thank you for your previous letters and having sent us samples of cotton prints. We find both quality and prices satisfactory and are pleased to place an order with you for the following items on condition that they will be supplied from your current stock at the prices as follows:

Quantity	Patter No.	Prices
500 yards	C-65	EUR €1 per yard CIFD3% Rotterdam
350 yards	D-98	EUR €0.95 per yard CIFD3% Rotterdam
200 yards	POLY-543	EUR €1.25 per yard CIFD3% Rotterdam

Our usual terms of payment are by D/P at sight and we hope that they will be acceptable to you. We expect to find a good market for these cotton prints and hope to place further and larger orders with you in the near future.

Sincerely yours,

Notes(注释)

1. previous *adj.* & *adv.* 早先的,先前的;在……以前

e. g. His previous shipment went to a Chinese importer, who paid 50% up front to acquire the wine. 他的上批葡萄酒发给了一家中国进口商,该进口商为购买这批葡萄酒预付了50%的费用。

Weekly movements of grains and soybeans by barge are trailing shipment patterns of the previous two years, while well below the five-year average. 谷物和大豆的每周驳船运量正在重现过去两年的走势,远远落后于过去五年来的平均运量。

Payment: By irrevocable L/C, payable by draft at sight. Other terms will be the same as our previous contract. 支付方式:凭即期汇票支付的不可撤销的信用证付款,其他条件与上笔合同相同。

2. print *n.* 印花布,印章;印刷

e. g. Many clients place the repeat order for our exotic print clothes. 许多客户都续购了我们这套体现异域风情的服装。

3. current stock 现有的库存

current *adj.* 最近的,现在的

current account 现金账户

current asset 流动资产

stock *n.* 库存

e. g. Currently we have red and blue stripe patterns in stock. 我们现有的库存型号是红色条纹和蓝色条纹两款。

We have to place the repeat order for these goods because their stock are getting lower and lower. 我们不得不再续订这些货物,因为它们的库存越来越少了。

4. yard *n.* 码,英制中表示长度的单位,1 码 =3 英尺

e. g. They sold the cloth at one pound a yard. 这种布他们每码售价一英镑。

She bought a yard of cooper wire. 她买了一码铜线。

Letter 2:

Dear Sir or Madam,

We are in receipt of your letter dated October 1st and pleased to place an order with you for the following goods.

Forty-five short tons of China sesame seed. The quality of the goods must in accordance to the revised terms as "China sesame seed/Moisture (max.)8%/Admixture (max.)2%/Oil content (wet basis ethyl ether extract) 52% basis". All the goods must be packed in new gunny bags.

We are arranging for the establishment of the relative letter of credit with the Citibank, Toronto Branch. As soon as it opened we shall let you know by E-mail.

As we are in bad need of the goods, we hope you will do everything possible to guarantee punctual shipment within the validity of the L/C.

Sincerely yours,

Notes(注释)

1. short ton *phr.* (词组)短吨,美吨(美制重量单位)

1 美吨 =907 千克

2. sesame *n.* 芝麻

3. in accordance to *phr.* (词组)根据

e. g. In accordance to your request, we are sending you the sample of our soap powder. 根据贵方的要求,现寄去我们的皂粉样品。

Issue payment in accordance to payment voucher amount. 按付款凭证上的金额支付现金。

4. revise *v.* 复核,校订,修正

e. g. In the light of present situation, we have to revise our purchase plan. 鉴于目前这种情况,我们不得不重新修订我们的订购计划。

Parties hereto may revise or supplement through negotiation matters not mentioned herein. 本合同如有未尽事宜,双方可协商修订或补充。

5. moisture *n.* 湿度,水分

moisture proof 防潮

moisture content 水分含量

6. admixture *n.* 混合物;掺和物

7. ethyl ether *n*. 乙醚

8. arrange *v*. 安排，整理

e. g. When arranging the shipment, we should allow for unforeseen circumstances. 我们在安排装运时应该考虑到可能发生的意外情况。

We put a lot of effort into arranging the exhibition. 我们为展览会的筹备花了大量的精力。

Our general manager is responsible for arranging this meeting. 我们的总经理负责安排此次会议。

9. establishment *n*. 建立,设立;商业机构或大型机关

e. g. With the establishment of major new markets, the economy is thriving. 随着主要的新市场的建立,经济越来越繁荣。

Our company is a well-run establishment. 我们公司是一家经营情况良好的企业。

What made you come and work in this establishment? 您到这个公司来工作的原因是什么?

10. guarantee *v*. 保证;担保

e. g. The excellent quality of your goods guaranteed successful conclusion of the business. 贵方商品的优良品质是此次交易成功的保证。

We guarantee prompt delivery of goods. 我们保证及时交货。

11. punctual *adj*. 准时的,守时的,按时的

e. g. The punctual arrival of the goods will help us to gain more market shares. 货物的准时到达将会帮助我们赢得更多的市场份额。

We possess of professional advanced design, keeping improving quality, favorable and reasonable prices, punctual delivery speed. 我们拥有专业前卫的设计、精益求精的质量、优惠合理的价格、快捷准时的交货速度。

Letter 3:

Dear Sir or Madam,

Thank you for your letter of April 5th . After examining your samples we found both the quality and the prices are up to our requirement. We are pleased to confirm having concluded with you a transaction of 350 metric tons of walnut meat at your revised price:

"Three hundred and fifty metric tons of walnut meat at GBP £5500 per metric ton CFR Helsinki, for shipment in May."

Enclosed please find our sales contract No. SC-7534 in duplicate. If you find everything in order, please sign and return one copy for our file. Our usual terms of payment are by confirmed, irrevocable letter of credit available by sight draft.

As the goods are urgently required by our customers, we find it necessary to stress the importance of making punctual shipment; any delay in shipment would result in our withdrawal of this order.

Sincerely yours,

Notes(注释)

1. conclude *v.* 缔结(条约等);结束

e. g. When buy the products concretely each time, both sides should conclude single contract. 在每次具体购买产品时,双方应缔结单独合同。

Could you lower your price a bit so that we can conclude the transaction? 贵方能否把价格稍稍降低一点,以便我们能达成交易。

2. duplicate *n.* 副本

短语:

in duplicate 一式两份;一式两份;一式两联

duplicate copy [印刷] 副本;复本;复制;复制本

duplicate invoice 副联;[会计] 发票副联;发货副单;[会计] 发票副本

duplicate part 备件;配件;备份零件

duplicate sample [贸易] 复样;[矿业] 副样;平行双样;[贸易] 复样品

3. file *n.* &*v.* 文档,档案;把……归档,存档

e. g. Where's the file of our recent letters? 我们近期的信件卷宗在哪里?

4. withdrawal *n.* 撤销,收回,取消

e. g. Voluntary withdrawal from the market by the manufacturer. 生产商自愿从市场上撤回有缺陷的产品。

The offer is subject to withdrawal without notice. 该报盘不经通知即可撤回。

Letter 4:

Dear Sir or Madam,

We appreciate your immediate response dated March 18 to our enquiry. The prices quoted in your fax gained favorable attention with us. Having studied your latest catalogues we found both the design and the workmanship are up to our requirement. We are enclosing herewith a copy of our order form No. 9876.

Quantity	Commodity	Catalogue No.	Packing	CIFC3%, Port of South Louisiana(USD)
2000 pieces	Ladies woolen garments	DK08W4	Packed in strong bale, covering with water-proof material.	230 per piece
2500 pieces	Gents woolen garments	BU39L7	Packed in strong bale, covering with water-proof material.	270 per piece

Shipment: Prompt shipment from Yokohama to Port of South Louisiana.

Payment: By T/T.

Please confirm upon receipt of this letter. If this first order is executed satisfactorily, we shall be happy to place repeat order with you in near future.

Sincerely yours,

Notes(注释)

1. response *n*. 回答;反应;响应

e. g. Your quick response to our enquiry will be highly appreciated. 您对我方的询盘如果能迅速做出回复,我们将不胜感激。

2. herewith *adv*. (尤用于商业函件)同此(函等)

e. g. We are pleased to send you herewith attached Sample-Cuttings of Cotton Shirting and Sheeting. 我方随函附上棉布衬衫衣料与被单料的剪样。

Thank you for your samples of striped coatings received today. Please make shipment in accordance with our Order No. 2602 enclosed herewith. 今天收到你们寄来的带条纹外衣料样品,谢谢。请按照信内附寄的第 2602 号订单发货。

3. waterproof *adj*. 防水的,不透水的

e. g. Waterproof material is usually used for inner packing. 内包装通常使用一些防水材料。

4. execute *v*. 履行,执行,贯彻,实行,实施;完成,实现,施行(法律等)

e. g. The two parties involved in a contract have the obligation to execute contract. 合同双方有义务履行合同。

Signatures on this Agreement received by the way of Facsimile, E-mail or Mail shall be deemed to be executed contract. 任何经由传真、邮寄及电子信件送达之合约,经签署后皆可视为可履行之契约。

Letter 5:

Dear Sir or Madam,

We are pleased to have received your order No. 1234 for car speaker and are sending you herewith our Sales Confirmation No. JH-8530 in two originals for your counter signature. Please send one copy back to us at your earliest convenience.

We appreciate you interest in our products which are of good quality and reasonable price. And our products have ready markets in many areas. We believe that you will be satisfied with what you bought.

Meanwhile, we are pleased to say that we have already made up your order No. 1234, and the goods will be delivered within seven days. We wish to stress that the stipulation in the relative L/C should strictly conform to the terms in our Confirmation. By this way, we can avoid subsequent amendments.

We hope this initial order will be the forerunner of our business.

Sincerely yours,

Notes(注释)

1. original *n*. 原件;正本 *adj*. 原始的,最初的

e. g. We will keep the original receipt for reference. 我们将保留原始收据以便参考。

Please copy out this letter and send the original to the ABC Company. 请把这封信抄打

一份，然后把原件交还给 ABC 公司。

2. counter-signature *n.* 会签

3. subsequent *adj.* 随后的，后来的

e. g. There have been further developments subsequent to our meeting. 在我们的会议之后又有新发展。

4. amendment *n.* （错误、毛病的）改正，纠正；（议案、法令、宪法等的）修正，修订，修改

e. g. Since you insist, we have to make the amendment of our letter of credit accordingly. 既然贵方坚持，我方只有对信用证做出相应的修正。

5. initial *adj.* 最初的，首次的

e. g. Our credit references will be provided if you can make an initial order. 首次订购时，我们将向您提供资信证明人。

You may be able to profit special terms on your initial order. 贵方的第一次订购可享特别优待。

Our client would like the initial order payment terms, L/C at sight. 我们的客人要求首次下单的付款方式为即期信用证。

Letter 6:

Dear Sir or Madam,

Thank you very much for your order No. 2345 dated August 11. We confirm having sold you the following goods on terms and conditions as below.

Name of Commodity: Embroidered Bed-Sheet

Article No.: AE-3950, AE-1046, UR-9576 and WP-5875.

Unit Prices (FOB New York): AE-3950 US $15 per piece

AE-1046 US $20 per piece

UR-9576 US $35 per piece

WP-5875 US $30 per piece

Please open the covering letter of credit in our favor immediately.

We are now arranging shipment of your goods; we will email you as soon as we have the definite date. Besides the embroidered bed-sheets we supply a wide range of beddings. We enclose our latest catalogue. If you are interested in some other items, please feel free to contact with us.

We believe this initial business will lead to further development of trade between us.

Sincerely yours,

Notes(注释)

1. embroidered *adj.* 刺绣的，绣花的

embroidered frock 绣花衫连裙

embroidered napkin 绣花餐巾

embroidered blanket 绣花被面

2. covering *adj.* 包含的，覆盖的

3. range *n*. （同类事物的）一系列；（在一定幅度内）变化

e. g. Net inns can offer merchandise ranging from the everyday to the esoteric. 网店出售的商品包罗万象，从日常用品到少数人使用的特别物品都有。

Letter 7：

Dear Sir or Madam,

We are delighted to inform you that your raincoats for kids have a steady market. We are herewith placing a repeat order as follows：

Specification No.	Quantity (piece)	Color	unit price(per piece, EUR)
2348	10000	Red	5.5
5432	10000	Orange	7
9863	10000	Blue	6.5

We hope that you can make delivery within two weeks on receipt of our order. As usual, the payment for above goods is going to be made by an irrevocable L/C open in your favor ten days after your acceptance of the order. Since we need these goods badly, please ship them by the first available vessel no later than the end of this month.

We are looking forward to the arrival of our order in time.

Sincerely yours,

Notes（注释）

1. repeat order 重复订单
2. badly *adv*. 非常，很；严重地，厉害地；恶劣地

Letter 8：

Dear Sir or Madam,

We have received the above shipment ex S. S. Red Star and we are satisfy with the quality of your canned peach. Because of the excellent quality and reasonable price, we believe we can sell additional quantities in our market. Please ship the goods according to the following requirements：

Commodity	Catalogue No.	Quantity(can)	Unit Price(US $, per can)	Packing
Canned Peach	688-PE	100000	8	20 CANS/CTN

Other terms and conditions are the same as are stated in Sales Contract No. PU9375. If the goods are not available from stock, we would appreciate that you inform us as soon as possible. Replacement goods which can be shipped from stock should be advised in advance, with full particulars of the specification.

Please make sure that the order will be punctually fulfilled.

Sincerely yours,

Notes(注释)

1. ex *prep*. (指货物等)从(船上、工厂等处)交货(不包括运给买主的费用)

ex warehouse price 仓库交货价

2. replacement *n*. 替代品

e. g. Replacement is guaranteed if the products are not up to the standard. 产品不合规格,保证退换。

We are engaged in the supply of small parts for replacement. 我们公司主营提供各种备用小零部件。

3. advise *v*. 建议;劝告,忠告;通知;警告

e. g. Please advise the date of shipment as soon as possible. 请尽快通知装货日期。

Please advise price breakdown and delivery term as soon as possible. 请尽早惠告价格细目表以及发货条件。

4. particular *n*. 详细说明

e. g. We should appreciate full particulars of your newly developed product. 如蒙赐寄贵公司新产品的详细资料,我们将深表感激。

And we hope you could send us a market report every week with full particulars on price changes. 此外,希望贵方能每周寄给我们一份市场报告,特别是有关价格变动的全部明细。

5. fulfill *v*. 履行(诺言、责任、义务等);做(要求的事情);按照……行动;完成(任务、计划等);尽(职)

e. g. Supplier ought to fulfill the order by dealer as possible as he can, and shall not refuse. 供货商应当尽其最大努力及时履行经销商的订购单,并不得无理拒绝。

Your company has to fulfill the terms of its obligation. 贵方公司必须履行合同条款。

Letter 9:

Dear Sir or Madam,

We have duly received your Sales Contract No. 5678 covering 100 metric tons walnut meat we have book with you. Enclosed please find one copy with our counter-signature for your file. Due to our mutual efforts, we are able to bridge the price gap finally and close the transaction successfully.

We are arranging the relative L/C with the Bank of China, Shanghai Branch and will send you an email as soon as it is established.

Thank you for your cooperation, and we hope this transaction will be a good beginning for our further business.

Sincerely yours,

Notes(注释)

1. duly *adv*. 如期地;适当地

e. g. The ordered goods were duly delivered. 所订购的货物已经按时交付了。

Enclosed is our contract No. 3456 in duplicate, of which please return us one copy, duly countersign. 随函附上我方第 3456 号合同一式两份，请及时会签并回寄一份。

短语：

duly countersigned 正式会签；会签；正式背签

duly endorsed 提单可以适当背书

duly handle 妥善处理

duly represent 交付地代表；正式代表

duly scheduled 排定

duly sign 正式签署

2. mutual *adj*. 共同的，相互的

e. g. We must pull together for mutual interest. 我们必须为相互的利益而通力合作。

Mutual interests tied us together. 互利关系把我们联系在一起。

3. bridge *v*. 在河面等上方架桥

bridge the gap *phr*. 缩短(悬殊的)距离

e. g. How can we bridge the gap between rich and poor? 我们要怎么做才能缩小贫富间的差距呢？

Letter 10:

Dear Sir or Madam,

Thank you very much for your order of May 10 for 1000 sets Icy air conditioner. We regret that we have to turn down your order because our present stock is not sufficient.

Because of the earthquake in Japan, we have difficulties to purchase the air-conditioning compressors. As we have not enough storage, we are not able to arrange production as before.

You may rest assured that whenever the supply position turns for the better, we shall revert to this matter and contact you by fax. We trust that our cordial relations will continue in spite of this loss of business, and that we shall be in the position to make a further order in the very near future.

Sincerely yours,

Notes(注释)

1. compressor *n*. 压缩机

2. position *n*. 处境，情势

e. g. We are really very sorry not to be in a position to accept your order, but hope you will understand our situation. 对于无法接受您的订单，本公司深表歉意，希望您能谅解我们的处境。

3. revert *v*. 恢复，重提

e. g. Reverting to our earlier question, can you deliver the goods before the end of this month? 回到我们之前的问题，您能在本月月底之前交货吗？

4. cordial *adj.* 衷心的

e. g. We'll fulfill our promise by rendering the trustworthy quality and requite your satisfactory smiles with our cordial service! 用我们的质量来履行我们的诺言,用我们的服务换取您满意的微笑!

Letter 11:

Dear Sir or Madam,

We acknowledge receipt of your order No. 2345. We are regretful to inform you that we have no option but to decline your order.

We have applied for import license to competent government but met with problem. The materials you ordered are usually prevented from entering our city due to the religious regulations.

As soon as we receive the authorized approval from our local government, we will deliver your goods promptly.

In spite of this loss of business, we hope to receive your order again in the near future.

Sincerely yours,

Notes(注释)

1. decline *v.* 婉拒,谢绝;减少,衰退

e. g. The company has gone into a decline because of falling demand. 由于市场需求减少,这家公司的生意每况愈下。

We must regretfully decline your kind invitation. 我们很抱歉,但不得不拒绝您的盛情邀请。

2. competent *adj.* 有权利的,有能力的

e. g. The contract was declared null and void by the competent authority. 主管部门宣布该合同无效。

短语:

competent authority [法]主管当局,主管部门

competent department 主管部门

3. regulation *n.* 法规;条例

e. g. The European Union has proposed new regulations to control the hours worked by its employees. 欧盟已经提出了新的法规来控制其雇员的工作时间。

短语:

administrative regulation 行政法规;行政管理规章

financial regulation 金融监管;财务监管

government regulation 政府法规,政府调控;政府监管

legal regulation 法律条例

market regulation 市场调节;市场监管;市场管理

regulation and control 调控

safety regulation 安全规则

Letter 12:

Dear Sir or Madam,

We are glad to receive your order of March 13th. Much to our regret that the pattern you order is not available because the demand for this article has fallen to such an extent that we have ceased to produce it.

Now we have a similar product in stock, Pattern No. HYT875, which we think you might be interested in. We enclosed a descriptive leaflet for your reference. They are of the same quality and the price almost the same. If you can book the complete stock, we can offer you 15%. In view of our long-standing business relationship, we are giving you this opportunity.

We are looking forward to your order.

Sincerely yours,

Notes(注释)

1. cease *v*. 停止,终了,结束

e. g. Rather than compromise on the core terms, we decided to cease the relationship with you. 我方宁可终止与贵方的合作,也不愿在核心条款上妥协。

2. leaflet *n*. 说明书;传单;小册子

e. g. In order to promote the sales of new product, ABC Company has series of activity, including: advertising and handing out leaflets. 为了促销新产品,ABC 公司举办了一系列促销活动,其中包括做广告和发传单。

7.5 Focal Words(焦点词汇及短语)

(1) order *n*. 订单

e. g. When do you want to place the order with us? 贵方何时向我公司下订单?

As our stocks are running short, we would advise your place the order as soon as possible. 因为我们的现货逐渐短缺, 我方建议贵公司尽快下订单。

If goods of inferior quality are delivered, we will not place our order with you again. 如果有劣质货物交付, 本公司将永远不再向贵方下订单了。

As price is steady rising, we'd advise you to place your order without delay. 因为价格正在稳步上升, 我方建议贵方早日下订单。

We regret that we cannot book the order at the prices we quoted six weeks ago. 非常抱歉,我们现在无法按照六周前所报的那些价格下订单。

We will take your order, and the order will be processed today. 我们会接下您的订单,所订货物今天就会处理出货。

v. 下订单;订购

e. g. This commodity has ready market. We recommend that you have to order them immediately. 这款商品很畅销,我们建议您迅速下单订购。

What type do you want to order? 贵方打算订购哪种型号的呢?

What we can order from you right now are cotton goods. 现在我们能向您订购的是棉织品。

短语:

order sheet/order form/order blank/order note 订单,订货单

order acknowledgement 订单确认书

duplicate order 重复订单

back order 欠交订单

firm order 确实已订购

first/initial order 首次订购

formal order 正式订购

fresh/new order 新订单

outstanding order/pending order 未完成订单

repeat order 续订

to accept/book/take/entertain/close an order 接受订单

to confirm an order 确认订单

to fulfill/execute/carry out/perform an order 履行订单;执行订单

to decline/refuse/turn down an order 取消订单

to cancel/withdraw/revoke an order 取消订单

(2) fulfill *v.* 履行;执行

e. g. You have to fulfill all the terms of our contract. 贵方必须满足我们合同里的所有条款的要求。

fulfill oneself *phr.* 充分发挥自己的能力和性格

e. g. She is able to fulfill herself through drawing. 她通过绘画能充分地发挥自己的才能。

fulfilled *adj.* 满意的,满足的

e. g. He doesn't feel really fulfilled in his present job. 他对自己目前的工作并非真正满意。

fulfillment *n.* 执行,履行;满意,满足

e. g. This contract is binding subject to the fulfillment of the following conditions. 本合同须满足下列条件方可生效。

(3) counter-sign *v.* 会签;连署签名

e. g. When Sales Contract has been signed by the seller, it will be counter-signed by the buyer. 销售合同经卖方签署后须经买方会签。

counter-signature, counter-signing *n.* 会签,连署签名

e. g. Please send us your sales confirmation in duplicate for counter-signing. 请将贵方的销售确认书一式两份寄给我们会签。

We are pleased to do business with you and are sending you our signed sales contract

No. 1234 in duplicate. Please return one copy with your counter-signature for our file. 我们很高兴能与贵方做生意,我们将已经签好的编号 1234 号销售合同一式两份寄给贵方。请会签后发回一份给我们以供我们存档。

(4) enclose *v*. 随函附上……

e. g. Referring to my conversation with you today, we now enclose an order sheet for hosiery as specified. 参照今日和贵方的谈判记录, 兹随函寄上订购袜子的详细订单,请查收。

Enclosed please find a set of samples herewith. 随函附寄上一套样品,请查收。

enclosure *n*. 附件(尤指信内的)

e. g. I received your enclosure with gratitude. 附件收到,十分感谢。

(5) price *n*. 价格

e. g. The price increase has had no perceptible effect on sales. 这次提价对销售没有产生明显的影响。

We'll buy everything you produce, provided of course the price is right. 当然了,倘若价格合适,我们将采购你们的全部产品。

The price increases were passed on by the firm to the consumers. 公司把上涨的费用转嫁到了顾客身上。

We are glad to inform you that business has been done at your adjusted price. 我们很高兴地通知您,我们愿意按您提出的价格同您做生意。

price、cost 和 charge 这三个词都有费用、钱数的含义,下面我们对这三个近义词进行区分:

price 一般指商品的售价;cost 则通常指服务收费或进行某程序所需要的费用;charge 指索取的费用,通常用于服务收费。

priced *adj*. 已标价的,有定价的

priced catalogue 定价目录

pricing *n*. 定价

pricing cost 定价成本

pricing method 定价方法

短语:

current price 现行价格,市价

competitive price 竞争性价格

closing price 收盘价

opening price 开盘价

retail price 零售价

wholesale price 批发价

reference price 参考价

7.6 Exercise(练习)

1. Multiple choice.

(1) With ________ to our Sales Conformation No. 1234 dated May 11, we regret to inform that your letter of credit has not reached us up to the time of writing.

A. refer B. reference C. regard D. regarding

(2) We have opened an irrevocable L/C ________ favor of your company for the amount of US $100000, with Bank of China, London Branch.

A. in B. for C. at D. with

(3) Which of the following goods can adopt "FAQ" to indicate the qualities? ________.

A. Jewelry B. Clothes C. Porcelain D. Soybeans

(4) We are pleased to confirm having ________ with you a transaction of 350 metric tons of walnut meat at your revised price.

A. done B. effected C. fulfilled D. concluded

(5) Which of the following goods cannot adopt the way of determining the quality of the goods by description & illustrations? ________.

A. Metal cutting machine tools B. Cars

C. Eggs D. Electrical appliances

(6) "We are pleased to inform you that your order No. 6789 for 1000 pieces table cloth has received our immediate attention. We promise to execute this order in strict accordance with your requirements." This is a(n) ________.

A. order B. acknowledgment

C. sales contract D. sales confirmation

(7) As there is heavy demand, we are sorry to inform you that ________.

A. the shoes are out of stock

B. the shoes can be supplied from stock

C. the shoes are in stock

D. the shoes are over stocked

(8) We enclose ________ a check for the amount of EUR €1200.

A. hereby B. herein C. herewith D. hereafter

(9) Enclosed is Sales Contract No. 2345 signed in Shanghai on May 25 in ________, a copy of which please sign and return.

A. twice B. two C. double D. duplicate

(10) You may rest ________ that we will execute your order to your entire satisfaction.

A. insured B. ensured C. assured D. sured

2. Put the following English phrases into Chinese or Chinese phrases into English.

(1) 销售合同
(2) 凭规格买卖
(3) 唛头
(4) 确认书
(5) 溢短装条款
(6) counter sign
(7) supplementary or additional marks
(8) net weight
(9) unit price
(10) FAQ (Fair Average Quality)

3. Translate the following Chinese sentences into English using the words or phrases in the brackets, and translate the following English sentences into Chinese.

(1) 如果贵方能够订购所有库存,我们将提供给贵方一个特别折扣。(book)

(2) 我们希望贵方能尽一切可能保证货物在信用证有效期内按时装船。(guarantee, validity)

(3) 付款方式必须与修改后的合同一致。(in accordance to)

(4) We have received the above shipment ex S. S. East Wind and we are satisfy with the quality of your goods.

(5) Please open the covering letter of credit in our favor immediately.

(6) Meanwhile, we are pleased to say that we have already prepared your order No. 1234, and the goods will be delivered within seven days.

4. Translate the following letter into English.

(1)

敬启者:

收到贵方于9月15日发出的发盘以及印花棉布的样品,十分感谢。在仔细验看样品后,我方认为无论是质量还是价格都符合我方的要求。我方非常高兴地向贵方首次订购以下商品。

商品名称:印花棉布

货物编号:IUT-64、HFD-975、JCE-368、NCY-74以及TK-7-V

单价(FOB纽约):

IUT-64	3.5美元/码
JCE-368	4.2美元/码
NCY-74	5美元/码
TK-7-V	3.8美元/码

数量：

IUT-64	1500 码
JCE-368	3000 码
NCY-74	1200 码
TK-7-V	2000 码

我们现在正在同中国银行上海分行办理相关的信用证，一旦开立成功，我们会第一时间以电子邮件通知您。由于我们急需这批货物，在信用证的有效期内按时转运是很重要的。除此之外，请注意货物必须与样品一致。

我们随信附上我们已经签了名的编号 3456 的销售合同一式两份，请查收。如果贵方审核无误，请尽快会签并退回一份，以便我方存档。

如收到此信函，请加以确认。如果第一次订单履行得令人满意，我们将十分高兴地向贵方进行续订。

谨上

（2）

敬启者：

我方十分高兴收到贵方 10 月 2 日发出的第 1357 号订单。订单中订购了大量我方于 8 月 31 日报盘中所列商品。

除了商品编号 ER-567：橘黄色带红色圆点这款库存不足外，其他的货物我们都可以现货供应。这款产品自上月起就脱销了。在收到贵方的来信之后，我们马上通知了工厂，要求他们加紧生产贵方所订购的这款商品。但由于我们的工厂正在忙于生产前几个月的订单，所以我们目前的状况无法接受你方的订单。

贵方在订单中提到急需这批货物。我们推荐一款贵方可能会感兴趣的类似产品——第 GTY-87 号产品。这款产品有着与 ER-567 号产品一样的设计和相似的质量，但在价格方面，这款产品便宜了 10%。这款产品在其他客户市场中有着极佳的市场表现，我们收到了大量订购此款产品的订单。

我们提出这一建议正是为了贵方的利益。希望能够收到贵方的订单。

谨上

Unit 8

L/C and Other Terms of Payment

信用证及其他支付方式

8.1 Study Aim(学习目标)

(1) 掌握主要支付方式的英文函电撰写表达方式。

(2) 掌握催开、审核、修改和展期信用证信函撰写的方法和注意事项。

8.2 Introduction(专业背景知识介绍)

在国际贸易活动中,买卖双方可能互不信任,买方担心预付款后,卖方不按合同要求发货;卖方也担心在发货或提交货运单据后买方不付款。因此需要两家银行作为买卖双方的保证人,代为收款交单,以银行信用代替商业信用。信用证(Letter of Credit)是国际贸易中最常见的支付方式。除了信用证之外,在国际贸易中另外两种重要的支付方式分别是汇付(Remittance)和托收(Collection)。与信用证不同的是汇付和托收都是以商业信用为基础的支付方式。汇付的方式有三种:电汇(Telegraphic Transfer,T/T),信汇(Mail Transfer,M/T)和票汇(Demand Draft,D/D)。托收可以分为光票托收和跟单托收,其中跟单托收可分为承兑交单(Documents Against Acceptance,D/A)和付款交单(Documents Against Payment,D/P),付款交单又可分为即期付款交单(D/P at sight)和远期付款交单(D/P after sight)。

1. 汇付(Remittance)

汇付是指付款人主动通过银行将款项汇交付款人的一种收付货款的方式。在进出口贸易中,通常是由进口人按合同约定的条件,将货款通过银行汇交给出口人。在通过银行办理汇付时,可分为3种方式。

(1) 电汇(Telegraphic Transfer,T/T)。电汇是进口人将货款交给进口地银行,填写电汇申请书,汇出银行电告汇入银行把货款付给出口人的一种汇款方式。

(2) 信汇(Mail Transfer,M/T)。信汇是进口人将货款交给进口地银行,由银行开具汇款委托书,通过信函寄交所在地银行,委托其向出口人付款的一种方式。

(3) 票汇(Demand Draft,D/D)。票汇是进口人向进口地银行购买银行汇票寄给出口人,出口人凭此向汇票上指定的银行取款的一种方式。汇出银行在开出银行汇票的同时,对汇入行寄发“付款通知书”,汇入行凭此验对汇票后付款。

汇付是单纯性支付(Clean Payment or Simple Payment)。也就是说,在汇付业务中,进口人付款与出口人交货(交单)不是对流进行的。代表货物的货运单据由出口人自行寄交进口人,银行并不经手,而进口人的付款也是自行进行的。虽然通过银行,银行只是提供服务而已。进口人的付款与出口人的发货是建立在商业信用的基础上的。在国际贸易中,汇付方式通常用于预付货款、货到付款、分期付款等业务。

2. 托收(Collection)

(1) 托收的当事人

托收是出口人开具以进口人为付款人的商业汇票,委托银行向进口人收取货款的一种方式。托收方式一般有4个当事人:委托人(Principal)、托收银行(Remitting Bank)、代收银行(Collecting Bank)、付款人(Drawee)。

(2) 托收的种类

根据是否随附货运单据,托收方式可以分成光票托收和跟单托收两大类。

光票托收是出口人仅开具汇票,委托银行收款,不随附任何货运单据。光票托收一般用于收取出口货款尾数、代垫费用、佣金、样品费等,不是托收的主要方式。

跟单托收是出口人发运货物后,开具汇票,连同全套货运单据委托银行向进口人收取货款的一种方式。国际贸易中,使用托收方式收取货款主要是采用跟单托收的办法。

托收属于商业信用,银行办理托收业务时,既没有检查货运单据正确与否或是否完整的义务,也没有保证付款人必须付款的责任。托收虽然是通过银行办理,但银行只是作为出口人的受托人行事,并不承担付款的责任,进口人不付款与银行无关。出口人向进口人收取货款靠的仍是进口人的商业信用。

如果遭到进口人拒绝付款,除非另外有规定,银行没有代管货物的义务,出口人仍然应该关心货物的安全,直到对方付清货款为止。托收对出口人的风险较大,D/A 比 D/P 的风险更大。托收对进口人比较有利,可以免去开证的手续以及预付押金,还有可以预借货物的便利。当然,托收对进口人也不是没有一点风险。如,进口人付款后才取得货运单据,领取货物,如果发现货物与合同规定不符,或者根本就是假的,也会因此而蒙受损失,但总地来说,托收对进口人比较有利。

3. 信用证(Letter of Credit)

信用证是国际贸易中最常见的支付方式,不仅适用于个别交易,也适用于系列交易。信用证的开证程序始于进口方。进口方通知开证行开立以出口方为受益人的信用证。信用证包含进出口双方达成交易的详细内容。信用证开出后,由开证行将信用证寄给出口方所在地的通知行。接到信用证后,银行和出口方会对信用证进行审核。根据审核无误的信用证,出口方就可备货装运。装运后,出口方就可以缮制符合信用证要求的单据,再据此向议付行交单议付,取得货款。信用证是银行应进口人的请求,开给出口人的一种银行有条件地保证付款的凭证。换句话说,在进出口业务中,信用证方式是指银行根据进口人的请求和指示,开给出口人的一种保证在出口人履行所规定的条件时,按期在指定地点支付货款的凭证。

信用证支付是在托收方式的基础上演变出来的一种比较完善的支付方式。在进出口贸易中,买卖双方相距遥远,互不了解,由于双方存在各自的经济利益,为维护各自的经济利益,在进出口货款如何收付这个焦点问题上,双方往往互不信任。为方便交易,避免商业信用的弊病,就产生了信用证支付方式,由银行作为第三者,居间保证付款。由于银行资金雄厚,信誉较好,所以信用证一经出现,便立即被贸易界广泛采用,成为当今国际贸易的主要支付方式。

(1) 修改信用证

信用证的特点决定了出口人的交单,必须与信用证规定完全一致。银行议付出口人的单据应严格遵守"单证一致"的原则。因此,单证不符,会影响出口人的安全收汇甚至整个交易的顺利进行。也就是说,信用证条款与合同规定是否一致,是出口人在信用证方式收取货款,顺利履行交货义务的前提。但在实际业务中,出口人收到的国外来证经常与合同不符,有的是由于开证人和开证银行的工作疏忽;有的是进口人出于不良动机而故意玩弄手段,投机取巧,制造障碍。因此,出口人必须对国外来证进行严格的审核,对其中不能接受的条款及时进行修改。信用证审核应该以买卖合同为基础,以出口国家的有关方针、政策为依据,参照国际商会制定的《跟单信用证统一惯例》第600号出版物来进行。

(2) 催开信用证

一般来说,当交易达成时,买方就有义务在合同规定的时间内通过其往来银行开立信用证。在实践中,习惯做法是在装运期前一个月开立信用证并到达卖方,以便给卖方充足的时间办理装运,如准备货物、预订舱位等。如果买方没有能够及时开立信用证,或买方开立的信用证没有能够及时到达卖方,卖方就必须和买方联系,催开信用证或弄清信用证的下落。撰写这类书信时,注意用词要得体,千万不要使用责怪和厌烦的口吻。应该有礼貌地说明所订货物已经备妥,但有关的信用证却没有收到。如果第一封信函没有回音,可以发第二封信函。这次,仍应克制不满情绪,但可以适当表示失望的心情。

(3) 展延信用证

有时,买方及时开来信用证,但卖方没能及时将货物备妥装运,或买方由于这样或那样的理由要求延迟装运,这时卖方将不得不要求展延信用证中的装运日期和到货日期。不管是要求修改信用证的信,还是要求展延信用证的信,在撰写时都要注意有礼貌,因为不论是修改还是展期,对对方来说都是件麻烦的事。

8.3 Writing Skills(写作技巧)

催证函的写作步骤如下:

(1) 用礼貌的语气提醒买家我方货物已备妥,但尚未收到相应的信用证。

(2) 礼貌地催促买方按时开立信用证,通过引用合同规定或者提醒买家不按时开立信用证的严重性。

(3) 表达期望并要求买方立即采取行动。

催证函的写作步骤及常见表达方式如表 8-1 所示。

表 8-1　催证函的写作步骤及常见表达方式

写作步骤	表达方式
1. 提醒买家我方货已备妥待运或交货期已临近,但尚未收到相关信用证	According to the stipulation of S/C No. 598, you should expedite the covering L/C, otherwise we shall be unable to effect shipment before May 10.(根据第 598 号销售确认书,贵方必须从速开证,否则,我们就不能在 5 月 10 日之前装船了。)
2. 向对方说明需及时开立信用证的原因或者重要性	We wish to remind you that it was agreed when placing the order, that you would establish the required L/C receipt of our Conformation.(我方提醒贵方注意,订货时按双方约定,一接到我方的确认书,贵方就开立信用证。)
3. 请对方及时开立信用证	As the goods have been ready for shipment for quite some time, you must expedite the covering L/C now.(货已备妥多日,贵方现在必须从速开证。)

修改或者延展信用证的信函写作步骤如下:

(1) 告知买方已经收到信用证,并感谢买方及时开立信用证。

(2) 礼貌地指出信用证出现的问题, 并详细解释需要做此修改的原因。

(3) 表达希望对方能积极配合。

改证或信用证展期信函的写作步骤及常见表达方式如表 8-2 所示。

表 8-2　改证或信用证展期信函的写作步骤及常见表达方式

写作步骤	表达方式
1. 告知对方我方已收到信用证	We wish to acknowledge receipt of the L/C NO. 066 for the amount of US $25000.(我方已经收到贵方金额 25000 美元的 066 号信用证。)
2. 指出信用证与合同不符需要修改的地方	The 200 pieces motors are scheduled to be loaded onto S. S. ZheHai on April 20. Please extend your L/C to the end of April.(200 台电动机定于 4 月20 日装上 ZheHai 号船。请延展贵方信用证到 4 月底。)
3. 希望对方予以配合	Please amend L/C NO. 526 allowing transshipment and partial shipment, so that we may effect shipment without delay.(请修改第 526 号信用证,允许转船和分装,以便我方能马上装船。)

其他付款方式信函的写作步骤和常见表达方式如下:

(1) 提示相关合同或者货物。

(2) 提出现在需要的付款方式,并解释原因。

(3) 表达希望能早日收到回复,并暗示希望未来建立持久的商业合作关系。

其他付款方式信函的写作步骤和常见表达方式如表 8-3 所示。

表 8-3　其他付款方式信函的写作步骤和常见表达方式

写作步骤	表达方式
1. 提示合同或相关的货物	We refer you to Contract No...(关于第……号合同) Referring to ...(关于……) With regard to our contract of...(关于我们……号合同) With reference to the contract of...(关于……的合同)

续表

写作步骤	表达方式
2. 提出具体付款的方式和理由	As you know...we suggest that...(正如你所知……我们建议……) As ...we shall be glad if you ...(因为……如果贵方……我们将不胜感激。)
3. 表示希望对方能够同意的意思和愿望	We wish you can accommodate us in this respect.(希望贵方在这方面给予照顾。) We hope to receive your favorable reply.(希望收到贵方的肯定答复。)

回复其他付款方式信函的写作步骤及常见表达方式如表 8-4 所示。

表 8-4 回复其他付款方式信函的写作步骤及常见表达方式

写作步骤	表达方式
1. 说明我方已经收到信函	Thank you for your letter of ...(感谢贵方的……来信。) We have received the letter of...(我方已经收到……来信。)
2. 说明自己是否同意,并阐明理由	We do not agree that...(我们不同意……) We want to make it clear that...(我们想澄清一点……) With regard to...,we regret being unable to accept...(关于……很遗憾,我们不能接受。)
3. 说明自己为此做出的努力以及愿意合作的意向	We hope that we can...sincerely.(我们诚挚地希望我们能……) Considering the long business relationship between us, we...(考虑到我们之间长期的业务关系,我方……)

8.4 Specimen Letters(样函)

Letter 1:

Dear Sirs,

We are pleased to inform you that the goods under your purchase contract No. TY213 are ready for dispatch .

According to the stipulations in the foregoing contract, shipment is to be made during May/June. The date of the shipment is approaching, however, we still have not received your covering L/C to date Therefore, we would like to ask you to rush the L/C so as to enable us to effect shipment within the stipulated time .

When establishing the L/C, please make sure that the L/C stipulations strictly conform to the terms of our contract to avoid subsequent amendments.

We look forward to your L/C soon.

Yours faithfully,

Notes(注释)

1. forgoing *adj.* 上述的,前面的
2. approach *v.* 接近,靠近

3. covering *adj.* 有关的，相关的
4. to date 到今天为止，迄今为止
5. conform to 跟……相一致，跟……相符

Letter 2：

Dear Sirs,

We have received your fax of April 12th, urging us to establish the L/C against our purchase contract No. TY213.

We are really very sorry for the delay in establishing the L/C, which was due to oversight of our staff. As soon as we are sure that it will reach you soon . We apologize again for the trouble we have caused you . We hope after receiving the covering L/C, you will ship the goods as early as possible. Thank you for your cooperation.

Yours faithfully,

Notes（注释）

1. oversight *n.* 疏忽，疏漏
2. instruct *v.* 指示，暗示

Letter 3：

Dear Sirs,

With reference to our sales confirmation No. 9816, we have contacted you several times to urge the establishment of the relevant L/C. To our great regret, however, the above L/C has not yet reached us up to the time of writing.

The goods you ordered have been ready for quite some time . But as you failed to establish the L/C in time, we have to cancel the shipping space we booked, which has Caused us much inconvenience . However, in view of our long—term business relations , we are prepared to wait for your L/C, which must reach us not later than November 23. If you again fail to send us the L/C in time, we shall cancel our sales confirmation and ask you to refund us the storage charges we have paid on your behalf .

We look forward to your early reply.

Yours faithfully,

Notes（注释）

1. with reference to 关于
2. relevant *adj.* 有关的，相应的
3. refund *v.* 退还，偿还
4. storage charges 仓储费

Letter 4：

Dear Sirs,

We have received your L/C No. 3310 covering Order No. 8210. On examination; we find the above L/C contains the following discrepancies:

1. As stipulated in our contract, transshipment and partial shipment are allowed, while your credit calls for "shipment by direct steamer".

2. The total amount should be US $20000 rather than US $2000.

3. The commission granted for this transaction should be 3% instead of 5%.

We therefore request you to instruct your bank to make the necessary amendment as early as possible, otherwise shipment will be delayed.

Thank you for your cooperation.

Yours faithfully,

Notes(注释)

1. discrepancy *n.* 差异,不同,不符点
2. transshipment *n.* 装运
3. partial shipment 分批装运
4. call for 要求

Letter 5:

Dear Sirs,

We very much appreciate the early arrival of your L/C No. 98642 issued by the bank of Sydney.

Upon checking the stipulations of the above credit, we regret to find the goods are required to be shipped "by direct steamer".

As direct sailings form our port to Sydney are few and far between, we expect you to allow us to ship the goods via Hong Kong. Therefore, please delete the clause" by direct steamer" and insert the Wording "transshipment is allowed".

We hope that this amendment will meet with your approval and thank you for your cooperation.

Yours faithfully,

Notes(注释)

1. few and far between 稀少
2. delete *v.* 删除,删去
3. insert *v.* 插入,加上
4. approval *n.* 赞成,承认,批准

Letter 6:

Dear Sirs,

We thank you for your L/C No. AX3326 issued through the Bank of Cyprus covering 2000 sets of microwave ovens.

We are afraid that we are not in a position to ship the goods by S. S "HuaHai" as scheduled, for sailing is cancelled because of serious damage it sustained while at the berth of

Hong Kong. However, we have contacted the shipping company and arranged for the shipment to be effected two weeks later. In this case, we earnestly hope that you will understand our situation and extend the letter of credit to the end of August.

We hope our request will not cause you much inconvenience. Your compliance with our request will be highly appreciated.

Yours faithfully,

Notes(注释)

1. schedule *v.* 计划,安排
2. sustain *v.* 承受,忍受,遭受
3. berth *n.* 停泊处,泊位
4. earnestly *adv.* 认真地,诚挚地

Letter 7:

Dear Sirs,

Thank you for being so prompt in delivering our last order. Now, we are considering placing further orders with you on the condition that you will change your terms of payment.

So far, all our purchases from you have been paid by confirmed, irrevocable letter of credit. After long years of satisfactory trading, we feel that we are entitled to easier terms of payment. Most of our suppliers allow us to pay by D/A at 60 day's sight. We shall be grateful if you could grant us the same terms.

We hope our request will meet with your agreement and look forward to your early reply.

Yours faithfully,

Notes(注释)

1. on the condition that 条件是,只要
2. confirmed, irrevocable letter of credit 保兑的,不可撤销信用证
3. entitle *vt.* 给……权利,给……资格

Letter 8:

Dear Sirs,

Thank you for your letter of July 21, in which you asked for an extension of the terms of payment.

In view of the pleasant business relationship we have had with you for many years, we have decided to make an exception to our rules and accept your suggestion. We shall, therefore, in the future draw on you at 60 day's sight, documents against acceptance.

We hope that our concession will lead to an increase in business between our companies. We assure you of our close cooperation at all times.

Yours faithfully,

Notes(注释)

1. extension *n.* 延长,扩充
2. in view of 鉴于,考虑到,由于
3. draw *v.* 开出(汇票)
4. concession *n.* 让步,妥协
5. at all time 一直

Letter 9:

Dear Sirs,

We thank you for your quotation dated May 24 for 1000 sets of Little Swan TX128 washing machines. We find your price as delivery date satisfactory; however we would suggest you alter your terms of payment.

We have been dealing with you in household electric appliances on the basis of irrevocable L/C payable at sight for quite a few years. Under this arrangement, it has indeed cost us a great deal, From the moment the credit is opened till the time our buyers pay us, the tie-up of our funds lasts about four months. This is currently a particularly serious problem for us in view of the difficult economic climate and the prevailing high interest rates.

With an eye to our long friendly business relations and our bright Cooperation prospects, we suggest you accept CAD on arrival of the goods.

Your favorable reply will be much appreciate.

Yours faithfully,

Notes(注释)

1. little swan 小天鹅
2. washing machine 洗衣机
3. alter *v.* 改变
4. household electric appliance 家用电器
5. quite a few 相当多的
6. tie-up 占压(资金)
7. currently *adv.* 现在,当前
8. prevailing *adj.* 流行的,主要的,占优势的
9. interest rate 利率
10. with an eye to 着眼于,考虑到
11. prospect *n.* 前景,前途
12. CAD(cash against documents)付款交单

8.5 Focal Words(焦点词汇及短语)

(1) foregoing *adj.* 上述的,前面的,上面的

e.g. We hope the foregoing terms of payment will be acceptable to you. 我们希望贵方

能够接受上述的付款条件。

Please let us know at an early date whether the goods we ordered can be shipped within the foregoing time of period. 请尽快告知我方，我们订购的货物能否在上述期限内到达我方。

(2) approach *v*. 接近，靠近

e. g. Since the sales season is approaching, we hope you can deliver the goods as early as possible. 因为销售季节即将来临，我们希望贵方能够尽早发货。

The date of shipment is approaching, but we haven't received your shipping instructions. 装运期将至，但我们仍未收到贵方的装运指示。

(3) to date 到今天为止，迄今为止，到目前为止

e. g. We haven't received any information from you to date. 迄今为止，我们未从贵方收到任何消息。

The captioned goods have not arrived at our end to date. 标题中提到的货物至今仍未到达我处。

(4) rush *v*. 匆忙，加速，快速

e. g. On receiving your letter, we have instructed our factory to rush production of your goods. 收到贵方来函之后，我们已经通知工厂加快生产贵方的产品。

We wish you will rush the relevant L/C so that we can effect punctual shipment. 我们希望贵方速开信用证，以便我方按时装运。

(5) subsequent *adj*. 后来的，随后的

e. g. This regulation applies to all subsequent transactions. 这项规定适用于以后所有的交易。

Subsequent to receiving your letter, we have contacted the shipping company, requiring about the shipping space. 接到贵方的来函之后，我们已经联系了船运公司，询问舱位的情况。

(6) urge *v*. 敦促，催促

e. g. We have written to urge the manufacturer to speed up production of your order. 我们已经写信敦促制造商加速生产贵方的订货。

On receiving your letter, we have contacted our bank and urged them to open the letter of credit. 一收到贵方来函，我们就联系了银行，催促他们开立信用证。

(7) due to 因为，由于

e. g. Due to our heavy commitment, we regret our inability to accept your order. 由于我方订单太多，很遗憾，我们无法接受贵方的订单。

Due to the recent shortage of raw materials, we have to cut down our production. 因为最近原材料短缺，我们不得不减产。

(8) on one's behalf or on behalf of sb. 代表某人，代替某人

e. g. Our contract is concluded on FOB basis, but we can offer to book the shipping space on your behalf. 我们的合同是在离岸价格的基础上达成的，但是我们可以代你们定

舱位。

(9) refund *v.* 退还,偿还,赔偿

e. g. The shipping company refunded the cost of the damaged goods. 船运公司赔偿了损坏的货物的损失。

You will have to refund us the the losses if you cancel your order. 如果贵方取消订单,您就要赔偿我们损失。

We will refund the goods to you if our customers are not interested. 如果我方客户不感兴趣,我们会把货物退还给你们。

(10) few and far between 稀少,很少

e. g. As direct steamers sailing to your port are few and far between, we have to ship the goods via Hong Kong. 因为开往贵港的直达船稀少,我们不得不经香港转运。

(11) discrepancy *n.* 差异,不同,不符点

e. g. The seller is liable for the refund of the extra cost because of the discrepancy in weight. 卖方应负责退还因重量差异而多收的货款。

There are several discrepancies between the clauses of the L/C and the terms of the contract. 信用证条款与合同条款有几点不符之处。

(12) on account of 因为,由于

e. g. On account of the recent earthquake, we are not able to deliver the goods before June. 由于最近的地震,我们无法在6月份之前交货。

We regret that the L/C didn't reach you in time on account of our fault. 很遗憾,由于我方过失,信用证未能及时到达贵方。

(13) postpone *v.* 推迟,使延期

e. g. Taking all these factors into consideration, we allow you to postpone delivering the goods. 考虑到这些因素,我们同意贵方推迟交货。

If you agree to postpone the establishment of the L/C until (or to) the next week, we shall be much appreciated. 如果贵方答应推迟到下周开立信用证,我们将不胜感激。

(14) exert oneself to do sth. 尽力做……

e. g. You can rest assured that we shall exert ourselves to comply with your request. 请放心,我们将尽力满足贵方的要求。

We promise to exert ourselves to rush the production of your order. 我们保证尽力加紧生产贵方的订货。

(15) draw *v.* 开出(汇票)

e. g. As agreed, we are drawing (a draft) on you for the value of this sample shipment. 按约定,我们将开出一张汇票向贵方索取这批样货的价款。

We are drawing on you at sight against your purchase of 200 sets of color TV sets. 对于贵方购买的200台彩电,我们将开出即期汇票向贵方索取货款。

(16) alter *v.* 改变,修改,改动

e. g. We have altered our terms of payment. 我们已经修改了我们的付款条件。

(17) prevailing *adj*. 流行的，主要的，占优势的

e. g. As we all know, the prevailing economic climate is not so good. 众所周知，当前的经济形势不佳。

The prevailing price of this kind of product is much higher than ours. 这种产品的市场价格比我们的价格要高得多。

(18) with an eye to 着眼于，考虑到，为了

e. g. We have lowered our price with an eye to closing this deal. 为了达成这笔交易，我们已经降低了我们的价格。

With an eye to our business prospects, we wish you will change your terms of payment. 为了我们彼此的贸易前景，我们希望您可以变更付款条件。

(19) Proforma Invoice 形式发票，是为了形式上的需要而由卖方出具给买方的一种发票，对买卖双方均无约束力，仅作为参考报价，便于买方办理一些必要的进口手续。除非另有说明，形式发票上所列价格往往要由卖方予以最后确认。

e. g. We hope the enclosed Proforma Invoice will help you to apply for the foreign exchange needed. 希望所附的形式发票将有助于您申请所需外汇。

Complying with the request in your letter of April 26th, we take pleasure in enclosing you our Proforma Invoice in quadruplicate. 根据您4月26日来函要求，我方高兴地随函附寄一式四份形式发票。

(20) despite *prep*. 不管，尽管，不论

e. g. Despite your delay in opening the relative L/C, we promise to ship the goods as early as possible. 尽管贵方信用证开立延迟，但是我们还是保证尽量早日发货。

Despite the fact that our manufacturer is heavily committed, we accept your order with a view to our long-standing business relationship. 尽管我们的制造商订单任务繁重，但考虑到我们长期的业务关系，我们还是接受贵方的订单。

(21) specify *v*. 指定，详细说明，明确规定

e. g. Terms of payment are specified in great detail in our contract. 我们合同中对付款条件有详细规定。

As specified in the L/C, the port of destination is New York. 信用证明确规定，目的港为纽约。

(22) at one's end 在……处，在……地

e. g. Please open the relevant L/C through a well-known bank at your end. 请通过贵地知名银行开立信用证。

Our representative at your end will go to visit your factory shortly. 我们驻贵地的代表不久将去参观贵方的工厂。

(23) amendment *n*. 修改，修正

e. g. Any amendment in the contract can be only made after having the consent of the two parties concerned. 只有在双方同意的情况下，才可对合同内容做出修改。

With regard to the present price level, we proposed an amendment in the contract we signed on May 1st. 鉴于目前的价格水平,我们建议对 5 月 1 日的合同内容进行修改。

(24) durability *n.* 耐久力,耐用性

durable *adj.* 耐用的,持久的

e. g. People often buy durable goods on installments in Western countries. 在西方国家,人们经常通过分期付款的方式购买耐用消费品。

(25) installment *n.* 分期付款

e. g. We shall reimburse you the total amount of the imported equipment by installments in 4 years. 我们将在四年内分期向贵方偿还进口设备的全部款项。

The cost of the machine you supplied may be repaid by 8 equal installments with the resultant products. 贵方所提供的机器的价款,可以用该机器生产出来的产品分八次等额偿还。

(26) sum *n.* 一笔钱(款项)

e. g. We can not accept the sums you proposed in your claim. 我们不能接受贵方的索赔数额。

As this transaction involves a very large sum, buyers have to think twice before deciding. 由于这笔交易数额巨大,买主在决定前必须再三考虑。

8.6 Exercise(练习)

1. Multiple choice.

(1) To our regret, your L/C was found not properly ________ on the following points in spite of our request.

A. amend B. to amend C. amending D. amended

(2) We hope that the stipulation of your L/C are in ________ with the terms of the contract.

A. conformity B. conform C. conformability D. comfort

(3) We have receive your L/C ________ the bank of China.

A. opened with B. open in C. opened through D. open at

(4) Please amend your L/C No. 1162 ________ transshipment and partial shipment.

A. allow B. to allow C. open D. can open

(5) We suggest that you ________ the covering letter of credit without the least possible delay.

A. will open B. shall open C. open D. can open

(6) A 4% discount will be granted only ________ at your order exceeds USD 2000.

A. depends on B. for condition that

C. on condition that D. subject to

(7) An exporter cannot receive payment until the goods on consignment ________

sometime in the future.

A. have offered for sale　　B. are quoted

C. arrive at destination　　D. have been sold

(8) We have made ________ that we would accept D/A at 60 day's sight for this order.

A. have offered for sale　　B. are quoted

C. arrive at destination　　D. have been sold

(9) ________ an order for one hundred pieces or more we allow a special discount of 5% for payment by L/C.

A. At　　B. In　　C. On　　D. From

(10) We find your terms ________ and now send you our order for 2 sets of generators.

A. satisfied　　B. satisfaction　　C. satisfactory　　D. of satisfaction

2. Put the following English phrases into Chinese or Chinese phrases into English.

(1) 预付货款

(2) 汇票

(3) 承兑交单

(4) 先交货后付款

(5) 寄售

(6) amendment advice

(7) exert oneself to do sth.

(8) out of the question

(9) deferred payment

(10) on one's behalf

3. Translate the following Chinese sentences into English using the words or phrases in the brackets, and translate the following English sentences into Chinese.

(1) 贵方6月11日来函收悉,得知贵方无法延展标题所指的信用证,我们感到很遗憾。(subject L/C)

(2) 很遗憾,由于贵方的信用证耽误,我们无法在3月份装运,请尽快解决此问题。(please attend to this matter with all speed)

(3) 只要贵方提出,我们愿意给你们60天的展期,并真诚希望这将有助于贵方摆脱当前困境。(help you out of your present embarrassment)

(4) We will draw on you by our documentary draft at sight on collection basis.

(5) In view of the small amount of this transportation, we are prepared to accept payment by D/P at 30 day's sight for the value of the goods shipped.

(6) To cover our shipment, we request you to establish a commercial letter of credit in

our favor for the contracted amount through an American bank.

4. Translate the following letter into English.

(1)

敬启者:

昨日收到了贵方第1123号订单下的6656号信用证。

我们遗憾地指出,信用证晚到了20天,这样一来,我们不得不要求贵方将装运期和信用证的有效期分别延长到5月2日和5月17日。另外,由于贵方开立信用证延迟,所以修改信用证的费用应该由贵方承担。我们等候贵方用电传把延长信用证期限的单证发给我们,以便我们可以发货,谢谢。

谨上

(2)

敬启者:

贵方9月29日来电收悉。在来电中,贵方要求将7796号信用证延期2周,因为贵方无法在规定日期内装运。

收到贵方来电后,我们联络了我们的客户。但是,他们说自己急需这些货物,不可能允许延期交货。所以,展证是不可能的。

因此,我们要求贵方尽力按原计划装运。如果贵方不能照办,我们将要求贵方赔偿我们所有损失。

盼早复。

谨上

Unit 9

Packing and Shipment

包装和装运

9.1 Study Aim(学习目标)

(1) 掌握常见的国际货物包装及运输方式的专业英语表述。

(2) 掌握有关货物包装与运输的信函的撰写技巧。

9.2 Introduction(专业背景知识介绍)

一般的,进入国际流通领域的货物不但要经过长途运输,而且要经过多次的转运和存储。包装条件和运输条件是进出口贸易合同的一项要件。进出口双方在签订合同时,一般对包装问题和运输方式等问题进行洽商,并做出具体的规定。

1. 包装(Packing)

在国际贸易中包装分为两大类:一类是运输包装(transport packing),是指将货物装入特定的容器,或以特定方式成件或成箱地包装。又称大包装或者外包装,是指将货物装入特定容器或以特定方式成件或成箱地包装。运输包装的作用在于保护货物在长时间和远距离的运输过程中不被损坏或者丢失,同时又可以方便货物的搬运,起到减少费用,节省租仓费的作用。另一类是销售包装(selling packing),又指小包装或者内包装,是指对制造出来的商品以适当的材料或容器进行初次包装。销售包装除了保护商品的品质外,还有美化商品,易携带商品的作用。目前商品的包装呈现小型化、透明化和实用化的倾向。

常见的运输包装有:

(1) 箱。如铁箱、木箱、板条箱、纸箱等;

(2) 桶。如木桶、塑料桶、铁桶等;

(3) 包,袋。如布袋、麻袋、纸袋、塑料袋等;

(4) 瓶。如长颈瓶、钢瓶等。

此外,也有少数商品不采用包装,仅仅采取散装(in bulk)和裸装(nude packed)方式。

关于包装的信函写的简明扼要。这类信函书写时,出口方可以向进口方详细描述其习惯包装方式(customary packing),同时也说明可以接受进口方的包装要求(packing instruction),但额外费用应由进口方承担。进口方也可以告知出口方其包装要求或对包装的担心,如果要更改有关包装责任的任何条款,都必须在装运前经双方协商同意后确定。

2. 装运(Shipment)

装运是国际货物贸易买卖合同中不可缺少的一项条款,合同签订以后,负责装运的一方必须履行安排运输的义务。在实际中,装运业务通常包括通关、租船订舱、缮制装运单据、发出装船通知等环节。

装运条款一般包括装运时间、装运港及目的港、装船时间、装运单据、分批装运或者转船装运等。装运时间通常是指将货物装上运输工具的时间或者期限。在按照 FOB、CFR、CIF 条件成交的情况下,卖方的装运时间以提单上签署的日期为依据。如果提单上的日期在合同规定的日期之内,那么卖方就算是履行了合同的交货义务。

在货物装运之前,有时买方会给卖方一个书面的通知,即装运须知,用来明确装运的要求、装船方式、包装规定和货物标记等。卖方完成货物装运之后,应履行合同的规定,并及时写信通知买方,即寄送装船通知。装船通知一般包括合同(或订单)号码、商品名称、数量、货值、船名及其起航日期等。寄送装船通知的目的是让买方及时办理保险并做好接货的准备。卖方完成发货后,必须向买方提供装运单据。装运单据是卖方履行合同及取得货款的重要依据。装运单据的种类和份数,由买卖双方根据每笔交易的具体情况协商决定。

在实践中,货运单据的种类很多,但可以把它分成两大类,即主要单据和辅助单据。主要的装船单据(shipping documents)包括:海运提单(ocean bill of lading)、商业发票(commercial invoice)和保险单(insurance policy)等。辅助单据包括:特定国家所需要的单据,如海关发票(customs invoice)、领事发票(consular invoice)、原产地证明书(certificate of origin)等;以及附属于商业发票的单据,如包装单(packing list)、重量体积单(weight and measurement list)、检验证明书(certificate of inspection)、其他单据(other documents)。

书写装运函的目的一般是敦促卖方尽快装运,修改装运条件,寄送装运通知,寄送装运单据等。此外,利用通知对方有关装运事项的机会,一方可以表达对与另一方进一步发展业务关系的愿望。

9.3 Writing Skills(写作技巧)

包装信函的写作步骤及常见的表达方式如表 9-1 所示。

回复包装信函的写作步骤和常见表达方式如表 9-2 所示。

表 9-1　包装信函的写作步骤及常见的表达公式

写作步骤	表达方式
1. 告知对方此次写信的目的,引起对方的注意	We thank you for the letter...(很高兴收到你方来信。) We wish to draw your attention to the following.(我们希望以下的问题能够引起贵方的注意。) We are now writing to you in regard to the packing of...(我方来函告知关于……的包装问题。)
2. 详细说明包装的要求和需要注意的问题	We are pleased to inform you that we shall pack our garments in...instead of in ...(我们很高兴通知您,我们的货物包装应该用……而不是……) As the goods are susceptible to be broken, these must be parked in ...(由于货物很容易受损,它们应该用……装运。)
3. 礼貌的结束语,并表示希望对方的配合,盼早日得到回复	We hope you will accept ...and assure you of our sincere cooperation.(我们希望您接受……,来确保我们真诚的合作能够达成。) We await your early reply.(期盼早日回复。)

表 9-2　回复包装信函的写作步骤和常见表达方式

写作步骤	表达方式
1. 感谢对方来函,并告知对方回信目的	Thank you for your letter of...(谢谢你关于……的来信。) We regret to inform you that...(我们很遗憾地告知你……)
2. 关于对方提出问题的解决方法和建议	In order to ..., we would like to make the following suggestions for your consideration(为了……我们特提出以下意见供贵方参考。)
3. 希望对方能确认包装意见和办法	We hope to have your confirmation on the packing.(希望得到贵方对此包装的确认。)

进口方给出口方的装运信函的写作步骤及常见的表达方式如表 9-3 所示。

表 9-3　进口方给出口方的装运信函的写作步骤及常见的表达方式

写作步骤	表达方式
1. 简要说明交易货物以及有关装运条件,敦促对方及时交货	We are very anxious to know about the shipment of ...(我们急切地想知道我们……的发运消息。) For some reason we request you to advance shipment of the consignment under order...from ...to...(出于一些原因,我们要求贵方将……订单下的货物装运期由……提前到……)
2. 陈述事实,说明理由	As we are in urge need of the goods, we find it necessary to stress the importance of making punctual shipment within the validity of the L/C.(由于我们急需这批货,所以我们认为有必要强调在信用证有效期内按时装运的重要性。)
3. 表明我方的观点及希望继续合作的愿望	We shall appreciate very much your close cooperation in this respect.(我们非常感谢贵方在这方面的积极配合。)

出口方给进口方的装运信函的写作步骤及常见的表达方式如表 9-4 所示。

表 9-4 出口方给进口方的装运信函的写作步骤及常见的表达方式

写作步骤	表达方式
1. 开头语	We have for acknowledgement your letter of November 20th, asking for definite news of shipment of the subject goods. (我方已经收到贵方12月20日的来信,要求明确关于主要货物最新的装运信息。)
2. 结束语	The shipment will reach you within 5 days. (货物将于5天内到达贵方。) We should be obliged if you would kindly understand the situation. (如果您能谅解我方的处境,我方将不胜感激。)

9.4 Specimen Letters(样函)

Letter 1:

Dear Sirs,

The 12000 chairs you ordered will be ready for dispatch by 17th September. Since you require them to be transported by sea, we are arranging for them to be packed in seaworthy containers.

Each chair is enclosed in corrugated carton, and 20 to a wooden case lined with plastics lining. A container holds 240 chairs; the whole cargo would therefore comprise 50 containers, each weighing 8 tons. Dispatch can be made from our works to Shanghai are US $80 per container, totally US $4000 for this consignment, excluding container hire, which will be charged for your account.

We hope that you will be satisfied with our packing arrangements and please let us have your delivery instruction at an earlier date.

Yours faithfully,

Notes(注释)

1. arrange for 安排
2. seaworthy *adj.* 适用于海洋运输的,经受得起航海的
3. container *n.* 集装箱
4. hire *n.* 租金
5. corrugated carton 瓦楞板纸箱
6. be lined with 衬有……,内衬……
7. lining *n.* 衬里,内衬
8. harbor *n.* 海港
9. freight charge 运费
10. exclude *vt.* 把……排除在外
11. for sb's account 记入……的账户,费用由……承担

Letter 2:

Dear Sirs,

Thank you for your letter of May 2, asking us to inform you of the packing requirements of Butterfly Brand Brown Sugar we ordered. After discussing this matter with our client, we are glad to advise you that our clients request as follows:

As brown sugar is moisture absorbent especially in hot rainy season, it should be packed in kraft paper bags containing 20 small paper bags of 1 kilogram net each, two kraft paper bags to a carton lined with waterproof paper。

We hope that the above packing requirements will be acceptable to you and thank you for your cooperation.

Yours faithfully,

Notes(注释)

1. butterfly *n.* 蝴蝶
2. brown sugar 红糖
3. client *n.* 顾客,客户
4. as follows 如下
5. moisture *n.* 潮湿,湿气
6. absorbent *adj.* 能吸收的
7. kraft *n.* 牛皮纸
8. waterproof *adj.* 防水的,不透水的

Letter 3:

Dear Sirs,

Enclosed we are returning for your file the counter-signed Sales Contract. No. CHJ886.

We wish to invite your attention to the marking. Please make sure that the port of destination. New York, should be clearly stenciled on the outer packing. Moreover, the case number should be clearly indicated . As these goods are precision instruments which cannot stand rough handing, the wording "HANDLE WITH CARE" should also be marked on the packing.

We appreciate your cooperation and please send us the shipping advice as soon as the goods are dispatched.

Yours faithfully,

Notes(注释)

1. counter-signed 会签
2. stencil *vt.* 用蜡纸印刷
3. precision *n.* 精密仪器
4. stand *v.* 持久,经受
5. rough handing 野蛮装卸
6. HANDLE WITH CARE 谨慎搬运

7. outer packing 外包装
8. the port of destination 目的港

Letter 4:

Dear Sirs,

We wish to call you attention to the fact that up to the present moment, no news has come from you about the shipment of our order for 2000 bales of cane.

According to the terms of our contract No. 55986, the shipment is to be effected by April 12,2004. When we placed the order, we explicitly point out that punctual shipment was of special importance because we are in urgent need of the goods.

We have to say that if the order is not executed within the stipulated time we shall be compelled to seek an alternative source of supply . Please understand how serious the situation is and take great efforts to get the goods dispatched with the least possible delay.

We look forward to receiving your shipping advice by fax within the next seven days.

Yours faithfully,

Notes(注释)

1. call one's attention to 提请……的注意
2. cane *n.* 藤条
3. explicitly *adv.* 明白地,明确地
4. punctual *adj.* 严格守时的,准时的
5. of special importance 非常重要,相当重要
6. urgent *adj.* 急迫的,紧急的,急切的
7. execute *v.* 执行,实行,完成
8. stipulate *v.* 规定,保证
9. compel *vt.* 强迫,迫使
10. dispatch *vt.* 分派,派遣,发送
11. shipping advice 装运通知

Letter 5:

Dear Mr. Green,

According to our purchase contract No. Tx-954 covering 6000 pieces Giant sewing machines, the shipment is scheduled for September 2004 . But yesterday our customer inform us that they needed the goods urgently to fulfill their orders with their buyers, so we venture to ask you to advance shipment to June 2004.

We realize that the change of delivery date will probably inconvenience you and we offer our sincere apologies. We know that you will understand that we would not ask for earlier delivery if we did not have compelling reasons for doing so.

In view of our longstanding cordial commercial relationship, we would be very grateful if you would make a special effort to comply with our request.

Thank you for your cooperation. We look forward to your early reply.

Sincerely yours,

Notes(注释)

1. purchase contract 购货合同
2. sewing machines 缝纫机
3. giant *n.* 巨人,大力士
4. schedule *n.* 计划,安排
5. fulfill *vt.* 履行,完成,实现
6. venture *v.* 冒昧,斗胆
7. advance *v.* 提前
8. delivery *n.* 交货
9. inconvenience *vt.* 给……带来麻烦,给……带来不便
10. longstanding *adj.* 长时间的

Letter 6:

Dear Mr. White,

We have received your letter dated 6th March requesting earlier delivery of goods under your purchase contract No. TX-954.

We have contracted our supplier with the request that they hasten their production of your contracted goods, But much to our regret, they are not in a position to do so, for they are heavily booked with orders for months ahead.

Under the present condition, we regret to inform you that we are not in a position to comply with your request, we will, however, make our greatest efforts to ensure that the goods will be shipped within the contract time.

Sincerely yours,
Ping Wang
Chief Seller

Notes(注释)

1. hasten *v.* 催促,加速
2. to one's regret 令……遗憾的是……
3. book *v.* 订货
4. ensure *v.* 保证

Letter 7:

Dear Sirs,

Thank you for your Letter of Credit No. 55876 in favor of Kee & Co., Ltd. We are pleased to inform you that we have delivered 20 metric tons of soybeans on board S. S. "Sunflower", which is scheduled to sail from Dalian on May 16 and due in New York on or about Jun 28.

To facilitate your taking delivery of the goods, we enclose one set of shipping documents comprising:

1. One non-negotiable copy of the bill of lading.
2. Commercial invoice in duplicate.
3. One copy of the certificate of guarantee.
4. One copy of the certificate of quantity.
5. One copy of the insurance policy.

We are glad that we have been able to execute your order as contracted . We hope the shipment will reach you in perfect condition and look forward to your further orders.

Yours faithfully,

Liang Zhang

Encl.

Notes(注释)

1. in favor of 以……为受益人
2. soybean *n.* 大豆
3. sail *v.* 起航,开船
4. facilitate *vt.* 使容易
5. enclose *vt.* 把……封在里面,随函寄去
6. comprise *v.* 包含
7. non-negotiable copy of the bill of loading 不可以议付(不能流通)的提单副本
8. certificate of guarantee 保证书,质量担保书
9. insurance policy 保险单
10. due *adj.* (车或者船) 应到的
11. in perfect condition 完好无损,状况良好
12. certificate of quantity 数量证明书

9.5 Focal Words(焦点词汇及短语)

(1) seaworthy *adj.* 适于海洋运输的,经得起航海的

e. g. We'd like to advise you that the packing of the goods must be seaworthy. 我们建议贵方货物的包装一定要适合海洋运输。

The goods are to be packed in seaworthy wooden cases. 货物将用适合海洋运输的木箱包装。

(2) exclude *vt.* 把……排除在外

e. g. The costs added up to US $2000, excluding the insurance premium. 除保险费用以外,费用合计为2000美元。

Having the goods insured is excluded from the sellers' responsibilities. 为货物投保不是

卖方的责任。

（3）stand *v*. 持久，经受

e. g. The packing of the goods must be strong enough to stand rough handling during transit. 包装必须结实，要能够经受得起运输途中的野蛮装卸。

We are afraid that the goods are perishable and cannot stand time-consuming ocean transportation. 我们担心货物容易变质，经受不起耗时的海洋运输。

（4）punctual *adj*. 严守时刻的，准时的

e. g. As we all know, punctual delivery of the goods is the basis for our good business relationships. 众所周知，准时交货是我们之间良好业务关系的基础。

If you can ensure punctual effectuation of this contract, we will consider placing repeat orders. 如果贵方能按期履约，我们将考虑再次向贵方订货。

（5）dispatch 分派，派遣，发运，有时也用 despatch

e. g. We confirm our cable of 8th and wish to inform you that the goods have been dispatched by S. S. "ANDES MARU". 现确认我 8 日电，并通知贵方货物已用"安第斯"轮发运。

We will arrange for the goods to be dispatched by the first available steamer upon receipt of your L/C. 我们一收到贵方信用证，就安排用最早的货船发货。

（6）sail *vi*. 起航，开船

e. g. The steamer on which we have booked shipping space is scheduled to sail from Qingdao to Boston on August 8. 我们订舱的货轮计划于 8 月 8 日从青岛开往波士顿。

We have already had the goods shipped by S. S. "Fortune", which is to sail for your port at the end of this week. 我们已经将货物装上了"幸运"号轮船，该轮将于本周末开往贵港。

（7）amendment *n*. 修改，修正

e. g. Any amendment in the contract can be only made after having the consent of the two parties concerned. 只有在双方同意的情况下，才可对合同内容做出修改。

With regard to the present price level, we proposed an amendment in the contract we signed on May 1st. 鉴于目前的价格水平，我们建议对 5 月 1 日的合同内容进行修改。

（8）fragility *n*. 脆弱，易碎

fragile *adj*. 脆的，易碎的

e. g. There is a mark "fragile, handle with care" on the box. 包装箱上有"易碎品，轻拿、轻放"的标志。

Glass is a matter of great fragility. 玻璃是一种易碎品。

（9）recovery *n*. 收回，收复

recover *vt*. 收回

e. g. The recovery of our investment is expected to be attained at the end of this year. 在今年年底我们就可有望收回投资。

Two years is not enough to recover the total cost. 两年内不足以收回所有成本。

(10) arise from 起源于……，由……引起，由……起源

e. g. Losses arising from inadequate packing should be assumed by the seller. 由于包装不当引起的损失应该由卖方承担。

All disputes arising from the fulfillment of this agreement should be settled through friendly consultation. 在履行协议过程中，如果双方产生争议，双方应友好协商解决。

(11) be in sb.'s interest to do sth. 做……对某人是有利的，还可以用

in sb.'s favor or in the favor/interest of sb. 以某人为受益人，为了某人的利益

e. g. It is in your interest to have the goods packed in cartons, which are cheaper. 使用便宜的纸箱包装对贵方是有利的。

It is in the favor of the buyer to effect an earlier shipment. 提前装运对买方是有利的。

(12) commit *vt.* 承担任务，接受订单，答应负责

e. g. As we are fully committed, we are not in a position to entertain any further orders. 由于我们订货已满，所以不能接受新的订单。

We wish to be able to ship the goods well ahead of the shipping schedule, but we cannot commit ourselves. 我们希望能早于装运日期交货，但是不能保证做到。

You are committed to open the L/C within this month. 贵方答应在本月开出信用证。

We cannot commit ourselves to meet your requirement. 我们不能保证一定能满足您的要求。

(13) press *vt.* 劝说，催促，敦促

e. g. Our customer pressed us to fulfill his order at an early date. 我们的客户催促我们早日履行订单。

The buyer is pressing us for the goods they have ordered. 买方催我们交货。

(14) at one's earliest convenience 在……方便时尽早

e. g. Please inform us of your decision at your earliest convenience. 请在你们方便的时候尽早告知我们您的决定。

The shipping company has promised to notify us of the earlier space available at its earliest. 货运公司答应在方便的时候尽早通知我们最早可以订到的舱位的情况。

convenience *n.* 方便，便利，便利的事物

(15) justify *vt.* 证明……是正当的

e. g. We believe you will agree that our request is justified. 我们相信，贵方也会认为我们的要求是合情合理的。

We hope you will justify why shipment of the goods has been delayed . 我们希望，对于发货延迟，贵方将会给出充分的理由。

Nothing can justify such careless mistakes. 如此粗心的错误不可原谅。

(16) entrust *v.* 委托，交托

e. g. We entrusted the goods to your care. 我们委托贵方照管货物。

We have entrusted our representative with the right to conclude a deal. 我们已经授予我们的代表达成交易的权利。

(17) It pays to do sth. 做……是上算的,做……是值得的,做……是有利的

e. g. Please rest assured that it pays to buy our products at the current price. 请放心,按现行价格购买我们的商品是很值得的。

It pays to advertise our products on TV. 为我们的产品在电视上做广告是值得的。

(18) assemble *vt*. 装配, 组装,其名词形式为 assembly

e. g. These products are assembled by a joint venture. 这些产品是一家合资企业组装的。

They imported parts and components and assembled them into cars. 他们进口零部件,把它们组装成汽车。

All parts must be strictly checked before assembly. 所有部件在装配前必须严格检查。

assembly line 装配线

(19) make compensation for sb. 's losses 补偿某人的损失

e. g. You should make compensation for our losses caused by the late delivery. 贵方应向我方赔偿由于晚交货给我们带来的损失。

(20) consignment *n*. 寄售的货物,委托代销的商品

e. g. As desired, we agree to ship our 500 pieces of bicycles to you on consignment. 按照贵方要求,我们同意以寄售的方式发给贵方 500 辆自行车。

You may sell the consignment at the prevailing market price. 贵方可按市价销售这批货物。

(21) be in a position to do sth. 能够

be not in a position/in no position to do sth. 不能做某事

be in a good position to do sth. 很有能力做某事,完全能做某事

be in a difficult position to do sth. 很难做某事

e. g. We are very sorry to say that we are not in a position to agree on your counter-offer. 我们很抱歉地向您告知,不能同意贵方的还盘。

We are in a position to offer you 50 metric tons of soybean, FAQ, 2002 crop. 我方可以报给贵方 50 公吨大豆,2002 年收成的大路货。

We are in a good position to meet your requirements. 我们完全可以满足贵方的需求。

9.6 Exercise(练习)

1. Multiple choice.

(1) The analysis of the 1st shipment is not satisfactory, ________ is certified by the China Commodity Bureau.

A. when　　B. which　　C. as　　D. that

(2) Fifty cases of Green Tea you sent us were found to be badly damaged. This was apparently attributable to ________ packing.

A. outer B. superior C. domestic D. faulty

(3) We have to file a claim against you ________ US $15000.

A. with the sum B. equal to

C. for D. to the amount of

(4) As it ________ only a small quantity, we hope you will have no difficulty in settling this matter.

A. involved B. involves C. involving D. involving

(5) We have ________ the drums one by one and found that most of them are leaking.

A. examined B. tested C. rolled D. traced

(6) We would like to ________ this claim to arbitration.

A. submit B. give C. put D. present

(7) We are prepared to make you a reasonable compensation, but not the amount you claimed because we ________ why the loss should be 50% more than the actual value of the goods.

A. cannot see B. are not certain C. cannot find D. know

(8) After the inspection of the above shipment, we found 5 cases ________.

A. missed B. lost C. missing D. lose

(9) If cargoes cannot be found within a few days, we will file our claim for the full ________ of them.

A. settlement B. solution C. solve D. answer

(10) We trust you will do your best to ________ this matter settled at once.

A. make B. place C. have D. let

2. Put the following English phrases into Chinese or Chinese phrases into English.

(1) 中性包装

(2) 适合海运的包装

(3) 包装不当

(4) 内包装

(5) 包装货

(6) immediate shipment

(7) shipment during March

(8) partial shipment

(9) loading port

(10) discharge port

3. Translate the following Chinese sentences into English using the words or phrases in the brackets, and translate the following English sentences into Chinese.

(1) 请贵方给予合作,将装运期提前到 9 月底,我们能够赶上圣诞节销售旺季。(cooperate with)

(2) 随函附寄一套有关这批货物的装运单据,请查收。(enclosed)

(3) 如能尽快装运,我们将不胜感激。(appreciate)

(4) We are very anxious to know about the shipment of our order for 8000 pieces Giant Bicycles.

(5) According to the stipulations of the contract, the shipment is to be made by the end of August.

(6) Due to a serious shortage of shipment space, we can not deliver these goods until October 11.

4. Translate the following letter into English.

(1)

敬启者:

贵方发来的 40 个纸板箱的钢螺钉我们已经收到。我们非常遗憾地通知你们:在 40 个纸板箱中,有 10 个纸板箱破碎,其中一些货物损坏,造成了一些损失。

我们承认这并非贵公司之过失,但希望能修改我们的包装要求,以免同类事件再次发生。我们要求,将每 500 克装在一个纸盒中,每 40 个纸盒装一木箱。

烦请告知我们贵方能否满足我们的要求,以及这些要求是否会引致价格上涨。

请尽快回信,不胜感激。

谨上

(2)

敬启者:

5 月 20 日要求提早装运第 954 号合约的来信收到。

我们已经联系了船运公司,得知 4 月 5 日前开往贵公司港口的船只已没有剩余货位。因此,很抱歉,我们无法满足你们的要求。

但请你们放心,我们一定会尽我们最大的努力,保证按时交货。

谨上

Unit 10

Insurance

保　险

10.1 Study Aim(学习目标)

(1) 熟悉经常发生的风险类别,了解保险单条款。
(2) 掌握关于投保、协商保险条款的常用词汇及句型。
(3) 掌握贸易双方进行投保、协议保险条款等信写作基本要点。

10.2 Introduction (专业背景知识介绍)

1. Definition of Insurance(保险的定义理解)

运输过程中的货物可能会面临各种各样的严重危险,甚至有时会遭受损失。保险则提供了一种补偿损失和所遭受损害的方式。换句话说,保险是一种为某人所遭伤害或损失而提供赔偿的合同,无论是损失的全部金额,还是损失的某一特定百分比。

2. Kinds of Insurance and Insurance Risks(保险的种类和险种)

在国际贸易中,人们习惯于针对运输过程中货物的风险进行投保。考虑到不同的运输方式,有四种基本的保险类别:海洋运输保险,陆路运输保险,航空运输保险,邮包运输保险。

在本章中,我们主要讨论海洋运输保险。

货物在海运中可能遇到的风险主要有两类。

(1) Perils of Sea,即海上风险,指自然灾害和意外事故;

(2) Extraneous Risks,即外来风险,包括由于偷窃、雨淋、短重、渗漏、破碎、串味、受潮、钩损、锈损等外部原因对货物造成损失的一般外来风险,以及由于战争、罢工、进口国拒绝进口或没收等外部原因造成的特殊外来风险。

海洋货物保险险别相应也分为两种,即基本险别和附加险别。

(1) Basic Risks(基本险)

基本险主要包括一切险(All Risks, AR)、平安险(Free from Particular Average,

FPA)、水渍险(With Particular Average, WPA = With Average, WA)。

(2) Extraneous Coverage(附加险)

附加险包括一般附加险和特殊附加险两类。

① 一般附加险包括偷窃及提货不着险(Theft, Pilferage and Non-delivery, TPND)、淡水雨淋险(Fresh Water & /or Rain Damage,FWRD)、短量险(Shortage of Weight)、混杂污损险(Intermixture and Contamination Risks)、渗漏险(Leakage Risks)、碰损破碎险(Clash and Breakage Risks)、钩损险(Hook Damage Risks)、锈损险(Rust Risks)、受潮受热险(Sweating and Heating Risks)。

② 特殊附加险包括战争险(War Risks)、罢工、暴动及民变险(Strike, Riot and Civil Commotions, SRCC)、交货不到险(Failure to Delivery Risks)、进口关税险(Import Duty Risks)、舱面险(On Deck Risks)、拒收险(Rejection Risks)。

3. Calculation on Insurance Value (保险费计算)

保险金额可按以下方式计算。

货物成本 + 运费 + 保险费 + 代表货物出售后的合理利润的总金额的百分之几

对于 CIF 的交易,根据中国人民保险公司 1981 年 8 月 1 日拟定的海洋运输货物保险条款,我们通常按发票金额的 110% 投保某种险别。有时候买方要求投保的金额超过 110%。在这种情况下,买方则需支付额外保险费。

10.3 Writing Skills (写作技巧)

买方关于保险信函的写作步骤及常见表达方式如表 10-1 所示。

表 10-1 买方关于保险信函的写作步骤及常见表达方式

写作步骤	表达方式
1. 列明相关交易背景信息(如合同号、订单号等);简单描述货物 Mentioning the relatively information of transaction (e. g. contract No., order No., etc). describe the goods simply	Referring to our S/C No. 20130820, which is the 3000 pairs of men's shoes, we are now asking for covering insurance for your account. 关于我方编号为 20130820 号合同项下 3000 双男鞋的货物,现特请求贵方办理保险。
2. 列明保险类型及投保险别要求 State the kinds of risk and other requirements	to insure the goods against All Risks 投保一切险 Please insure FPA. 请投保平安险。 We have insured the goods WPA. 请给这些货物投保水渍险。
3. 说明保费及分担 Note the responsibility of the premium	for one's account/to be borne by/to be responsible 由……负担 The extra freight is to be for buyer's account. 额外运费由买方负担。 As a rule, the extra premium involved will be for buyer's account. 按常规,额外保险费应由买方负责。

续表

写 作 步 骤	表 达 方 式
4. 希望对方同意并希望对方尽早发货 Wishing the reader to accept and ship the goods early	We wish you can accommodate us in this respect. 希望贵方在此方面给予照顾。 We hope to receive your favorable reply. 希望早日收到贵方答复

卖方关于保险信函的写作步骤及常见表达方式如表 10-2 所示。

表 10-2 卖方关于保险信函的写作步骤及常见表达方式

写 作 步 骤	表 达 方 式
1. 说明收到信函 Stating that you have received their letter	We are pleased to confirm receipt of your letter of 21st Aug,2013, asking for covering insurance of the captioned goods. 贵方 2013 年 8 月 21 日请求为所述货物办理保险的信函,我方确认已收到。
2. 说明自己的意见(同意或不同意)及其理由 Giving your reply of agreeing or refusing and your reasons	We agree to...我们同意…… We want to make it clear that...我方想澄清一点…… With regard to... we regret being unable to accept... 关于……很遗憾不能接受……
3. 说明会立即发货等 Stating the goods will be sent soon, etc.	We sincerely hope that we can...诚挚地希望我们能…… We have insured the goods...我们已经为货物投保……

10.4 Specimen Letters(样函)

Letter 1:

Dear Sirs,

Insurance

We thank you for your letter of May 10th, quoting us 100 metric tons of Wool on CIF terms. We regret, however that we prefer to have your quotations and/or offers on CFR terms.

For your information, we have taken out an open policy with the Lloyd Insurance Company, London. All we have to do when a shipment is made is to advise them of the particulars. Furthermore, we are on very good terms with them. We usually receive from our underwriters quite a handsome premium rebate at regular intervals.

In the meantime, we should be obliged if you could supply us with full details regarding the scope of cover handled by the People's Insurance Company of China for our reference.

We look forward to hearing from you at an early date.

Yours faithfully,

Notes（注释）

1. take out 通过申请而取得；办理（保险）手续

take out insurance（=cover insurance）投保，洽办保险

e. g. Have you taken out insurance for us on these goods? 贵方为我方的货物办理保险了吗？

2. policy *n.* 保（险）单

部分常用词组：

insurance policy 保（险）单

open policy 预约保（险）单，船名未确定保单，流动保单

general open policy 预约总保单

floating policy 流动保单

voyage policy 航程保单

marine insurance policy 海上水险单

specific policy 单独保单，船名确定保单（以别于船名未定的流动保单）

time policy 定期保险单

transferable policy 可转让的保单

3. Lloyd Insurance Company, London 伦敦劳埃德保险公司

4. on good terms with sb. 与某人关系良好

e. g. We are on good terms with the firm mentioned. 我们与该商号关系良好。

5. underwriter *n.* 保险商

underwriters 可与 insurance company 及 insurers 通用，但 underwriters 主要指专保水险的保险商

e. g. Underwriters decline to insure against inherent vice. 保险商拒绝承保内在缺陷险。

underwrite *v.* 保险

通常作及物动词，宾语一般为险别。

e. g. Insurers here will not underwrite this risk. 保险公司不会承担该风险。

6. handsome *adj.* 相当大的，可观的

e. g. He received quite a handsome sum of money as a gift. 他收到了一笔相当可观的钱作为礼物。

7. premium *n.* 保（险）费；较高价格

e. g. The extra premium is for buyers' account. 额外保费由买方负担。

This kind of additional risk is coverable at a premium of 2‰. 此种附加险的保费是 2‰。

During Christmas, walnuts are selling at a premium. 在圣诞节期间，核桃正按高价售出。

8. rebate *n.* 回扣

freight rebate 运费回扣

interest rebate 利息回扣

insurance rebate 保险回扣

tax rebate 减税

rebate system 回扣制,运费回扣制

e. g. There is a 5% rebate on freight. 运费有 5% 的回扣。

Letter 2:

Dear Sirs,

Re: S/C No. 3200

Regarding S/C No. 3200 covering Cotton Cloths, we would like to inform you that we have established with the Bank of China in a confirmed, irrevocable L/C No. 2132 amounting to Stg 330000 with validity until 1st May.

Please see to it that the above-mentioned goods are shipped before 31st May and insured against All Risks for 110% of the invoice value. We know that according to your usual practice, you insure the goods only for full invoice value, therefore the extra premium will be for our account.

Please arrange the insurance as requested and in the meantime, we await your shipping advice.

Notes(注释)

1. regarding *prep.* 关于;等于 concerning 或 about,也可以写作 with regard to、in regard to 或 as regards

e. g. I send you a fax this morning regarding order No 1234. 我今天早晨给您发了一个关于 1234 号订单的传真。

We would appreciate receiving details regarding the commodities. 如能告知该商品的详细情况,则不胜感激。

2. amount to 总计,金额达……

e. g. The total expenses amount to ￥500.00. 全部费用合计为 500 元。

Our loss amounts to $1000. 我们的损失达 1000 美元。

3. Stg *n.* 等于 Sterling,英镑

4. validity *n.* 有效期

e. g. The validity date of the L/C should be extended to July 30. 信用证有效期应延长到 7 月 30 日。

The offer is valid for 5 days. 报价在五天内有效。

5. see to it that 确保

e. g. Please see to it that the L/C extension should reach here before June 30. 请注意信用证展期通知应于 6 月 30 日之前到达我处。

Please see to it that the goods we ordered are shipped as soon as the covering letter of credit reaches you. 请确保一收到有关的信用证,就马上装运我们所订的货物。

6. insure *v.* 投保,保险

e.g. Please insure the goods against breakage. 请给货物投保破损险。

Please insure for 10% above invoice value. 请按发票金额的 110% 投保。

insurance *n.* 保险

e.g. We will arrange insurance on your behalf. 我们会代表贵方安排保险。

We shall provide such insurance at your cost. 我们会提供这样的保险,费用由您负担。

We shall cover the insurance ourselves. 我们会自己进行投保。

7. extra *adj.* 额外的

8. premium *n.* 保费

e.g. The extra premium is for buyer's account. 额外的保费由买方承担。

9. for our account 由我方负担

10. shipping advice 装运通知,指卖方发货后向买方发出的通知,其内容包括货物名称、数量、金额、载货船名和开航日期等

Letter 3:

Dear Sirs,

Re: Your Order No.1009 for 500 cases Toys

This is to acknowledge receipt of your letter of 20th July requesting us to effect insurance on the captioned shipment for your account.

We are pleased to inform you that we have covered the above shipment with The People's Insurance Company of China against All Risks for $2000. The policy is being prepared and will be forwarded to you by the end of the week.

For your information, we are making arrangements to ship the 500 cases of toys by S. S. "Jinan", sailing on or about the 11th August.

Sincerely yours,

Notes(注释)

1. acknowledge receipt of 等于 be in receipt of,但较正式,意思是收到

e.g. We acknowledge receipt of your letter of April 3,2002. 我们收到贵方 2002 年 4 月 3 日的来信。

2. effect *vt.* 意思同 make

e.g. Payment should be effected within three months after shipment. 付款应在发货后三月之后履行。

3. forward *vt.* 转去;意思同 pass on

e.g. We will forward your decision to the buyers. 我们会把您的决定转告买方。

Your communication of the 24th May addressed to our sister corporation in Shanghai has been forwarded to us for attention. 贵方 5 月 24 日寄到我们上海公司的信已经转交给我们了。

4. make arrangement to do sth. 安排做某事

e. g. We have made arrangements with Bank of Japan, Tokyo, to open a credit in your favor. 我们已经与东京的日本银行安排开立以贵方为受益人的信用证。

We trust that you will make all necessary arrangements to deliver the goods in time. 我们相信贵方会及时作必要的装运安排。

5. case *n*. 箱子

6. sail *v*. 起航,开航

e. g. The ship is scheduled to sail for Hong Kong on the 23rd of this month. 该轮将于本月 23 日驶往香港。

Letter 4:

Dear Sirs,

We have received your letter of May 8th,2013 asking us to arrange All Risks cover for a consignment of Little Swan brand, automatic washing machine, valued at RMB 1000000 to be shipped from Dalian to Port London, UK by ABC liner LTD.

All Risks Generally we cover insurance WPA and War Risk, in the absence of definite instructions from our clients. If you desire to cover All Risks, we can provide such coverage at a slightly higher premium . Breakage is a special risk, for which an extra premium will have to be charged. The present rate about 9% . we note that you wish us to insure shipments to you for 10% above invoice value, which is having our due attention.

We trust the above information will serve your purpose and await your further news.

Notes(注释)

1. consignment *n*. 运送的货物
2. Little Swan brand, automatic washing machine 小天鹅牌自动洗衣机
3. ABC liner LTD. ABC 轮船运输有限公司
4. required coverage 所要求险种
5. in the absence of definite instructions from our clients 在没有接到我方客户明确指示前提下
6. at a slightly higher premium 以稍稍高一点的保费

Letter 5:

Dear Sirs,

Re: order No. 8119

We wish to refer you to our Order No. 8119 under S/C No. 1018 for 6000 MP3, MP4, MP5 respectively, from which we have noticed that the goods are to be covered against AR for 110% of the invoice value.

As your offer is on CIF basis, the shipment should be insured at your end according to the contract. In order to make the goods safer and prevent pilferage in transportation, we shall be pleased if you will arrange to insure the goods on our behalf against All Risks and

Additional TPND at 130% of the Invoice value.

We sincerely hope that our request will meet with your approval.

Yours faithfully,

Notes(注释)

1. refer sb. to 请某人参看
2. on CIF basis 以 CIF 价
3. at your end 在贵方
4. on our behalf 代表我方
5. insure the goods on our behalf against All Risks 代表我方为货物投保一切险
6. meet with your approval 得到……的同意,得到……的批准

Letter 6:

Dear Sirs,

In reply to your letter of June 1st concerning Order No. 8119 under S/C No. 1018, we wish to give you the following information:

For transactions finalized on CIF basis, we usually make insurance with PICC against All Risks, as per Ocean Marine Cargo Clauses of PICC dated January 1th, 1981.

We also can effect insurance against any additional risks if you do desire, and the extra premium is to be for your account.

Usually, the insurance amount is 110% of the invoice value. However, if you require higher percentage and any additional risk, we may do accordingly but you have to stand the additional premium as well.

We hope that all the information will serve your purpose and look forward to your reply.

Yours faithfully,

Notes(注释)

1. for transactions finalized on CIF basis 对于按照 CIF 达成的交易
2. if you do desire 确实想
3. extra/additional premium 额外的保费

Letter 7:

Dear Sirs,

Re: your L/C No. TK 309

We thank you for your letter of December 6 and your L/C No. TK 309 for RMB 25000 issued by the Bank of Singapore, advised through the Bank of China, Hong Kong.

On going through the stipulations of your credit, we regret to find that in addition to FPA and War Risks, you require insurance to cover TPND and SRCC which were agreed upon by both parties during our negotiations at the First Beijing International Fair.

Under the ordinary circumstances, no loss or theft of such merchandise as mild steel flat bars is likely to occur during transport or after arriving at its destination.

Therefore, it is our practice to cover FPA for such commodity. Since you desire to have your shipment insured against TPND, we can arrange such insurance at your cost.

With regard to SRCC, we wish to state that the People's Insurance Company of China, from now on, accepts this special coverage, and will fall in with the usual international practice.

We hope you will see your way to arrange with your bank for an amendment to your L/C to increase the amount in order to cover the extra premium under advice to us.

We assure you that as soon as your amendment reaches us, we shall, of course, make the necessary arrangements for the shipment.

Yours faithfully,

Notes(注释)

1. on going through 浏览
2. stipulations *n.* 条款,规定
3. FPA 平安险

War Risks 战争险

TPND 偷窃及提货不着险

SRCC 罢工、暴动及民变险

4. First Beijing International Fair 首届北京国际博览会
5. merchandise *n.* 商品

表示商品的单词有:good、product、commodity、item、article。

6. mild steel 低碳钢,软钢

flat bars 扁平钢条

7. at your cost 计入贵方成本,由贵方承担成本
8. fall in with 与……保持一致,与……一样
9. see your way 贵方能否

see sb.'s way (clear) to doing sth. 觉得可能或便于做某事

e.g. I can't see my way to finishing the work this year. 我看我今年做不完这项工作。

Could you see your way to lending me $10 for a couple days? 您能不能借给我10美元,过两天还您?

10. extra premium 额外的保费

Letter 8:

Dear Sirs,

In reply to your letter of March 20, we would like to give you a further explanation for the sale of all kinds of canned foods that we prefer to close business on CIF basis as we are well connected with the Shipping Company and Insurance Company here and they can offer you very good service of transportation and insurance. Of course, transaction can be concluded at a price of CFR if you hope to arrange insurance yourselves.

Usually we cover insurance WPA & WAR Risks in the absence of definite instruction from buyers. Please be sure that we can assist to arrange all kinds of coverage according to desire of the customers.

We have learnt from your letter that you wish to insure the goods for 110% of the invoice value. 10% above invoice the value is the usual practice in international trade. We shall serve you the same.

Yours truly,

Notes(注释)

1. further explanation 进一步地解释

2. close business 进行交易

close *v*. 结束

close a deal with sb. 同意交易协定的条款,成交

3. on CIF basis 以 CIF 价为基础上

4. We are well connected with the Shipping Company and Insurance Company here. 我们与当地的船舶公司和保险公司保持有良好的合作联系。

5. In the absence of definite instruction from buyers. 没有买方的明确指示。

6. arrange *v*. 安排

7. coverage *n*. 保险范围,险别

Letter 9:

Gentlemen,

Re: Our Order No. 642

20 cases of Brother Sewing Machines shipped by the S. S. "Goddess" arrived here yesterday. We had the cases opened and the contents examined by a local insurance surveyor in the presence of the shipping company's agents. But much to our regret we have to inform you that four sewing machines in two cases of them were badly damaged. Obviously, the damage was caused by rough handling during transit.

We enclose the surveyor's report and the shipping agent's statement. As our order was placed on a CIF basis and you effected the insurance, we should be grateful if you would submit the insurance claim for us with the insurers. We expect to be compensated for the loss sustained in due course.

We hope no difficulty will arise in connection with the insurance claim and thank you in advance for your trouble on our behalf.

Yours faithfully,

Notes(注释)

1. Brother Sewing Machines 兄弟牌缝纫机

2. S. S. "Goddess" "女神号"轮船

3. contents *n*. 所容纳之物,所含之物,内容,信中指箱内的缝纫机产品

4. local insurance surveyor 本地保险调查员

5. in the presence of the shipping company's agents 在船舶公司代理商在场的情况下

6. much to our regret 非常遗憾

7. rough handling during transit 运输过程中的粗暴装卸

8. shipping agent's statement 船运代理商的声明

9. in due course（习语）在适当时机，最终

e. g. Your request will be dealt with in due course. 你的要求将在适当时机予以处理。

10. in connection with（习语）与某人或某事有关

e. g. I am writing to you in connection with your job application. 此信是有关你求职一事的。

11. in advance（习语）预先，提前，事先

12. on our behalf 为我方利益

（习语）

on behalf of sb. /on sb. 's behalf 为了……的利益；代表……

（US）in behalf of sb. /in sb. 's behalf 做某人的代表或代言人，为某人之利益

e. g. On behalf of my colleagues and myself I thank you. 我代表我的同事以及我自己向您表示谢意。

Ken is not present, so I shall accept the prize on his behalf. 肯不在场，所以我代表他领奖。

The legal guardian must act on behalf of the child. 法定监护人应该维护这个孩子的利益。

Don't be uneasy on my behalf about me. 不要为我担心。

10.5 Focal Words（焦点词汇及短语）

（1）The People's Insurance Company of China 中国人民保险公司

China Insurance Clause, CIC 中国人民保险公司制定的中国保险条款

Institute Cargo Clauses 协会货物条款

Institute, Institute of London Underwriters 伦敦保险学会

CIC 中的海洋运输货物保险条款所包括的三个基本险别为：

FPA（Free from Particular Average）平安险

WPA（With Particular Average）水渍险

All Risks 一切险

（2）insure *v.* 保险，投保，通常用作及物动词，宾语一般为所保的货物

e. g. Please insure the goods against all risks and war risk. 请将此货投保一切险及战争险。

The insurance company here insures this risk with 5% franchise 此保险公司保此种险有5%的免赔率。

有时也用作不及物动词，如：

Please insure against breakage. 请投保破碎险。

过去分词 insured 作定语构成的部分常用词组：

insured amount(=insurance amount) 保(险)额

insured cargo 或 insured goods 投保的货物

insured 还可作名词用，前面加定冠词，即 the insured，作“被保险人”解。

e. g. In international trade by transportation insurance we mean that the insured, who is usually the importer or the exporter, covers insurance on one or several lots of goods against certain risks for a certain insured amount with the insurer. i. e. the insurance company, at an agreed premium. 在国际贸易中，我们所说的货物运输险，是指被保险人，通常即进口商或出口商，对一批或若干批货物向保险人，即保险公司，按一定的保额和约定的保费投保一定的险别。

insure the goods for the buyer's account 由贵方负担保险费

insure the goods on behalf of the buyers 代为买方投保

insure the goods with an insurance company 向保险公司(投保)

insure the goods for the sum of US $100 (投保)金额为 100 美元

insure the goods for 110% of the invoice value against All Risks 按发票金额的 110% 投保一切险

(3) insurance *n.* 保险

insurance company 保险公司

insurance agents 保险代理人

insurance policy 保险单

insurance premium 保险费

insurance certificate 保险凭证

insurance coverage 保险范围

insurance amount 保(险)额

insurance declaration 保险声明书，保险通知书

air transportation insurance 航空运输保险

marine insurance 水险，海上保险，海运险

ocean marine cargo insurance 海洋运输货物保险

overland insurance 陆运保险

overland transportation insurance 陆上运输保险

parcel post insurance 邮包保险

to arrange insurance 投保，洽办保险

to cover insurance 投保，洽办保险

to effect insurance 投保，洽办保险

to provide insurance 投保，洽办保险

to take out insurance 投保，洽办保险

即：provide/effect/cover/arrange/take out insurance 为货物投保。

说明保险情况时，insurance 后接介词的一般用法。

表示所保的货物,后接 on,如 insurance on the 100 tons of wool;

表示投保的险别,后接 against,如 insurance against all risks;

表示保额,后接 for, 如 insurance for 110% of the invoice value;

表示保险费或保险费率,后接 at,如 insurance at a slightly higher premium, insurance at the rate of 5‰;

表示向某保险公司投保,后接 with,如 insurance with the People's Insurance Company of China。

e. g. We have covered insurance on the 100 metric tons of wool for 110% of the invoice value against all risks. 我们已将 100 公吨羊毛按发票金额的 110% 投保一切险。

(4) cover *n.* (保险业)保险

insurance cover 保险

e. g. We have arranged the necessary insurance cover. 我们已安排了必要的保险。

Does your policy provide adequate cover against breakage? 你们的保险单是否提供适当的破碎险?

v. 保险, 投保

及物动词,宾语除可为所保的货物和投保的险别外,还可以是 insurance 和被保险人。

+goods: 直接跟投保的货物或东西

e. g. We have covered these goods against All Risks. 我们已经为这些货物投保了一切险。

+risk: 直接跟投买的险别

e. g. Please cover the glassware against Clash & Breakage Risks. 请对玻璃器皿投破碎险。

We shall cover FPA(平安险)for you. 我们将为您投平安险。

Please cover WPA(水渍险)on the above goods. 请对以上货物投水渍险。

+insurance on...for...against...with 对某人就某物投保某险别

e. g. We shall cover insurance on your goods for 110% of the invoice value against All Risks with the PICC. 我们将会对您的货物按发票金额的 110% 向中国人民保险公司投保一切险。

cover [effect, arrange, take out, ...] insurance on (sth.) for (amount) against (risk) with (company) 向(某公司)将(某货物)按(多少金额)投保(某险别)

e. g. We have covered insurance on the shipment on the shipment for 110% of the invoice value against All Risks with the PICC. 我们已向中国人民保险公司将这批货按发票金额的 110% 投买了一切险。

coverage *n.* 保险范围

e. g. We want broader coverage to include some extraneous risks. 我们需要投保范围广泛的保险,包括一些附加险。

coverable *adj.* 可投保的,可承保的

e. g. Please let us know the premium at which breakage is coverable by the insurers on your side. 请告知贵处保险人承保破碎险的保费。

10.6 Exercise(练习)

1. Multiple choice.

(1) Generally we cover insurance against A. R. ________ definite instructions from our clients.

A. in absence of　　B. in the absence of

C. in no absence of　　D. in all absence of

(2) In ________ with your request, we have issued our Endorsement No. AB/201 to this effect together with the relevant debit note for an additional premium of RMB 200.00.

A. compliance　　B. complaints　　C. complement　　D. compliment

(3) We had the case opened and the contents examined by a local insurance ________ in the presence of the shipping company's agents.

A. surveyor　　B. survivor　　C. server　　D. servant

(4) The case was invoiced as containing ten typewriters, eight of ________ were badly.

A. that　　B. it　　C. what　　D. which

(5) As you hold the insurance policy, we should be ________ if you would take the matter up for us with the insurers.

A. gradual　　B. gradable　　C. grateful　　D. graceful

(6) We hope no difficulty will ________ in connection with the insurance claim and thank you in advance for your trouble on our behalf.

A. rise　　B. raise　　C. arise　　D. arouse

(7) We cannot grant you insurance ________ for 150% of the invoice value, because the contract stipulates that insurance is to be ________ for 110% of invoice value.

A. covered, coverage　　B. coverage, covered

C. coverage, coverage　　D. covered, covered

(8) In the ________ of damage, to be surveyed by Johnson Survey Co. and claims payable at Shanghai.

A. even　　B. evident　　C. evidence　　D. event

(9) For your information, we have ________ an open policy with the Lloyd Insurance Company, London.

A. made out　　B. turned out　　C. worked out　　D. taken out

(10) In the meantime, we should be obliged if you could supply us with full details ________ the scope of coverage ________ by the People's Insurance Company of China For our reference.

A. regarding, handled　　B. Regarded, handled

C. regarding, handling D. regarded, handling

2. Put the following English phrases into Chinese or Chinese phrases into English.

(1) insurance coverage
(2) Rejection Risks
(3) premium
(4) insurance policy
(5) insurance clause
(6) 投保人
(7) 承保人
(8) 一切险
(9) 碰损破碎险
(10) 中国人民保险公司

3. Translate the following Chinese sentences into English using the words or phrases in the brackets, and translate the following English sentences into Chinese.

(1) Regarding insurance, the coverage is for 110% of invoice value up to the port of destination only.

(2) We ask you to insure our goods for US $10000 against All Risks with the ABC Insurance Company.

(3) We will effect insurance against All Risks, as request, charging premium and freight for the consignees.

(4) 请为我们的下列货物投保。(insure sb. on sth.)

(5) 保险费根据保险范围的不同而变化。如果投保附加险,额外的保险费由买方支付。(vary with;for sb's account)

(6) 我们想为这批货物投保破碎险。(cover)

4. Translate the following letter into English.

(1)

敬启者:

事由:我方的第1001号订单项下的2000台洗衣机

希望贵方参看我方的第1001号订单项下的2000台小天鹅牌全自动洗衣机,从订单上贵方可注意到此批货物是以CFR价订购的。

现在我方希望在贵地为货物的运输安排保险。如果贵方能够按照发票金额人民币1000000元再加成10%,即为货物投保人民币1100000元的一切险,我们将感激不尽。

当然,一旦收到贵方的借据通知单,我们将偿还保险费用。如果贵方愿意,也可以给我们开立所需金额的汇票。

我们真诚地希望贵方能同意我们的要求。

谨上

(2)

敬启者:

久仰贵公司在保险行业的信誉,我们想由贵公司为我们的小天鹅牌全自动洗衣机投保金额为1000000元人民币的一切险,该货物将由ABC运输公司从大连运往英国伦敦。

预期货物将于5月底备妥待运,我们将安排货物于6月6日左右通过大连起航的“胜利”号船装运。

如果贵方能迅速办理此事,我们将感激不尽。

谨上

Unit 11

Complaints and Adjustments

索赔与理赔

11.1 Study Aim(学习目标)

(1) 了解索赔的定义和种类。

(2) 掌握关于索赔与理赔的常用词汇及句型。

(3) 能够通过信函对合同中的不同意见进行申诉,对损失进行索赔,或者进行理赔。

11.2 Introduction(专业背景知识介绍)

1. Definition of Complaints and Claims(投诉与索赔的定义理解)

在国际贸易中,经常会发生合同的缔约方之一违反合同的情况,另一方则有权为了保护自己免受损失而向违约方提出赔偿。投诉是指对于某种不满意、无法接受或者某人错误处理某事的状态的一种陈述。索赔是按照保险单条款要求进行赔偿的申请。

2. Reasons and Kinds of Complaints(索赔的原因和种类)

投诉和索赔通常是由遭受损失的买方对卖方提出。提出索赔的原因主要有以下方面:①拒绝交货;②错误交货;③货物到达延迟或损坏;④缺货;⑤劣质;⑥不良包装,等等。

有时,卖方也会针对买方提出投诉和索赔,主要是因为:①买方拒绝开立信用证;②买方迟开信用证;③ 没有令人满意或充分的理由不履行合同,等等。

买方提出的投诉和索赔有两种:真诚的投诉和索赔与虚假的投诉及索赔。

通常情况下,买方基于错发货物、劣质、质量与要求不符、不良包装、数量不足、迟发货物等原因提出的索赔为真诚的索赔。虚假的索赔通常发生在以下情况:一是买方故意挑出货物的问题并以之为借口逃避履行合同;二是买方不想要这批货物因为找到更廉价的货物渠道。

3. Tips for Making Complaints and Adjustments(索赔和理赔信函写作注意事项)

进行索赔和理赔时,需要注意以下事项。

首先,对于买方来说,写索赔信的目的是为了得到更好的服务或者合理的赔偿,而不是指责他人。因此,投诉或索赔信应该以一种克制、言语得体的方式进行写作。

其次,对卖方而言,所有的赔偿要求,无论是正当或者不正当,都应该严肃对待,并且进行细致调查。

11.3 Writing Skills(写作技巧)

索赔信的写作步骤及常见表达方式如表 11-1 所示。

表 11-1 索赔信的写作步骤及常见表达方式

写作步骤	表达方式
1. 详尽陈述事实,说明出了什么问题	We regret having to inform you that ...arrived in...很遗憾通知您……到达…… It was found that upon examination...检查后发现……
2. 说明此差错带来的不便或损失,以使索赔更有力	The materials are quite unsuited to...货物很不适合…… These goods are entirely useless to us...这些货物对我们毫无用处…… This has caused us much inconvenience...这给我们带来了很大不便……
3. 表明希望对方如何解决问题,如不知道哪种解决方式为宜,可敦促对方采取必要的行动	We wish to get your early reply. 希望早日收到贵方答复。 We look forward to your settlement at an early date. 盼早日收到您的解决方案。

在回复索赔信时,卖方可以根据自己的调查结果同意赔偿或拒绝赔偿。同意索赔的信函的写作步骤及常见表达方式如表 11-2 所示。

表 11-2 同意索赔的信函的写作步骤及常见表达方式

写作步骤	表达方式
1. 对给对方带来不便表示歉意	We wish to express our deepest regret over the unfortunate incident...对这个不幸事件我们希望表达我们深深的歉意…… We are extremely sorry for the late delivery of...我们为迟交……感到非常抱歉
2. 解释问题出现的原因并表示同意索赔	Another thorough check-up reveals that...再次彻底检查发现…… The wrong pieces may be returned...发错的货可以退回…… We are prepared to make you a reasonable compensation. 我们准备给贵方合理的赔偿。
3. 表示希望继续与对方的合作关系	We hope this will not affect our friendly relationship. 我们希望这不会影响我们的友好关系。 We wish to be able to serve you in future businesses. 我们希望能够在将来的生意上为你方提供服务。

有时卖方不得不拒绝客户的索赔,比如不能接受指控或只同意部分接受,这时回信应谨慎,不要让对方觉得你在表达其要求无理,而是使对方相信你们确实认真考虑了他们的投诉,并用具体事实说服对方接受你的立场。

拒绝索赔的信函的写作步骤及常见表达方式如表 11-3 所示。

表 11-3 拒绝索赔的信函的写作步骤及常见表达方式

写作步骤	表达方式
1. 对给对方带来不便表示歉意	We wish to express our deepest regret over the unfortunate incident...对这个不幸事件我们希望表达我们深深的遗憾…… We are extremely sorry for the late delivery of...我们为迟交……感到非常遗憾。 We regret the inconvenience you have experienced...我们对贵方经历的不便表示遗憾……
2. 解释问题出现的原因并表明自己的立场	After a check-up we found that...检查后我们发现…… The shipment you complained...贵方抱怨的货物…… We are of the opinion that...我们的意见是…… In order to settle the claim quickly...为了尽快解决索赔……
3. 直接拒绝或建议可能的解决办法	We regret being unable to accept your suggestion to...很遗憾不能接受贵方……的建议。 As this is a matter concerning insurance, we hope you will refer it to...由于这事关于保险,我们希望您与……联系。
3. 希望表示继续与对方的合作关系	We hope this will not affect our friendly relationship. 我们希望这不会影响我们的友好关系。 We wish to be able to serve you in future businesses. 我们希望能够在将来的业务中为您提供服务。

11.4 Specimen Letters(样函)

Letter 1:

Dear Mr. Smith,

We have recently received a number of complaints from customers about your clocks. The clocks are clearly not giving satisfaction and in some cases we have had to refund the purchase price.

The clocks complained about are part of the batch of five hundred supplied to our order No. 908 of 2nd April. This order was placed on the basis of a sample clock left by your representative. We have ourselves compared the performance of this sample with that of a number of the clocks complained about and there is little doubt that many of them do not tell the right time.

The complaints received relate only to clocks from the batch referred to. Clocks supplied before these have always been satisfactory. We are therefore writing to ask you to accept return of the unsold balance, amounting to 503 clocks in all, and to replace them by clocks of the quality our earlier dealings with you have led us to expect.

Sincerely,

Notes(注释)

1. complaint *n*. 抱怨,不满

e. g. We received your letter of complaint of 12 June with regret. 收到贵方6月12日的投诉信,甚歉。

Recently we received many complaint from our customers. 最近我们收到许多客户的投诉。

complain *v*. 抱怨,投诉

e. g. Many customers complain about products. 许多客户投诉我们的产品。

claim *n*. 索赔

register one's claim with sb. /against sb. 提出索赔,也可以用 file/lodge/raise/make a claim with/against you

e. g. Claims are payable only for that part of the loss, that is over 5%. 损失只赔超过5%的部分。

We register our claim with you as follows: …我们就下列问题向你们提出索赔:……

Claims for shortage or incorrect material must be made within 30 days after arrival of the goods. 对短重或错发的索赔必须在货到后30天内进行。

Your claim on this cargo has been settled. 贵方对这批货的索赔要求已经解决。

We lodge a claim with you for the short-weight. 我们就短重向贵方提出索赔。

We lodge a claim with you on fertilizer. 我们向您提出关于化肥的索赔。

2. giving satisfaction 令人满意,意思同 satisfactory

satisfaction *n*. 满意

e. g. The pens are not giving satisfaction. 这些钢笔很令人不满意。

The first shipment of pens has turned out to the satisfaction of the users. 第一批运送的钢笔令客户们非常满意。

3. in some cases 有时候

e. g. In some cases, the goods are returned to us. 有时货被退回来了。

4. refund *v*. 偿还,归还(款项)

e. g. We have had to refund the purchase price. 我们不得不退回货款。

The sellers promise to refund the buyers the full invoice value of the goods. 卖方答应按货物发票的金额偿还买方。

We will refund the transportation expenses. 我们会退回运费。

5. batch *n*. 一批货

6. on the basis of 在……基础上,以……为依据

e.g. On the basis of the SCIB's Survey Report, we lodge a claim with you for the short-weight. 根据商检局的检验报告,我们对贵方短重提出索赔。

7. compare *v.* 比较

compare something with... 把某物与……相比; compare something to... 把某物比作……

e.g. When we compare the goods with the samples you sent, we found that... 当我们把货物与您寄来的样品比对时,我们发现……

8. performance *n.* 性能,表现

e.g. The performance of the machine is not satisfactory. 机器的运转令人不满意。

9. there is little doubt 意思同 there is no doubt,毫无疑问

e.g. There is little doubt that it is caused by rough handling. 毫无疑问,这是由于粗暴搬运造成的。

There is little doubt that he is in trouble. 毫无疑问,他有麻烦了。

10. relate to 与……相关;与……有关

e.g. This is a problem relating to pollution. 这是一个与污染有关的问题。

The loss is related to his negligence. 损失与他的疏忽有关。

11. unsold balance 没卖出去的货物,balance 指剩下的部分

12. in all 总共

e.g. Your claim for shortage of weight amounts to 84.82 tons in all. 贵方短重索赔共计 84.82 吨。

Letter 2:

Dear Sirs,

Thank you for your letter of 20 May.

We agree with you that our shoes should last longer than one month. If they do not, we like to know the reason why.

We have carefully examined the pair you returned to us. Our production manager reports that the shoes have been thoroughly soaked and then dried by heat. Even the best quality shoes will not withstand this treatment .

For this reason, we regret that we cannot agree to your request for a replacement pair.

Yours sincerely,

Notes(注释)

1. agree with 同意某人的意见

e.g. We agree with you on this point. 在这点上我们同意您的观点。

We agreed that we will give you an increase in commission. 我们同意给贵方增加佣金。

agree to 同意或接受(建议、办法、条件)

e.g. We agree to your proposal. 我们同意您的建议。

agree on(upon)双方同意或商定

e. g. L/C terms were agreed on(upon).以信用证付款是双方商定的。

agreement *n*. 协议,协议书。用法有 come to an agreement、reach an agreement

e. g. We are glad that we have come to an agreement on this matter. 很高兴我们已经就这个问题达成一致。

2. last *v*. 持续

e. g. The game lasts for 4 hours. 比赛持续了 4 小时。

adj. 上一个

e. g. Our last class was not very interesting. 我们对上一节课不太有兴趣。

3. thoroughly *adv*. 彻底地,全面地

e. g. The police checked the room thoroughly. 警察彻底检查了屋子。

thorough *adj*. 彻底的,全面的

e. g. After a thorough examination, we found that...彻底调查之后,我们发现……

4. soak *v*. 浸泡

5. dry *v*. 烘干

e. g. We dry our clothes near the fire. 我们在火边烘干衣服。

6. withstand *v*. 承受,禁得住

e. g. We have made it clear that the packing must be strong enough to withstand rough handling...我们已经说明了包装必须足够结实以经得起粗鲁装运。

7. treatment *n*. 待遇,对待

e. g. His treatment of the animal was cruel. 他对待这只动物很残忍。

8. for this reason 由于这种原因

e. g. For this reason, we cannot accept your request for a replacement. 由于这种原因,我们不能接受贵方换货的要求。

Letter 3:

Dear Sirs,

Our order No. 098 of 9 March for plastics has now been delivered. We have examined the shipment carefully and, to our great disappointment, find that they are not of the quality we ordered.

The materials do not match the samples you sent us. The quality of some of them is so poor that we feel that a mistake has been made in making up the order. The goods do not match the requirements of our company. We have, therefore, no choice but to ask you to take the materials back and replace them with materials of the quality we ordered.

We are very keen to resolve this matter amicably. If you can replace the materials, we are prepared to allow the agreed delivery time to run from the date you confirm that you can supply the correct materials.

We look forward to your early reply.

Yours sincerely,

Notes(注释)

1. to our great disappointment 令人非常失望的是

用 great 表示强调。有时也用 much 强调,如 much to our disappointment。类似的说法有: much to our surprise、to our regret 等。这种短语一般用于句首。

e. g. To our great regret, we learn that you are not satisfied with goods. 很遗憾地得知贵方对货物不满意。

Much to our disappointment, we found that many cases are broken. 我们很失望地发现许多箱子都破了。

2. match *v.* 匹配,相符

e. g. These shoes do not match; one is large and the other is small. 这双鞋不相配,一只大,一只小。

3. make up 准备,凑足

4. have no choice but... 别无选择,只能……,后面接动词不定式

e. g. We have no choice but to give up. 我们别无选择只能放弃。

He has no choice but to accept their advice. 他别无选择,只能接受他们的建议。

5. are very keen to 非常希望

e. g. Although we are keen to meet your requirements, we regret being unable to satisfy your request for a reduction in price. 虽然我方想满足贵方要求, 但很抱歉不能按照贵方要求降低价格。

6. amicably *adv.* 友好地

e. g. We hope this will be settled amicably. 我们希望友好地解决这件事。

7. are prepared to 准备好做某事

e. g. Are you prepared to accept their terms and conditions? 您准备好接受他们的交易条件了吗?

We are prepared to give you a 6% discount if you place a large order. 如果贵方订货量大的话,我们准备给你们 6% 的折扣。

8. run *v.* 开始计算

Letter 4:

Dear Sirs,

Your letter of July 12 has been received, and we were very sorry to hear about the problem you experienced with our Color TV sets.

We maintain rigid inspection standards, but occasionally an imperfection does slip by, as it unfortunately did in the case of your Color TV sets.

We have entered a replacement order to be shipped to you at once. Your satisfaction is extremely important to us and we apologize for the inconvenience you have been caused.

Thank you for purchasing our products.

Yours sincerely,

Notes（注释）

1. experience *v.* 经历

e. g. We regret the inconvenience you have experienced...我们对您经历的不便表示遗憾……

He has experienced the war. 他经历过战争。

2. maintain *v.* 维持，保持，持续

e. g. The sales are maintained in the first quarter. 第一季度销量保持不变。

The situation is maintained. 形势没有变化。

maintenance *n.* 维修，维持

e. g. Our maintenance staffs are the fastest. 我们的维修是最快的。

3. rigid *adj.* 严格的

e. g. Our products have to experience rigid examination. 我们的产品必须经过严格的检查。

4. inspection *n.* 检查，检验

Commodity Inspection Bureau 商检局

5. standard *n.* 标准

e. g. It is required that the equipment and technology to be provided by you should be up to advanced world standard. 贵方所提供的设备和技术应达到国际先进水平。

We feel it necessary to inform you that your last delivery of our order is not up to the usual standard. 我们有必要通知你们，上次交货标准与以往不一样。

6. occasionally 有时候，不时地

e. g. We have to occasionally tell them to watch for errors. 我们不得不不时地提醒他们注意错误。

Occasionally, we encounter difficulties. 我们不时遇到困难。

7. imperfection *n.* 不完美

e. g. Imperfection is common in writing letters. 瑕疵在信函撰写的过程中是常见的。

8. slip by 悄悄地溜过，没被注意到

9. in the case of 在……情况下

e. g. We shall do our best to satisfy you in the case of shipment. 在装运方面，我们会和贵方合作。

in this case 如果这样，在这种情况下

e. g. In this case, we will not fail to cable you an offer. 如果这样，定去电给你报盘。

in no case 决不，后面句子倒装

e. g. You may rest assured that in no case will the L/C be delayed. 您可以放心，信用证绝不会迟开。

such being the case 情况既然这样

e. g. Such being the case, we regret being unable to make you an offer at present. 情况

既然这样，抱歉我们目前无法报盘。

10. replacement 换货

e. g. We will send you the replacement as soon as possible. 我们会尽快给贵方寄去换货。

11. extremely *adv.* 非常

e. g. We are extremely satisfied with you. 我们对你们非常满意。

He is extremely interested in the art. 他对艺术非常感兴趣。

12. apologize for 为……致歉

e. g. We apologize for the inconvenience caused. 我们为引起的不便表示歉意。

He has apologized for his negligence. 他为他的疏忽表示歉意。

13. hear about 听说

e. g. We hear about the news from a friend. 我从一个朋友那里听说这个消息。

Letter 5：

Dear Sirs,

Re：Claim on Mountain Bikes

The captioned goods you shipped by S. S. "Yellow River" on May 18 arrived here today.

On examination, we have found that many of the Mountain Bikes are severely damaged, though the cases themselves show no trace of damage.

Considering this damage was due to the rough handling by the steamer ship company, we claim on them for recovery of the loss, but an investigation made by the surveyor has revealed the fact that the damage is attributed to improper packing. For further particulars, we refer you to the surveyor's report enclosed.

We are, therefore, compelled to claim on you to compensate us for the loss of US $35000, which we have sustained by the damage to the goods.

We trust that you will be kind enough to accept this claim and deduct the sum claimed from the amount of your next invoice.

Yours truly,

Notes(注释)

1. due to 出于
2. rough handling 粗鲁装卸
3. for recovery of the loss 弥补所受损失
4. be attributed to 归因于……
5. deduct *v.* 扣除，减掉

Letter 6：

Dear Sirs,

We have received your letter of May 21th, informing us that the mountain bikes we shipped to you in a damaged condition on account of improper packing.

Upon receipt of your letter, we have given this matter our immediate attention. We have studied your surveyor's report very carefully.

We are convinced that the present damage was due to extraordinary circumstances under which they were transported to you. We are, therefore, not responsible for the whole damage; but as we do not think that it would be fair to have you bear the loss alone, we suggest that the loss should be divided between both of us, to which we hope you will agree.

Notes(注释)

1. give this matter one's immediate attention 立即调查此事
2. surveyor's report 鉴定报告
3. extraordinary circumstances 不正常情况
4. responsible for 对……负责任
5. bear the loss 承担损失

Letter 7:

Dear Sirs,

Referring to our previous letters and cables in respect of our order of January 22th for 1000 metric tons of Zinc Sheets, we have to call your attention to the fact that so far we have not had any definite information from you as to when we may expect delivery, although these goods were contracted to be shipped before the end of June.

Needless to say, we have been put to no little inconvenience through the delay. It is therefore imperative that you inform us by cable immediately of the earliest possible shipment for our consideration, without prejudice to our right, to cancel the order and/or lodge claims for losses thus sustained.

Please look the matter up at once and let us have your cable reply by the earliest opportunity.

Yours faithfully,

Notes(注释)

1. in respect of 关于某事
2. zine sheets 锌皮
3. expect *v.* 期望,预期

e. g. Please let us know when we may expect delivery of the goods ordered on July 15th,2003. 请告知我方 2003 年 7 月 15 日订货可望何时交货。

We expect that the consignment will be ready for shipment at the end of this month. 我方预计该货本月底可备妥待运。

We do not expect to be able to place further orders at this same high level price. 我方不想再按这样高的价格订货。

Whereas ABC Co. is expecting to minimize the cost for the production of the plant by utilizing XYZ Co. 's technology…,we…鉴于 ABC 公司希望利用 XYZ 公司的技术,把工厂的生产费用降低到最低限度……,我们……

4. be put to 使遭受

5. no little 意思同 many,许多

6. to lodge a claim against(on,with)…

to make a claim against (on, with)…

to file a claim against (on, with)…

to raise a claim against (on, with)… 向……提出索赔

e. g. This guarantee shall be valid only for claims lodged with this bank on or before September 30, 2003. 本担保在 2003 年 9 月 30 日或之前向银行提出索赔有效。

The goods are short-landed by 1000 kilos; therefore we raise a claim against you. 货物到达时短缺 1000 公斤,因此我们向贵方提出索赔。

We have raised a claim on ABC Trading Company on account of damage. 我方因货物破损向 ABC 贸易公司提出索赔。

7. look up 查询;(价格)上涨;(情况好转)

e. g. The prevailing opinion is that price are looking up. 当前人们普遍认为价格看涨。

Letter 8:

Dear Sir,

Our Order No. 145

We duly received the documents and took delivery of the goods on arrival of the S. S. "Lucky" at Shanghai.

We are much obliged to you for the prompt execution of this order, everything appears to be correct and in good condition except in case No. 1-92. Unfortunately when we opened this case we found it contained completely different articles, and we can only presume that a mistake was made and the contents of this case were for another order.

As we need the articles we ordered to complete deliveries to our own customers, we must ask you to arrange for the dispatch of replacements at once. We attach a list of the contents of case No. 1-92, and shall be glad if you will check this with our order and the copy of your invoice.

In the meantime, we are holding the above-mentioned case at your disposal.

Please let us know what you wish us to do with it.

Yours faithfully,

Notes(注释)

1. duly received 如期收到

2. on arrival of the S. S. "Lucky" at Shanghai "幸运"号货轮到达上海

3. be obliged to 感激

e. g. We are much obliged to you for your help. 非常感激您对我们的帮助。

4. prompt *adj.* 迅速的

prompt execution of this order 订单的迅速执行

5. presume *v.* 推测

6. arrange for 安排

arrange for the dispatch of replacements at once 立即安排替换商品并且发运

7. attach *v.* 附加,随附

e. g. We attach a catalogue of our commodities for your consideration. 随附我方商品的目录单一份,供贵方考虑。

attachment *n.* 附件

8. in the meantime 在此期间

9. above-mentioned case 上述箱子

10. disposal *v.* 处理,处置

at sb. 's disposal 由某人做主,听某人之便,由某人支配

put (or leave) something at sb. 's disposal 把某事交某人自由处理

e. g. We will leave the case No. 1-19 at your disposal. 我们将把 1 ~ 19 号箱的货交贵方自行处理。

Letter 9:

Dear Sirs,

Your Order No. 145 per S. S. "Lucky"

Thank you for your letter of we were glad to know that the consignment was delivered promptly, but it was with great regret that we heard case No. 1-92 did not contain the goods you ordered.

On going into the matter we find that a mistake was indeed made in packing, through a confusion of number, and we have arranged for the right goods to be dispatched to you at once. Relative documents will be mailed as soon as they are ready.

We will appreciate it if you will keep case No. 1-92 and contents until called for by the local agents of World Transport Ltd., our forwarding agents, whom we have instructed accordingly. Please accept our many apologies for the trouble caused to you by the error.

Yours faithfully,

Notes(注释)

1. consignment *n.* 托运的货物,装运的货物;托运,运送;委托,托管

2. on going into the matter 经调查此事

3. call for sth. 需求,需要,要求某事物

e. g. We will appreciate it if you will keep case No. 1-92 and contents until called for by the local agents of World Transport Ltd. 如果贵方能够保存编号为 1 ~ 92 的箱子及其所装商品,直到世界运输有限公司当地的代理商需要该批货物,我方将十分感激。

4. forwarding agent 运输代理

forwarding order 托运单

forwarder *n.* 运输商

5. accordingly *adv.* 照着(办、做等);相应地

e. g. We must ascertain the actual conditions and arrange accordingly. 我们必须了解具体情况,做出相应的安排。

Our contract stipulates that the goods should be packed in seaworthy packing, so you must act accordingly. 我方合同规定货物包装应为适于海运的包装,贵方必须照办。

11.5 Focal Words(焦点词汇及短语)

(1) claim *n.* 索赔

与 claim 搭配的动词如下。

① 提出索赔: lodge/make/file/raise a claim

② 考虑并接受索赔: entertain a claim

③ 接受索赔: accept a claim

④ 拒绝索赔: decline/refuse a claim

⑤ 撤回/撤销索赔: withdraw a claim

⑥ 解决索赔,理赔: settle a claim

与 claim 搭配的介词如下。

① against/with/on sb.: 索赔的对象

② for/on reason: 索赔的原因

③ for amount: 索赔的金额

④ on/against goods: 索赔的货物

e. g. They have raised a claim against the insurance company. 他们已经向保险公司提出了索赔。

We lodged a claim against you on this shipment for short weight. 因为这批货重量短少,我们向您提出索赔。

On the basis of the Survey Report, we file a claim with you for GBP 1000. 根据检验报告,我们向您索赔 1000 英镑。

We are prepared to lodge a claim against the exporter on the 200 metric tons of black tea under S/C No. 123 for inferior quality for USD 2000. 我们打算因质次对第 123 号合同项下的 200 公吨红茶向出口商提出 2000 美元的索赔。

Claim must be made within 30 days after the arrival of the goods at the destination. 索赔必须在货到目的地后 30 日内提出。

(2) complain *v.* 抱怨,申诉(常与 about 连用)

complaint *n.* 抱怨,申诉

file/lodge/make a complaint against somebody about something 就某事对某人提出不满意见

(3) compensate *v*. 偿还,补偿

compensate sb. for sth. 因某事向某人赔偿

e. g. You are asked to compensate us for the damage. 贵方需因损害向我方赔偿。

You should compensate us for the delay of shipment. 贵方需因运输延误向我方赔偿。

(4) 与 claim 相关的常用词汇及表达方式

claim for short weight 由于短重而索赔

claim for damage 由于损坏而索赔

claim for loss and damage of cargo 货物损失索赔

claim for inferior quality 由于质量低劣而索赔

claim against carrier 向承运人索赔

claimant 索赔人

claims assessor 估损人

claims settling agent 理赔代理人

claims surveying agent 理赔检验代理人

claiming administration 索赔局

claims department (commission board) 索赔委员会

claim letter 索赔书

claims documents 索赔证件

claim report 索赔报告

claims statement 索赔清单

claims settlement 理赔

claims settling fee 理赔代理费

claim indemnity 索赔

claims rejected 拒赔

insurance claim 保险索赔

11.6 Exercise(练习)

1. Multiple choice.

(1) We lodge a claim ________ you ________ the short-weight.

A. with…with　　B. for…for　　C. with…for　　D. for…with

(2) You can file a claim with the insurance company in your area, who will ________ the loss incurred.

A. compensate　　B. compensate for

C. compensate to you　　D. compensate you

(3) We have already ________ a claim against the insurance company for $310 for damage in transit.

A. raised B. arisen C. risen D. praised

(4) I'll write to our home office to ________ our claim immediately.

A. waive B. wave C. weave D. wait

(5) Considering this damage was due to the ________ handling by the steamship company, we claimed on them for recovery of the loss.

A. tough B. rough C. though D. thorough

(6) An investigation made by the surveyor has revealed the fact that the damage is ________ to improper packing.

A. contributable B. attributive C. attribution D. attributable

(7) We are, therefore, ________ to claim on you to ________ us for the loss of $27500, which we have sustained by the damage to the goods.

A. compensate, compelled B. compensated, compelled

C. compelled, compensate, D. compel, compensate,

(8) We trust that you will be kind enough to accept this ________ and deduct the sum ________ from the amount of your next invoice to us.

A. aim, claimed B. claimed, claimed

C. aim, claim D. claimed, claim

(9) As we do not think that it would be fair to have you bear the loss alone, we suggest that the loss ________ between both of us, to which we hope you will agree.

A. are divided B. be divided C. is divided D. to be divided

(10) Unfortunately when we opened this case we found it contained completely different articles, and we can only ________ a mistake was made and then contents of this case were for another order.

A. resume B. resume C. preserve D. propose

2. Put the following English phrases into Chinese or Chinese phrases into English.

(1) claim letter

(2) claimant

(3) short-weight

(4) inferior quality

(5) claim documents

(6) 理赔

(7) 拒赔

(8) 撤销索赔

(9) 放弃索赔

(10) 不正确包装

3. Translate the following Chinese sentences into English using the words or phrases in the brackets, and translate the following English sentences into Chinese.

(1) We've given your claim our careful consideration.

(2) We lodged a claim with you on fertilizer yesterday.

(3) We filed a claim with(against) you for the short-weight.

(4) 中方代表与贝克先生商谈了索赔问题。(discuss)

(5) 我们已经收到了内容详尽的索赔信件。(receive)

(6) 有时候,船公司或保险公司应负责赔偿。(be responsible for)

4. Translate the following letter into English.

(1)

××先生:

有关上周发运的第 343 号订单的来信收悉。

对于货物在运送途中破损的事宜,本公司感到遗憾。本公司一向特别小心包装货物,然而不当的运输方法亦会引致损坏。

本公司将按照贵公司开列的破损货物清单更换新货,不日将运抵贵处。

已就有关损失向保险公司索偿,烦请保留破损货物供保险公司检查。

不便之处,敬希见谅。

谨上

(2)

先生们:

很遗憾必须通知贵方,贵公司上次运来的货物不符合贵方平常的标准。货物看起来太粗糙。兹分别寄上这批货的样品,以便与原样做比较。贵方可以了解这批货物品质的低劣情况。

我方非常信赖贵方货物的品质,但这次使我们相当失望,因为我们必须将这批货提供给新客户。请立即告诉我方解决此困难的办法。

谨上

第三篇

经贸函电实用部分

Practical Usage of Business Correspondences

Unit 12 Complete Business Cases

完整的业务案例

为了更好地体现外贸函电在国际商务活动中的运用,本章节将国际贸易活动中常用的贸易术语与国际结算方式进行不同的组合,设计贸易流程图,并按照流程图箭头的走向,列出流程中出现的函电。贸易术语主要选择《2000 年国际贸易术语解释通则》中的 CIF 术语和 FOB 术语;国际结算方式主要选择 L/C、D/P、D/A、T/T before Shipment、T/T after Shipment 五种方式。

12.1 CIF + L/C (1)

CIF + L/C 如图 12-1 所示。

1. 建立业务关系函

Dear Mr. Li,

We have obtained your address from Internet and are now writing to you for the establishment of business relations.

I know you are very well connected with all the major dealers of female clothes and feel sure we can purchase large quantities of products if we get your offers at competitive prices.

Please let us have all necessary information concerning your products for export.

Yours faithfully,

Tina Wong

Answer to above.

Dear Miss. Wong,

We thank you for your letter and shall be pleased to enter into business relations with you.

As requested, we are sending you by another mail our latest catalogue and price-list of our exports.

If you find business possible, please write to us.

Yours sincerely,

Ping Li

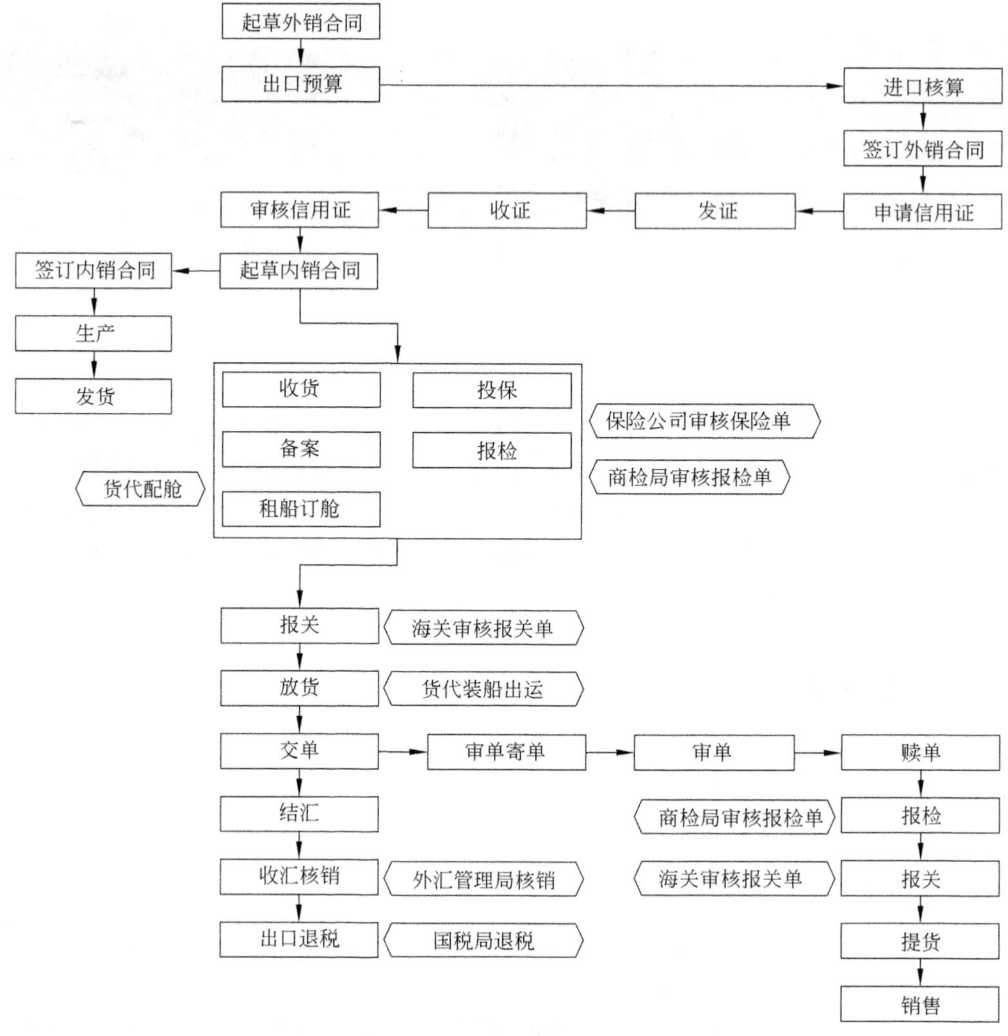

图 12-1　CIF + L/C

2. 资信调查函

Dear Sir or Madam,

Will you please be kind enough to obtain for us all information possible respecting the financial condition and business standing of Xiguateng Export Company of Wuhan?

As we are on the point of transacting some important business with them, we should like to know exactly how their credit stands. I shall feel under great obligation if you will advise me confidentially respecting the reputation they enjoy in this line.

Any information you may give us will be treated as strictly confidential.

Truly yours,

Tina Wong

Answer to above.

Dear Miss. Wong,

We inform you that we can give favorable information about the Xiguateng Export Company. Though they had not been long established, they stand pretty well and enjoy the fullest respect and unquestionable confidence in the business circle.

Please consider this information for which we accept no responsibility as strictly confidential.

Sincerely yours,
Jessica

3. 询盘函

Dear Sir or Madam,

We are looking for companies who can help us distribute our products in new markets. We manufacture all-style female clothes and shoes. At present we export to Europe, but we would like to export to your country.

Please find enclosed our brochure, which gives details of our products.

We look forward to hearing from you.

Sincerely yours,
Ping Li

Encl.

4. 发盘函

Dear Miss. Wong,

In order to start a concrete transaction between us, we take pleasure offer you firms as follows, subject to your reply reaching us by the end of this month.

300 pieces "Natural Beauty" Brand female cotton shirts at USD 100 per piece CIF Shanghai. The shipment will be made during August. We require payment by confirmed irrevocable letter of credit payable by draft at sight.

This is the best offer we can make at present and we trust that you will accept this offer without loss of time as the demand for our cotton shirts is heavy.

Yours very truly,
Ping Li

5. 还盘函

Dear Mr. Li,

We are in possession of your letter last Friday offering us 300 pieces "Natural Beauty" Brand female cotton shirts USD 100 per piece CIF Shanghai.

While appreciating the quality of your lines, we made a careful study of your offer. We find your prices are too high to be acceptable. In order to make your products more competitive in our market, we suggest that you reduce prices by 10%. If you will agree to our counter-suggestion, regular orders for large numbers will be placed. Otherwise, we will conduct our business elsewhere.

Please let us have your E-mail confirmation at your earliest convenience.

Yours faithfully,

Tina Wong

6. 接受函

Dear Miss. Wong,

I'm sorry to learn from your letter that you find our prices too high. We do our best to keep prices as low as possible without sacrificing quality and are constantly enquiring into new method of manufacture.

But regarding our long term of business relationship, we decide to accept your counter-offer. We will send you some samples if they are to your satisfactory please place your order at your convenient.

Sincerely yours,

Ping Li

7. 订购函

Dear Mr. Li,

We thank you for your letter of last Friday. We are glad to inform you that your samples are satisfactory. Enclosed please find our order No. 001 for three of the items.

All these items are urgently required by our customers. We, therefore, hope you will make delivery at an early date.

Yours faithfully,

Tina Wong

Encl.

Order No. 001

Quantity	Item	Catalogue No.	CIF Shanghai
100	Female cotton shirt blue	123	USD 90 each
100	Female cotton shirt red	124	USD 90 each
100	Female cotton shirt yellow	125	USD 90 each

Packing: in cotton cloth bales.

Shipment: During August

Payment: By irrevocable L/C available by draft at sight.

8. 订立合同函

Dear Miss. Wong,

We have booked your Order No. 001 for female cotton shirts and are sending you herewith our Sales Contract No. 001 in duplicate. Please sign and return one copy to us for our file.

It is understood that a letter of credit in our favor covering the above-mentioned goods, will be established immediately. We wish to point out that the stipulations in the relevant credit should strictly conform to the terms sated in our Sales Contract into order to avoid subsequent amendments. You may rest assured that we shall effect shipment with the least possible delay upon receipt of the credit.

We appreciated your cooperation and look forward to receiving your further orders.

Yours faithfully,

Ping Li

9. 催证函

Dear Miss. Wong,

With reference to the goods under our Sales Contract No. 001, we wish to inform you that the goods are ready for dispatch.

The date of delivery is approaching, but we have not yet received the covering L/C to date. Please do your utmost to expedite the L/Cs, that we may execute the order smoothly. In order to avoid subsequent amendment, please see to it that the L/C stipulations are in exact accordance with the terms in the Contract.

Hope to hear favorably from you soon.

Yours truly,

Ping Li

10. 发证函

Dear Mr. Li,

Attach to Sales Contract No. 001 we have made arrangements the Bank of China, Shanghai, to open a credit in your favor. The credit is valid until Sep. 30th and will be confirmed to you by the Bank's London office, Queen Street. It is understood that the goods will be shipped before August.

Bales containing the goods should be marked N. B. The amount of our credit has been fixed to provide adequate cover for your invoice, Which should provide for all charges.

Please notify us when the goods are shipped.

Yours faithfully,

Tina Wong

11. 改证函

Dear Miss. Wong,

We are in receipt of your letter on last Friday requesting us to ship all the goods during August. Unfortunately we are unable to comply with your wishes.

When we offered the goods, it was expressly stated that shipment would be effected during August. If you desire early delivery, we can only make a partial shipment of half amount of goods in July and remaining others in August. We hope this arrangement will be agreeable to you. Should this be so please amend the covering credit to allow partial shipment under advice to us.

Please cable us your confirmation so that we can request the manufacturers to expedite delivery.

Yours faithfully,

Ping Li

12. 包装函

Dear Mr. Li,

We accept your amendment to the shipment, you could arrange your manufacture and shipment smoothly owe to we change the L/Cs items about partial shipment.

As to the packing, we are not sure whether cartoon bales could provide the goods from damage during the shipment. Do you have any good advice?

Yours faithfully,

Tina Wong

13. 包装接洽函

Dear Miss. Wong,

With reference to your last letter we are glad that you accept our amendment to the shipment. As the goods are susceptible to be broken, the goods be packed in wooden cartoon could be better.

We trust that the above instructions are clear to you and that the shipment will give the users entire satisfaction.

Yours faithfully,

Ping Li

14. 装运及保险函

Dear Miss. Wong,

We have arranged all the insurance and delivery about the Sales Contract No. 001. The insurance company is the People's Insurance company London Branch and the shipping company is the Ocean Shipping Company Mary voyage No. 555, we will deliver the goods on July 30th. If the goods arrive at the port of Shanghai they will contact you.

About the claim and settlement we conform to the Sales Contract No 001.

Yours faithfully,

Ping Li

12.2 CIF + L/C (2)

1. 建立业务关系函

Dear Sirs,

We have obtained your address from Alibaba and are now writing to you for the establishment of business relations.

We are very well connected with all the major dealers here of computer, and feel sure we can sell large quantities of computer if we get your offers at competitive prices. We would like you to send us details of various ranges, including sizes, colors and prices, and also samples of the different qualities of material used. Meanwhile, please quote us the lowest price CIF Shanghai, inclusive of our 3% commission, stating the earliest date of shipment.

We look forward to your prompt reply.

Yours faithfully,

Brown

2. 资信调查函

Dear Sirs,

We have received a large order from Angel Computer Imp. & Exp. Co. Shanghai. We would therefore appreciate it if you would provide us information about the financial condition and business standing of the previously mentioned firm.

The reference we have obtained is the ICBC, Shanghai. Will you please be good enough to obtain for us the information we need?

Any information that you may provide us will be treated in strict confidence.

We thank in advance.

Yours faithfully,

Bob

资信调查函回复如下。

Dear Mr. Bob,

Referring to your letter of Sep. 10th, 2013, we wish to inform you that we have obtained the information you require from the ICBC, Shanghai Branch.

The subject company was established in January 1998 with a capital of US $70000. Do business as importers and exporters in various kinds of computers. Their balance sheets of recent years enclosed will show you that their import business in this line has been managed and operated under satisfactory condition.

Please note that the information is provided with strict confidence and without any responsibility whatsoever on the part of this Bank.

Yours faithfully,

Susan

3. 报盘函

Dear Sirs,

Thank you very much for your letter of Sep. 10th, 2013, we are pleased to send you samples and all the necessary information on Dell under separate cover.

At your request, we are pleased to make you an offer, subject to your final confirmation, as follows:

Commodity: Dell Computer XPS 14

Size: 160cm ×90cm (inch 14)

Color: Black, White, Red, Yellow

Price: US $1800 each set CIF Shanghai inclusive of 3% commission.

Shipment: During Sep. /Nov.

Payment: By 100% confirmed, irrevocable L/C in our favor payable by draft at sight to reach the sellers one month before shipment, and remain valid for negotiation in China till the 15th day after shipment.

We look forward to hearing from you.

Sincerely yours,

Bob

4. 接受函

Dear Sirs,

We are glad to have received your letter of Sep. 11th offering us Dell Computer inch 14 at CIF Shanghai USD 1800 per set.

In reply, we accept your offer, but we suggest that for this trial order, we wish to order 50 sets. If there is a promising market in our area, we will increase the order. Please delivery on time.

Encl: S/C No. 2453

Sincerely yours,

Brown

5. 请求开立信用证函

Dear Sirs,

Thank you for your order No. 2543. In order to execute it, please open an irrevocable L/C for the amount of USD 90000 in our favor. This account shall be available until Sep. 30th. Upon arrival of the L/C we will pack and ship the order as requested. And we will cover All Risks at invoice value plus 10%, that is USD 9900.

We look forward to hearing from you early.

Yours faithfully,

Bob

回复函如下。

Dear Sirs,

Thank you for your letter of Sep. 12th enclosing details of your terms. According to your request for opening an irrevocable L/C, we have instructed the ICBC, Shanghai to open a credit for USD 90000 in your favor, valid until Sep. 31th, the L/C No. is 256874AS. Please advice us by fax when the order has been executed.

We look forward to your prompt reply.

Sincerely yours,

Brown

6. 租船订舱函

Dear Sirs,

Result from we have business with Angel Computer Co. Shanghai, so we want to book the shipping space, which sail to Shanghai during Sep./Nov.. We will ship 50 sets computers, as the goods are susceptible to be broken, must be packed in wooden cases capable of withstanding rough handling.

We look forward to receiving your shipping advice soon.

Yours faithfully,

Bob

租船订舱回复函如下。

Dear Sirs,

We have received your letter of Sep. 15th, from which we understand that you have booked our order for 50 sets computers.

Our confirmation of order will be forwarded to in three days. As our purchase is made on CIF basis, we have arranged shipment with our forwarding agent, SPEED Company, Shanghai, who is going to take care of shipping those goods. Once the shipping space is booked, we will inform you of the name of the ship and time.

We are looking forward to the satisfactory arrival of the goods.

Sincerely yours,

July

7. 装船通知函

Dear Sirs,

We are pleased to advise you that we have completed the shipment of your order 0405. The ship is scheduled to sail from Sydney on Sep. 20th and the estimated time to arrive at Shanghai is Nov. 1st, we have mailed to you by fax this morning the documents. The details are as follows:

Our Contract No.: S123

Your Order No.: O123

Commodity: Dell Computer

Quantity: 50 sets

Invoice Amount: USD 258.80

Vessel: HERO

B/L No.: V0408

L/C No.: 123456B

Invoice No.: F2356

Insurance Policy No.: BY2564

Packing List No.: CT8524

We trust this consignment will reach you in sound condition and look forward to cooperation with you before long.

Yours faithfully,

July

8. 投保函

Dear Sirs,

Re: Your Order No. 2543 for 50 sets computers

This is to acknowledge receipt of your letter dated Sep. 10th, requesting us to effect insurance on the captioned shipment for our account.

We are pleased to inform you that we have covered the shipment with the People's Insurance Company of China against All Risks for USD 9900. The policy is being prepared accordingly and will be forwarded to you by Next Tuesday.

Yours truly,

Bob

9. 装运通知函

Dear Sirs,

Your order has been shipped. The name of ship is HERO, which is owed to SEEPED Company, it will arrive at Shanghai on Nov. 1st, please receive the goods on time.

We look forward to cooperating with you before long.

Yours faithfully,

Bob

12.3 FOB + L/C

FOB + L/C 如图 12-2 所示。

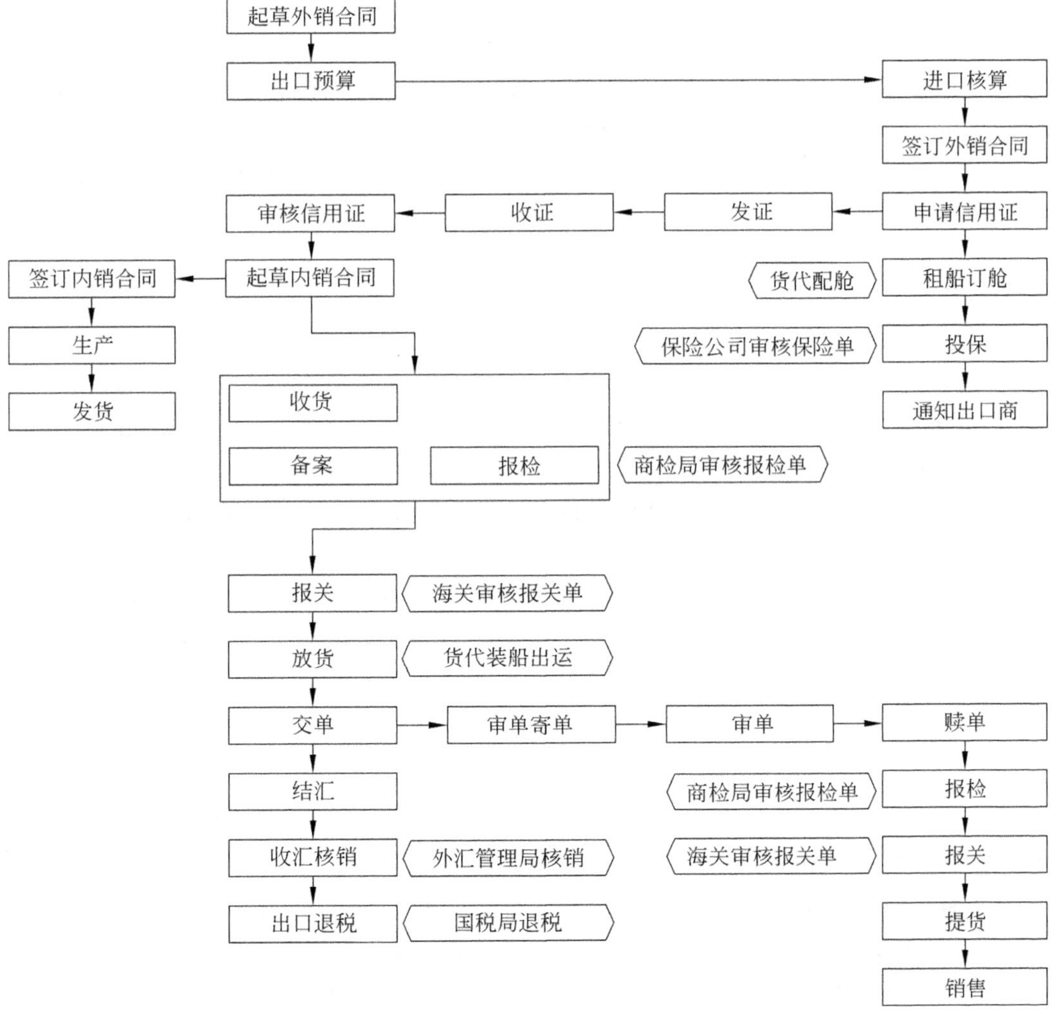

图 12-2 FOB + L/C

1. 建立业务关系函

Dear Mr. Li,

We have obtained your address from Internet and are now writing to you for the establishment of business relations.

We are keenly desirous of buying various styles of clothes and feel sure we can buy large quantities of clothes if we get your offers at competitive prices. If you can supply these goods, kindly airmail us a sample, please enclose your pricelist and suitable illustrations.

We await your early reply.

Truly yours,

Xi Sun

建立业务关系函回复如下。

Dear Miss. Sun,

We thank you for your letter and shall be pleased to enter into business relations with you. In compliance with your request, we are sending you our latest illustrated catalogue and price list and the samples you need by mail.

Sincerely yours,

Li Li

2. 资信调查往来函

Dear Sirs,

We have received a large order from Only & Co. We would therefore appreciate it if you would provide us information about the financial condition and business standing of the previously mentioned firm.

The reference we have obtained is ICBC, will you please be good enough to obtain for us the information we need?

Any information we receive from you, of course, will be held in strict confidence.

Yours faithfully,

Xi Sun

资信调查回复函如下。

Dear Miss. Sun,

Thank you for your inquiry about the business standing of Only & Co. We are pleased to supply you with the following information obtained from ICBC.

The subject company was established in January 1982, with a capital of RMB 1000000. Do business as importers in various kinds of clothes. Their balance sheets of recent years enclosed will show you that their import business in this line has been managed and operated under satisfactory condition.

We hope that we have been of assistance to you, and that you will recognize the importance of keeping this communication strictly private.

Yours faithfully,
Feng Wu

3. 询盘函

Dear Sirs,

We have been informed by the chamber of commerce that you are one of the leading exporters of clothes. And that you wish to export kinds of clothes to our market.

We are considering the purchase of your clothes, you will be pleased to note that our corporation is one of the leading importers of clothes, having over 30 years' history and high reputation.

We shall be able to give you considerable orders, if the quality of your products is fine and the prices are moderate. Please let us have your lowest FOB price, together with your terms of business.

Please let us know by return of post whether you would be interested in such an order.

Yours faithfully,
Xi Sun

4. 发盘函

Dear Miss. Sun,

Thank you for your enquiry and for your interest in our products.

We are enclosing our quotation sheet covering different size and colors of our clothes that can be supplied from stock . Delivery will be with 20 days after your placing an order to us . Payment of the purchase is to be effected by an irrevocable L/C at sight in our favor.

We hope you will find our quotation satisfactory and look forward to receiving your order not later than the end of next month . Enclosed detailed information.

Yours faithfully,
Li Li

5. 还盘函

Dear Sirs,

We are glad to have received your letter covering detailed information.

In reply, we don't deny the quality of the clothes, but I should like to point out that your choice in color and style is limited and that the shades that are now fashionable are missing. To step up the trade, we counter-offer you that the price should be cut down by 10%. If you will agree to our offer suggestion, regular order for large numbers will be placed . Otherwise we will conduct our business elsewhere.

It is hoped that you would seriously take it into consideration and let us have your reply very soon.

Sincerely yours,
Xi Sun

6. 接受函

Dear Miss. Sun,

We have received your letter of counter offer . It is regretful for us to see that you cut down the price of our clothes too sharp, but regarding our long term of business relationship, we decide to accept your counter offer on condition that cash must be paid within three months of date of delivery, or you must sign the contract for 3 years and the price according to the market level.

Sincerely yours,
Li Li

7. 订购往来函

Dear Sirs,

Re: Our Order No. 456

Please ship the following merchandise:

Trouser

Quantity	size	color	Price	Pattern No.
200	26	red	100	1
260	27	black	100	2
400	28	blue	100	3
200	29	white	100	40

Skirt

Quantity	Size	Color	Price
100	S	white	120
100	M	white	120
100	L	white	120
100	S	blue	120
100	M	blue	120
100	L	blue	120
100	S	red	120
100	M	red	120
100	L	red	120

Delivery: During September

Payment: By L/C to be opened in accordance with our agreement.

Packing: Usually packing in strong bales, with gunny bags cover and waterproof material.

Please acknowledge this order immediately on receipt and inform definite delivery date. Thank you.

Yours faithfully,

Xi Sun

订购回复函如下。

Dear Miss. Sun,

Re: Your Order No. 456

We have booked your order No. 456 for skirts and trousers and are sending you here with our Sales Confirmation No. 123 in duplicate. Please sign and return one copy to us for our file.

Those you have ordered have been popular with the old, the young and are selling well in several countries. We appreciate the business you have able to give us and assure you that your order will receive our most careful attention.

We are arranging for the establishment of the relative Confirmed Irrevocable Letter of Credit through the bankers and shall inform you by fax as soon as it is opened.

We appreciate your cooperation and look forward to receiving your further order.

Yours faithfully,

Li Li

8. 催证函

Dear Miss. Sun,

Please open a credit of \$214000 with your correspondents in favor of the ABC bank, to be available to the Company until August 25th against a shipment of goods by sea leaving London for China on August 10th.

We wish to remind you that it was agreed when placing the order, that you would establish the required L/C upon receipt of our confirmation. Most important of all, the skirts and trousers are seasonal, so we should take it into consideration seriously and open the L/C in time.

As the goods have been ready for shipment for quite some time, it behooves you to take immediate action, particularly since we cannot think of any valid reason for further delaying the opening of the credit . Moreover, any problem the credit caused you must understand.

Yours faithfully,

Li Li

9. 改证函

Dear Miss. Sun,

We wish to acknowledge receipt of the L/C No. 3450 for the amount of USD 5000 covering your Order No. 456 requesting us to deliver the skirts and trousers during September. Unfortunately we are unable to comply with your wishes.

When we offered the merchandise, it was expressly stated that shipment would be effected in September. If you desire early delivery, we can only make a partial shipment in August and the remaining in September. We hope this arrangement will be agreeable to you. Should this be so, please amend the covering credit to allow partial shipment under advice to us.

Please cable us your confirmation so that we can request the manufacture to expedite delivery.

Yours faithfully,

Li Li

10. 包装方式洽谈函

Dear Miss. Sun,

We are now writing to you in regard to the packing of garment.

The relative clause should be stated that goods shall be packed in cartons instead of in wooden cases, which will prevent skillful pilferage, and is fairly fit for ocean transportation. Besides our carton are well protected against moisture by plastic lining and are comparatively light and compact to be easy to handle.

We hope you will find it in order and pay special attention to the packing.

Yours faithfully,

Li Li

包装方式回复函如下。

Dear Sirs,

We have received your letter with pleasure and immediately informed our workers about our packing. After talking about it, they will have no objections to your packing of the garments in cartons if you can guarantee that all the loss the packing leads to the insurance company must undertake.

We think you will understand that our candid statements are made for our mutual benefits as packing is a sensitive subject, which often contribute to some problems.

We appreciate your cooperation.

Yours faithfully,

Xi Sun

11. 保险函

Dear Sirs,

We have known that your company is the largest insurance company in China with branches and sub-branches throughout the country. We wish to insure with your company a shipment of garments valued at $214000 on board the vessel HeXie against All Risk, bound from London to Shanghai sailing on August, 10.

We shall appreciate it if the goods could be insured at favorable rate and awaiting your early reply.

Yours truly,
(Signature)

保险回复函如下。

Dear Miss Sun,

We have received your letter of August 5 in regard to insurance. In reply, we would like to inform you of readiness to insure with us a shipment of garments from London to Shanghai by sea.

The prevailing rate for the proposed shipment against All Risks is 0.8%, subject to our own Ocean Cargo Clauses. Copies thereof are enclosed herewith for your reference.

If you find our rate acceptable, please let us know.

Yours truly,
(Signature)

12. 装运函

Dear Miss. Sun,

We are pleased to notify you that the cargo has been shipped by the vessel HEXIE, which will sail today from London to Shanghai. The details are as follows.

Our contract No.: XM647832

Our order No.: 345

Our L/C No.: SX4560

Invoice No.: FQ562089

B/L No.: vs050086

Invoice amount: USD 214000

We have taken every care in packing and handling goods, so that they will reach you in good order and condition. In order to facilitate your checking the goods, all the cartons have been marked with number, which are corresponding to those indicated in the packing lists, where the color and size assortments have also been stated.

We trust that this consignment will turn out to your entire satisfaction, and hope that we shall have many opportunities in future to demonstrate our ability to handle orders promptly and carefully.

Yours truly,
(Signature)

13. 索赔函

Dear Sirs,

Re: S/C No.: XM647811

We have informed by our agents in WUHAN, to our regret, 10% of the packages were seriously damaged with big hole and the garments are painted.

We immediately invited the surveyors to spot to look into the case, and they found this was due to poor packing. A detailed result will be enclosed to you.

In accordance with the stipulations of the Sales Confirmation, we are obliged to hold you are responsible for the damage and claim on you for the compensation for the loss.

We are awaiting your prompt reply.

Yours truly,
(Signature)

12.4 FOB + D/P

FOB + D/P 如图 12-3 所示。

1. 建立业务关系往来函

Dear Mr. Peng,

We are writing to you at the suggestion of our Commercial Counselor's Office of the Embassy in your country. We take the liberty to introduce ourselves as exporters of silk cloth, which we have been exporting to Japan and Europe. We are specialized in the above business. We are desirous of establishing direct business relations with your corporation, knowing that you are the importer of silk piece goods. We shall be grateful if you will let us know whether you are interested in the above items. Awaiting your prompt reply.

Sincerely yours,
Jane

建立业务关系回复函如下。

Dear Miss. Jane,

We thank you for your letter and shall be pleased to enter into business relations with you.

Please send us your samples of your exports.

Awaiting your prompt reply.

Sincerely yours,

Yu Peng

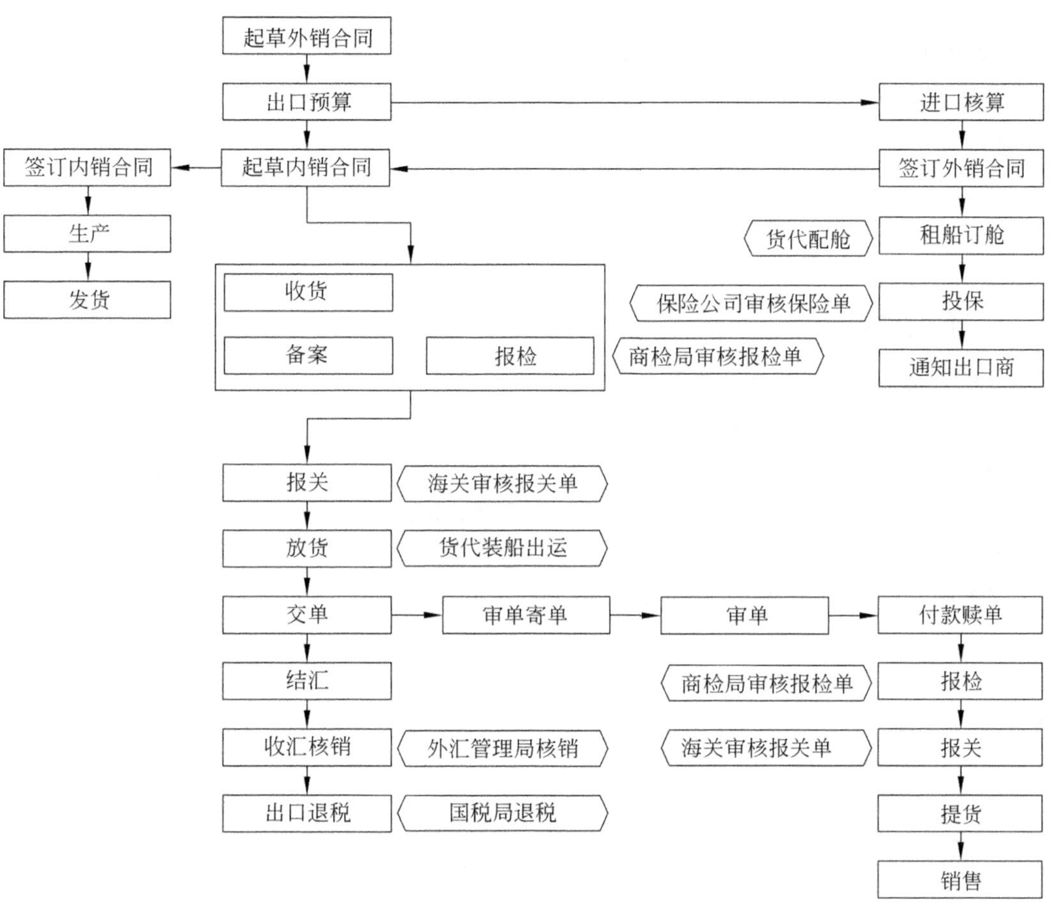

图 12-3 FOB + D/P

2. 资信调查往来函

Dear Mr. Lin,

Will you please be kind enough to obtain for us all information possible respecting the financial condition and business standing of Yali Co., Ltd.?

As we are on the point of transacting some important business with them, we should like to know exactly how their credit stands. I shall feel under great obligation if you will advise me confidentially respecting the reputation they enjoy in this line.

Any information you may give me will, of course, be treated as strictly confidential.

Truly yours,

Jane

资信调查回复函如下。

Dear Miss Jane,

We inform you that we can give nothing but favorable information about the firm in question. Though they had not been long established, they stand pretty well. They command considerable funds and an unlimited credit, and the executives are thorough business men. The firm enjoys the fullest respect and unquestionable confidence in the business world.

Please consider this information for which we accept no responsibility as strictly confidential.

Sincerely yours,

Kai Lin

3. 询盘往来函

Dear Mr. Peng,

Thank you for your prompt reply.

We have sent the samples to you today. I guess you will receive them in three days.

But we have to mention that the design and working on them are for one of our previous customers.

Please inform us of your own designs on the boards when you send us an order.

Sincerely yours,

Jane

Dear Jane,

Thank you for your massage. Just yesterday we received your samples. Thanks. And we will work on the order and get back to you.

Truly yours,

Yu Peng

Dear Mr. Peng,

In your previous e-mail you agree to work on the order and get back to me, but so far we haven't received your order.

Do you still need these silk piece goods? If so, we can guarantee the best quality and the most competitive prices, because we have our own factory with advanced equipment. We also have long and stable relationship with silk suppliers, and we can get the best prices from them. So we know how to cut cost without affecting the quality and delivery date.

I'm sure our first deal will be successful!

Sincerely yours,

Jane

Dear Jane,

Our designs are ready. We have sent them to you today by courier.

Will you please quote us your best prices for it?

Please also state your items of payment.

Please reply as soon as possible.

Truly yours,

Yu Peng

4. 发盘函

Dear Mr. Peng,

Thank you for your prompt reply. The following is our quotation for the quantity of silk cloth:

Length × width

10m × 10m: USD 19.00/piece 100 pieces FOB Hamburg

9m × 13m: USD 20.00/piece 500 pieces FOB Hamburg

Each one has yellow, red, green, blue and white. Payment by D/P

I believe the above is acceptable.

Awaiting your favorable reply.

Truly yours,

Jane

5. 接受函

Dear Jane,

I confirm your offer of yesterday. The silk cloth:

Length × width

10m × 10m: USD 19.00/piece 100 pieces FOB Hamburg

9m × 13m: USD 20.00/piece 500 pieces FOB Hamburg

Payment by D/P

When is your best delivery date?

Awaiting your reply.

Truly yours,

Yu Peng

6. 包装装运函

Dear Mr. Peng,

The cloth we offered are packed in cartons of 20 pcs each, with inner boxes. Our bank is: Bank of China, Hangzhou Branch No. 37 Zhoushan Road, Hangzhou, China.

Our delivery date will be 20 days after we receive your money.

Truly yours,

Jane

7. 索赔函

Dear Jane,

I'm sorry to say that some of the cloths were caught in the rain. Our Survey Report stated the damage was attributed to improper packing. And we can't use it. We must therefore lodge a claim against you for the amount of USD 3000.

We hope the matter will call your best attention.

Truly yours,

Yu Peng

8. 理赔函

Dear Mr. Peng,

Thank you for your letter. It was great regret that we hear this affair. We will make payment for it.

We hope this matter will not affect our good relations in our future dealing.

Truly yours,

Jane

12.5 FOB + D/A

FOB + D/A 如图 12-4 所示。

1. 建立业务关系往来函

Dear Sir or Madam,

We have obtained your name and address from the Internet, and we are writing to enquire whether you would be willing to establish business relations with us.

Now we are keenly desirous of enlarging our trade in light industrial products, and would appreciate your catalogues and quotations. If your price are competitive, we would expect to transact a significant volume of business.

We await your early reply.

Truly yours,

Qing Ye

建立业务关系回复函如下。

Dear Miss. Ye,

We have received your letter with thanks. We are glad to inform you that we would like to supply light industrial products. We are confident that our products will meet the requirements of your market. We are sending you our latest illustrated catalogue and price list covering our export range.

If you find business possible, please write to us.

Sincerely yours,

Daiy

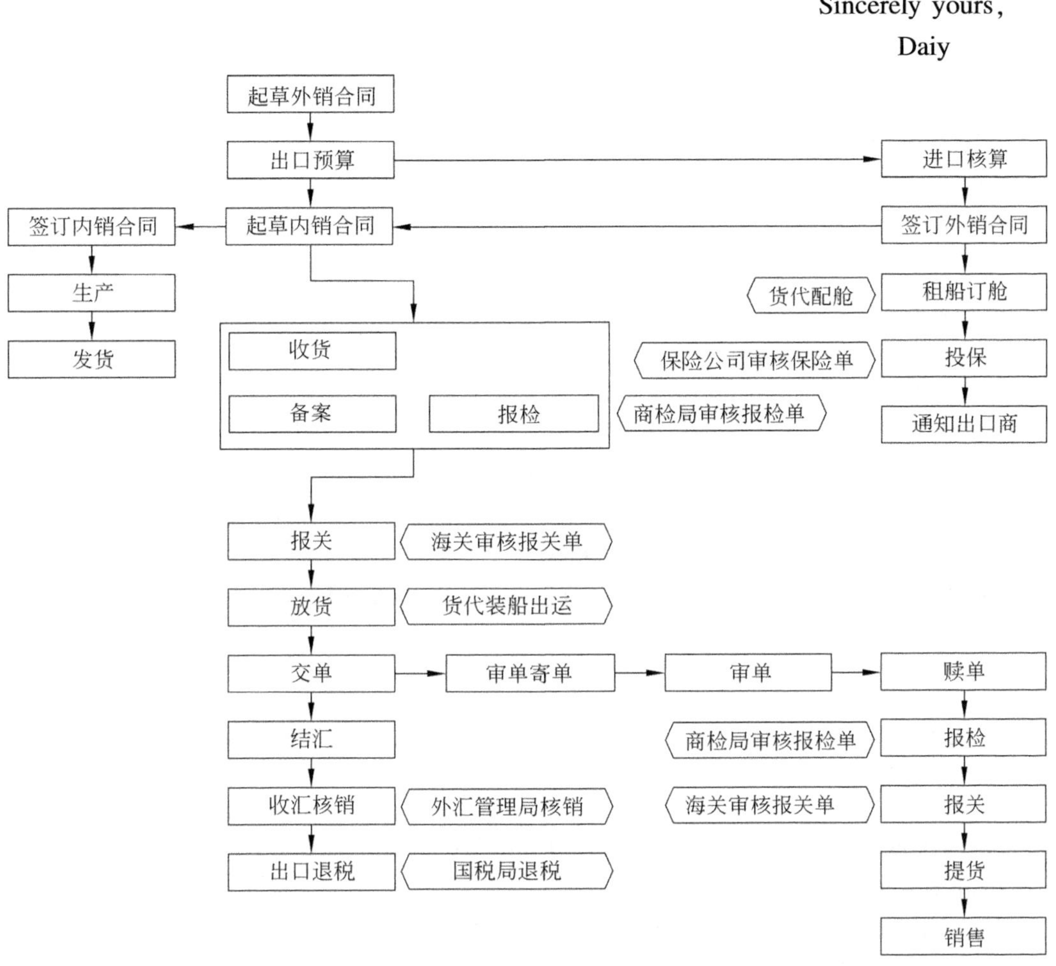

图 12-4 FOB + D/A

2. 资信调查往来函

Dear Sir or Madam,

We have received a large order from ABC IMP. & EXP. Co., We would there appreciate it if you would supply us information about the financial condition and business standing of the previously mentioned firm. The reference we have obtained is the ABC Bank. Will you please be good enough to obtain for us the information we need? Any information that you may provide us will be treated in strict confidence.

We thank in advance.

Yours faithfully,

Daiy

资信调查回复函如下。

Dear Daiy,

In reply your letter of September 16th, 2013, we are pleased to tell you the subject company has never failed to meet their obligation. The credit report of recent years enclosed will show you that import business has been doing well.

Please note that the information is furnished at your request without any responsibility on our part and should be held strictly confidential.

Yours Truly,
Yezi

3. 询盘函

Dear Sir or Madam,

We have received you reply and learned from the Internet that you are exporters of light industrial products and willing to establish business relations with you. We are satisfied with the products on the catalogue and hope that the products will meet our need. Meanwhile, please quote us the lowest price FOB Wuhan.

Should your price be found competitive, we shall place a large order with you.

Yours truly,
Qing Ye

4. 发盘函

Dear Miss Ye,

Thank you for your letter of September 18th. We are gratified to receive your request for light industrial products.

At your request, we are pleased to make you an offer, subject to your final confirmation, as follows:

Commodity: "HYGIENIX FACIAL TISSUE"

Quantity: 50000 bags

Price: US $3.5 each bag FOB Wuhan

Quality: Selected

We are sure that you can get benefit from our products.

We look forward to your prompt reply.

Your faithfully,
Daiy

5. 还盘函

Dear Sir or Madam,

We are glad to have received your letter offering us Hygienix facial tissue.

In reply, we regret to inform you that your price is too high; Market information tells us that some products have been sold in other companies at a level about 5% lower than yours. We do not deny the quality of your products, but the difference in price is a wide gap. To step up the trade, we counter-offer you 60000 bags Hygienix facial tissue FOB Wuhan.

It is hoped that you would seriously take it to consideration and let us have your reply very soon.

Sincerely yours,

Qing Ye

6. 接受函

Dear Miss Ye,

We have receipted of your letter. And we are sorry that you find our price too high. We do our best to keep prices as low as possible without sacrificing quality. Considering the quality of the goods offered, we don't feel that the price we quote are at all excessive, but bearing in mind the special character of your trade, we have decided to accept your counter-offer. We make this allowance because we want to establish a long business with you.

At least we hope this revised offer will now enable you to place an order.

Sincerely yours,

Daiy

7. 订购函

Dear Sir or Madam,

We thank you for your account, and place an order following:

Order No. 108

Please ship the following merchandise:

Commodity	Quantity	Catalogue	Price
Hygienix facial tissue	60000 bags	27	USD 3.2 each

Delivery: Before October

Payment: By D/A before shipment

Packing: Usually packing in carton, with waterproof material. Please acknowledge this order immediately.

Your faithfully,

Qing Ye

8. 付款函

Dear Sir or Madam,

Thank you for your letter.

When the goods purchased by us are ready before shipment, you cable us and we will pay you the full amount by D/A. We hope you will agree our request. We look forward to your confirmation of our order and your affirmative reply to our arrangement of payment.

Your faithfully,

Qing Ye

付款回复函如下。

Dear Miss Ye,

We are pleased to acknowledge your order for our products. The arrangement you supposed to meet outstanding accounts are quite satisfactory. All items included in your order can be supplied from stock and will be packed and shipment immediately.

Your faithfully,

Daiy

9. 保险函

Dear Sirs,

Knowing that your company is the largest insurance company in China with branches and sub-branches throughout the country. We, ABC Import and Export Corporation, wish to insure with your company value at USD192000.00 against All Risks.

We shall appreciate it if the goods could be insured at favorable rate.

Yours truly,

Qing Ye

保险回复函如下。

Dear Miss Ye,

We are pleased to receive your letter.

The prevailing rate for the proposed shipment against All Risks including War Risks is 5%, subject to our own Ocean Cargo Clauses and Ocean Marine War Risk Clause.

If you find our rate acceptable, please let us know.

Yours truly,

Damon

10. 装运函

Dear Miss Ye,

Re: Your order No. 108

We received your letter requesting us to ship the goods. For your information, we have get in touch with the COSCO and have now succeed in booking the required shipping spaces on S. S. Mary sail to Wuhan before October.

We trust that everything is now in order.

Your Truly,
Daiy

12.6 CIF + T/T before Shipment

CIF + T/T before Shipment 如图 12-5 所示。

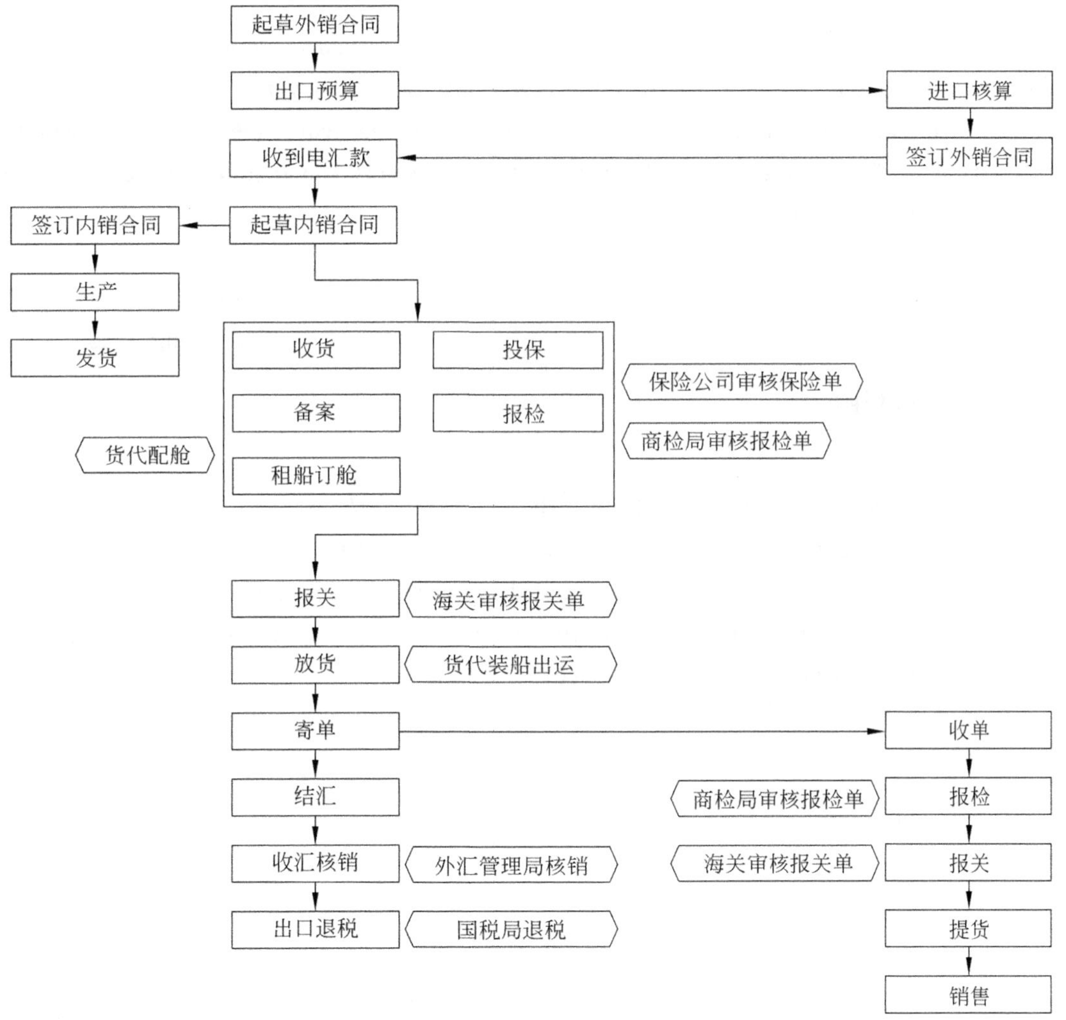

图 12-5 CIF + T/T before Shipment

1. 建立业务关系函

Dear Sirs,

We owe your name and address to the Commercial Counselor's Office in Beijing who have informed us that you are in the market for cheongsam.

We wish to buy some quality cheongsam and with different style. Also please enclose your pricelist and all suitable illustrations.

We look forward to receiving your enquiries soon.

Yours faithfully,
Sweet

建立业务关系回复函如下。

Dear Sweet,

We have received your letter with thanks. We are very glad to inform you that we can supply quality cheongsam and different style with fully decorated with flowers and or other designs. We are confident that our products will meet the requirements of the market. Enclosed please find a catalogue and pricelist of the products you require. We are sending you by mail the samples you need.

Waiting for your order.

Sincerely yours,
Ming Xiao

2. 资信调查函

Dear Sir,

We have received a large order from ABC Company. We want to know if you would provide us information about the financial condition and business stand of the previously mentioned firm. The reference we have obtained is the Royal Bank, USA, Will you please be good enough to obtain for us the information we need? Any information that you may provide us will be treated in strict confidence.

Yours faithfully,
Ming Xiao

资信调查回复函如下。

Dear Mr. Xiao,

Referring to your letter of June 25th, 2013, we wish to inform you that we have obtained the information you require from the Royal Bank, USA. The subject company is with a capital of 100000 dollars. Their balance sheets of recent years enclosed will show you that their import business in this line has been managed and operated under satisfactory condition. Please note that the information is provided with strict confidence and without any responsibility whatsoever on the part of this bank.

Yours faithfully,
Hong Zhang

3. 具体询盘函

Dear Mr. Xiao,

We are glad to note from your letter of 1 July. You will be please to note that our company is one of the leading importers of cheongsam products, having over 30 years' history and high reputation. Sample cheongsam and all necessary information are regarding these goods so as to acquaint us with the quality and workmanship of your supplies. Meanwhile please quote us your lowest price. CIF California, stating the earliest date of shipment.

Should your price be found competitive and delivery date acceptable, we intend to place a large order with you.

We trust you will give us an early reply.

Yours faithfully,

Sweet

4. 发盘函

Dear Sweet,

We acknowledge with thanks the receipt of your letter dated July. 10th, showing your interest in the cheongsam product and extending the wish to place orders with us. In reply, we are offering you as follows, subject to our final confirmation:

Commodity: cheongsam

Packing: In bales or in wooden cases, at seller's option

Quantity: 300 PCS

Price: USD 300 CIF California

Shipment: August,2013

Under separate cover, we have sent you samples of various sizes and the brochure required. Because of the excellent quality and favorable price, you may be assured that our products will no doubt help you expand your market.

As the price of raw material has gone up steadily since June, we hope you will let us have your order before further rise in costs.

Yours sincerely,

Ming Xiao

5. 还盘函

Dear Mr. Xiao,

We refer to your quotation for the captioned article, the samples and catalogues enclosed. We have contacted our clients, who find the quality and delivery time acceptable but the price so greatly different from those quoted by other supplies that it is unacceptable to them. Market information tell us that some cheongsam in other place sold at a level about 30% lower than yours, We hope the above offer is acceptable to you and await with keen interest your trial order.

Sincerely yours,
Sweet

6. 接受函

Dear Sweet,

We conform having your T/T of July 23th, asking us to make a 10% reduction in our price for cheongsam.

Much to our regret, we find it intolerable to comply with your request because ours is the best possible price if you take the quality into consideration. However, in order to develop our market in your place, we have decided to accept your counter as an exceptional case.

We hope we can conclude a contract before long and await your prompt reply.

Yours truly,
Ming Xiao

7. 订购函

Dear Mr. Xiao,

We are pleased to place the following order with you if you can guarantee shipment at Beijing to California by Oct. 25th.

300 PCS cheongsam

Kindly confirm acceptance of our order by return and send advice of shipment. We will send the bank draft upon receipt of them.

Yours sincerely,
Sweet

8. 结算方式

Dear Mr. Xiao,

We are pleased to acknowledge your order for our cheongsam.

The arrangements you proposed to meet outstanding accounts are quite satisfactory. All items included in your order can be supplied from stock and will be packed and shipped immediately your remittance by T/T is received.

Yours sincerely,
Sweet

9. 投保函

Dear Sweet,

This is to acknowledge receipt of your letter of 27th, July requesting us to effect insurance on the captioned shipment for your account.

We are pleased to inform you that we have covered the above shipment with The People's Insurance Company of China against All Risks for $200000. The policy is being prepared and will be forwarded to you by the end of the month.

For your information, we are making arrangements to ship the 300 PCS cheongsam by S. S. "Tsinan", sailing on or about the 11th, August.

Sincerely,

Ming Xiao

12.7 FOB + T/T after Shipment

FOB + T/T after Shipment 如图 12-6 所示。

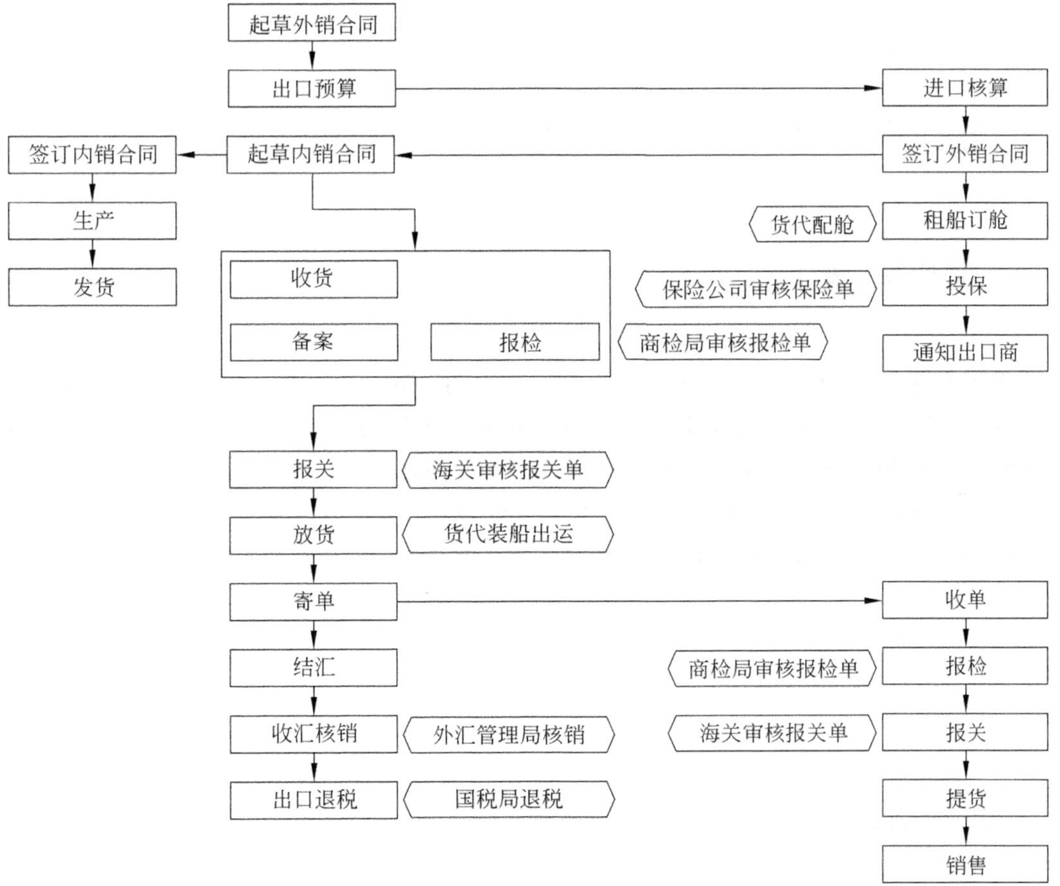

图 12-6 FOB + T/T after Shipment

1. 建立业务关系函

Dear Sirs,

We have obtained your company's name and address from internet and now writing to you for the establishment of business relations.

We wish to buy kinds of women's dress with high quality and good design. If you can supply this type of garments. Please enclose your pricelist and all suitable illustrations.

We await your early reply.

Sincerely yours,
Ann Cooper

建立业务关系回复函如下。

Dear Madam,

We thank you for your letter and shall be pleased to establish business relations with you.

At requested, we are sending you our latest illustrations and pricelist of our merchandise.

If you find it possible, please write to us for detail information.

Yours faithfully,
Yang Liu

2. 资信调查函

Dear Sirs,

We intend to enter into business relations with the Fair Lady Garment Corporation Ltd. Will you please be kind enough to obtain for us all information possible respecting the financial condition and business standing of the company?

We should like to know exactly how their credit stands. I shall fell under great obligation if you will advise me confidentially respecting the reputation they enjoy in this line.

Any information that you may provide us will be treated in strict confidence.

We thank you advance.

Truly yours,
Ann Cooper

资信调查回复函如下。

Dear Madam,

The subject company you inquired about in your letter of September 11th, 2013. The information we have obtained from the 1 +2 Equity Bank.

Though the company had not been long established, they stand pretty well, They command considerable funds and an unlimited credit. The company enjoys the fullest respect and unquestionable confidence in the business world.

Please note that the information is provide with strict confidence and without any responsibility whatever on the part of this bank.

Yours faithfully,

Peng Chen

3. 询盘函

Dear Sirs,

We learn with pleasure from your letter of September 14th, 2013.

At present, we are interested in women's dress and shall be pleased if you will send us different design samples. So as to acquaint with material and workmanship of your replies

Meanwhile, please quote us the lowest price FOB shanghai which the payment is T/T after shipment.

Should your price be found competitive and the delivery time acceptable, we shall make a large order with you.

Sincerely yours,

Ann Cooper

4. 发盘函

Dear Madam,

Thank you for your enquiry of September 16th, 2013 for women's dress and are pleased to quote a special offer. Which subject to our final confirmation, as follows:

Art No: 110342 women's dress

Specification: 32/28/34, 30/30/36

Quantity: 1300 PCS of all

Packing: in cartons

Price: 15 yuan per pc FOB Shanghai

Payment: by T/T after shipment

We trust you will find our quotation satisfactory and look forward to receive your order.

Truly yours,

Yang Liu

5. 还盘函

Dear Sirs,

Thank you for the samples you send in response to our enquiry of September 11th. But I should like to point out that your choice in color and pattern is very limited and that the shapes that are now fashionable are missing.

In reply, we suggest that you could perhaps make some allowance on your quoted price at a level about 10% lower than yours that would help to introduce your goods on this market. So as to the delivery time, consider to the time market, we hope that you can delivery within 60 days after receipt the order.

We hope you take our suggestion into consideration and give us your reply as soon as possible.

Sincerely yours,

Ann Cooper

6. 接受函

Dear Madam,

I am sorry to learn from your letter of September 18th that you find our kinds of women's dress too few and cut down the price at the offer's level 10%. We have done our best to keep the price as low as possible.

But regarding to building a long term of business relationship with you, we decide to accept your counter-offer. On condition that the goods must be delivered within 60 days after receipt the order and cut down 10% lower at the price.

Yours faithfully,

Yang Liu

7. 订购函

Dear Sirs,

We are in receipt of your letter of September 12th and are pleased to place an order with you for the following goods.

Re: our order No. 1103

Please ship the following merchandise.

Quantity	Pattern No.	Catalogue	Unit price	Price term
500 PCS	12	9	RMB 15	FOB Shanghai
500 PCS	13	8	RMB 15	
300 PCS	14	6	RMB 15	

Delivery: during November

Payment: By T/T after shipment

Packing: usually packing in strong bales with gunny bags cover and waterproof material.

All these item are urgently required by our customers. We therefore hope you will make delivery at an early date.

Sincerely yours,

Ann Cooper

订购回复函如下。

Dear Madam,

Re: Your order No. 1103

We are pleased to confirm your order which we have accepted on the term.

We confirm with you the following order for the women's dress at the terms stated in your letter:

Quantity	Pattern No.	Catalogue	Unit price	Price term
500 PCS	12	9	RMB 15	
500 PCS	13	8	RMB 15	FOB Shanghai
300 PCS	14	6	RMB 15	

Delivery: during the last ten day of November

Payment: By T/T after shipment

Packing: usually packing in strong bales with gunny bags cover and waterproof material.

For the above order, we enclose our sales confirmation No. 315 in duplicate. Please sign and return one copy for our file at your easiest convenience.

We are arranging for producing the goods, we thank you again for the above order and hope that this will lead to a long-term cooperation between us.

Yours faithfully,

Yang Liu

8. 包装函

Dear Sirs,

We are writing to you in regarding to the packing of our garments and we would like you to have the goods packed in cartons instead of in gunny bales. As packed in cartons have the following advantages.

It will prevent women's dress from water,

It is fairly fit for ocean transportation.

It is convenient to handle.

It is us that take in detail conditions into consideration make the decision, we hope you will accept our carton packing and assure you of our long cooperation.

Yours faithfully,

Ann Cooper

包装回复函如下。

Dear Madam,

Thank you for your packing instruction. At request, we immediately approached our client about the packing. But we regret to inform you that the supplier have completed the package. If change the package, it will increase the cost of the goods and it will extremely inconvenient.

Meanwhile, they also thought that pack in gunny bales will be safely. In other world trade which shipment of ocean transportation, the garments usually packing in gunny bags. Because the ship will provide prevent measure. It is also convenient to handle.

We appreciate your cooperation.

Yours faithfully,
Yang Liu

9. 保险函

Dear Sirs or Madam,

We have known that your company is the largest insurance company in China. Our YIYUANMEIYING Garment Ltd. wish to insure with your company a shipment of Chinese porcelain valued at RMB 19500 on board against All Risks bond from Shanghai to Chicago sailing on November 28th.

We shall appreciate it if the goods could be insured at favorable rate.

Yours faithfully,
Ann Cooper

保险回复函如下。

Dear Sirs or Madam,

We have acknowledged receipt of your letter of Sep. 28th and are pleased to note your garments to insure with us a shipment of Chinese porcelain from Shanghai to Chicago by sea.

The prevailing rate for the shipment against All Risks including War Risks is 0.5%, subject to Ocean Marine cargo clauses and Ocean Marine War Risks clauses. Copies there are enclosed herewith for your reference.

We trust the information will serve your purpose and await your further news.

Yours truly,
Lily Sung

10. 装运函

Dear Sirs,

We refer to our previous letter in respect of our order No. 1103 of September 11th for 1300 PCS women's dress, which was stipulated for shipment at the last ten days in November 2013. We are anxious to know about the shipment of our order for 1300 PCS women's dress.

As we are in argent need of the goods, because the garment is goods of time season, so we find it necessary to stress the importance of shipment. If you have completed product the garments please inform us as soon as possible. Please note that we will shipment at the port of Shanghai.

We should appreciate prompt shipment and hope to establish a regular connection for the future if this consignment proves to conform to the samples supplied.

Yours faithfully,
Ann Cooper

装运通知(出口商)函如下。

Dear Madam,

Re: Your order No. 1103

We have received your letter of November 24th reminding us to ship the goods in time. At requested, we have completed the production of women's dress and prepare for shipping.

Our shipment information of the order will be forwarded to you in a few days. Since the purchase is made on FOB basis. You can ship the goods from Shanghai port. As soon as the shipping space is booked. We shall inform you to ship the garments at November 28th 12 AM 2013. Shanghai port. Please prepare for shipment in time.

We trust that everything is now in order.

Truly yours,
Yang Liu

11. 付款函(出口商提醒)

Dear Madam,

We are pleased to acknowledge that you have control the goods and arranged the shipment. According to the items, which include in your order can be shipped in time. It will be paid after shipment by T/T.

Now we have completed the order and take the garments into your control. Enclosed the shipment documents and other documents our bank account is at ABC bank China and our accounting number is 123456.

We are looking forward to your early payment.

Yours faithfully,
Yang Liu

付款函(进口商支付)如下。

Dear Sirs,

We are in receipt of your letter of November 28th.

At requested, we are pleased to acknowledge that we have prepared the money, today we have received the garments and we are satisfied with the women's dress, we will remit by T/T at tomorrow. According to the items, pay to the ABC bank China and its accounting number is 10678211, which will suit your requirement.

Looking forward to next cooperation.

Sincerely yours,
Ann Cooper

12. 索赔函

Dear Sirs,

Re: our order No. 1103 for 1300 PCS women's dress.

We have received the women's dress this afternoon. We are regret to find that according to the order we need pattern No. 12 is 500 PCS, but now it is just only 300 PCS. And we need 300 PCS pattern No. 14 instead of 500 PCS. It wills influent our outstanding achievement and it is aloes for us which you can check up your dispatch bill.

In view of our long-standing business cooperation in future and consider for the good quality and time limited of the garments. We will make the payment by T/T for RMB 19500, which cut down RMB 500.

We trust that the arrangement we have made will satisfy you and look forward to next cooperation.

Yours faithfully,

Ann Cooper

13. 理赔函

Dear Madam,

We have checked up the dispatch bill, we should be sorry to say it is really a mistake of us. In consideration of the garments' time season and exchange for the women's dress is not convenient, it is also a lose for us.

Meanwhile, we are pleased to see that the measures you take both of us are satisfied with the fair and reasonable decision. On the other hand, in view of this mistake, we decide to give you a 3% discount for next order. We agree with you.

We really appreciate your cooperation and expect further development of business between us.

Sincerely yours,

Yang Liu

Unit 13 Introduction of Foreign Trade English in the Export Sales Staff Exams

外销员考试中的外经贸英语简介

13.1 Introduction the Examination for Export Sales Staff (外销员考试简介)

外销员资格考试是对外贸易经济合作部(以下简称“外经贸部”)统一组织的全国性考试,采取全国统一命题、统一考试时间和统一阅卷的方式进行,是绝密级的考试。

所谓外销员,是指在具有进出口经营权的企业从事进出口贸易活动的工作人员。持有外销员资格证书,是在外经贸企业上岗、从事进出口业务人员的必备条件,是外经贸部在招聘我国驻外大使馆经济商务处工作人员时优先考虑的重要因素。

1989年,外经贸部决定对全国外经贸行业的外销员进行岗位培训,并组织全国统一考试,向考试合格者颁发外销员岗位证书。1997年7月1日,外经贸部决定,在全国外经贸行业统一实行外销员资格证书制度,代替原来的外销员岗位证书与外销员水平证书,并将外销员资格考试扩大到社会。

随着国际贸易方式日趋多样化、复杂化,外销员所从事的工作涵盖货物贸易、技术贸易和服务贸易的出口、进口、招标、谈判、承包等各个方面。外销员资格考试的内容依据实际业务的最新发展做出调整。不同于由人事部与外经贸部共同组织的国际商务师考试这一专业技术职称考试,外销员资格考试是一种行业资格考试,侧重于外经贸业务所应具备的基本理论和基本技能,增加考试中的实际案例,强化对外语口语的要求,强调实用性和可操作性。

外销员考试科目由外贸综合业务和外经贸外语两科组成,每科60分为及格。其中,外贸综合业务包括《中国对外经济贸易理论与政策》、《国际贸易》、《国际贸易实务》、《国际金融》、《国际经济法》、《国际营销学》和《国际经济合作》七门课程的内容;外经贸外语由英语、日语、俄语三个语种任选其一,外经贸外语分笔试和口试,口试含听力和商业英语会话。从2000年开始,统一口语考试时间、统一口语考试命题。按照规定,报考当年度外销员资格考试的考生,单科通过成绩可以保留两年,外贸综合业务、外经贸外语笔试和口试成绩均合格者,方可颁发资格证书。

外销员考试每年举行一次,以往考试时间设在每年9月的第二个星期六、星期天。以当年公布的报名时间、考试时间为准。

13.2 Introduction of Foreign Trade English Examination Part (外经贸英语考试部分介绍)

外销员考试中的外经贸外语部分,考生可从英、日、俄语中任选一个语种进行报考,主要考查外贸术语、外经经贸信函翻译、信用证的审核和修改、中外经贸短文互译等。以下我们以外经贸英语考试为例,对外经贸英语笔试的评价目标、考试内容与试卷结构、命题原则作具体介绍,并说明外经贸英语口试的考试目标、能力要求、考试内容、考试程序和成绩评定标准。

1. Written Examination of the Foreign Trade English(外经贸英语笔试)

(1) 评价目标

外销员考试是一种从业资格考试,其中的外经贸英语考试旨在考查考生的英语基础知识、运用英语理解和表达进出口业务和相关的经贸内容的水平,性质上兼顾水平测试和资格考试,是一种"基础"与"专业"相结合的综合性考试。该考试重点考查应试者运用英语理解和表达外经贸常用知识的能力。为达到上述目标,考试对应试者的词汇量、语法知识、经贸知识以及理解和表达能力提出如下要求。

① 词汇量:要求考生认知词汇应达到5000个以上,掌握运用的词汇和词组(包括国际商务词汇术语)应达到2500个以上。

② 语法知识:要求考生熟悉主要的词法、句法和其他基本语法规则,规范地使用单词及词组、英语句子的结构和常用句型、各种时态、主动和被动语态、简单句和各种从句。

③ 阅读理解能力:应试者应能综合运用英语语言知识理解外经贸专业的一般性业务内容的英语书面材料。能够掌握所读材料的主旨、事实和细节;利用上下文猜测某些词汇和短语的意义;根据所给信息进行判断,并完成选择、翻译等试题。

(2) 考试内容与试卷结构

外经贸英语考试共有六种题型,包括外贸术语英汉互译、单项选择题、商务信函翻译、填制合同、审证和改证、汉英经贸短文互译。

① 外贸术语英汉互译(translate the following terms):包括外贸术语英译汉和外贸术语汉译英两部分。其中,外贸术语英译汉共10题;外贸术语汉译英共5题。要求掌握常用的外贸术语及其缩写,包括国际商务各个环节经常用到的术语,涉及贸易磋商、价格、运输、保险、付款、单证、包装、商品品质、数量等,与外汇、关税、商检有关的术语,各种贸易政策和贸易方式,以及国内外主要的经贸机构的名词及其缩略词等。

② 单项选择题(choose the best answer for each of the following question):共25小题。该题型涉及各种词语的运用、句子结构、习惯用法等一般语言现象和经贸英语中常见的语言现象,内容涵盖外贸实务的大部分流程和环节。

③ 国际商务信函汉译英(translate the following into an English letter in a proper form):考核一封信函翻译。要求考生掌握国际商务英语信函的组成部分、基本格式、常

用语句的多种表达方式。内容方面，要求考生能够把汉语撰写的对外商务信函的要点翻译成比较规范的英语信函；其中一部分考查内容是英语信函的组成部分和格式。

国际商务信函的考试内容主要体现在询价及答复、发盘及还盘、推销、订单及其执行、付款条款、保险、装运、索赔等基本业务环节中的简短信函，一般说来为一信一事。

④ 填制合同(fill in the contract form with information gathered from the following correspondences)：要求考生熟悉并理解销售合同的基本格式和规范，要求能根据成交凭证(如中文合同或往来函电等)，用简单明了、正确无误、符合用法习惯和国际惯例的英语填制合同。

⑤ 审证和改证(write a letter in English asking for amendments to the following letter of credit by checking it with the given contract terms)：要求根据汉语或英语所给信息审核信用证，找出不符点，如信用证的种类、金额、商品品质、数量、价格、包装、装运、保险、付款、有效期等细节，并用英文写出改证函。

⑥ 汉英经贸短文互译(translate the following passages)：这个部分一般分作两个小题：英译汉(From English into Chinese)一篇；汉译英(From Chinese into English)一篇。英译汉取材一般是国外报刊有关国际经济和贸易的一般性文章；汉译英取材多为国内报纸杂志中大经贸范畴下的政策概述、形势综述、业务常识、专业介绍、个案分析、中国企业和外贸公司的对外宣传材料等。

(3) 命题原则

外销员考试命题的广度和难度根据考试大纲规定的范围及对应试者能力的要求而确定。命题原则主要如下：

① 外贸术语英汉互译

这部分的考试形式，主要采用英汉互译的方式，不要求解释，只要给出对应的词语即可。术语范围以“全国国际商务专业人员职业资格考试(从业资格)”《国际商务英语》收录的术语为主，但是并不局限于此。

英语中有些术语的汉语表述可能不止一种；同样，汉语中一些术语或其他概念可能有两种甚至两种以上的英语对应词。对此，不作硬性规定。

译文要求书写规范，不允许出现拼写错误、错别字、大小写错误等。

② 单项选择题

一般而言，一道题只有一个考查点，它既可以是介词、连词、名词或其他词类的用法，也可以是关系词等从句的前后协调，少数情况下还涉及进出口业务中的习惯表达方式。

③ 国际商务信函汉译英

译写信函要求完整、准确、规范，并无语法错误，符合英语用法习惯和外贸习惯。

④ 填制合同

要求考生熟悉并理解销售合同的基本格式，能够正确填写相关内容，如合同号码、买卖双方名称、商品名称、规格、数量、价格、包装、保险、装运、支付等。

⑤ 审证和改证

考试中除了审核信用证与合同的不符点外，改证函的撰写应格式规范，语言正确，表达清楚、简洁。

⑥ 汉英经贸短文互译

本题的英译汉部分在200个英语单词左右,汉译英部分一般都在120~200个汉字之间。本题属于提高题性质,因此翻译难度较高。

考试应当合理安排各个测试项目的层次结构和难度结构。本考试题目的难易程度分为比较容易、较难、难三个等级,试卷中各种难易程度的题目各占一定比例。

2. Oral Examination of the Foreign Trade English(外经贸英语口试)

(1) 考试目标

外经贸英语口试考查应试者的一般口语表达能力、语言技巧以及经贸类会话的熟练程度。应试者应在规定的时间内(约10分钟),阅读试题,熟悉内容,并回答考官提出的相应问题。

(2) 能力要求

具体要求为: 朗读流畅、发音准确、回答问题反应敏捷、具备一定的经贸口语表述能力、中外互译基本准确。

(3) 考试内容

朗读、汉译英、英译汉、自由会话

(4) 考试程序

外经贸英语口试试题共有十套题目,其余语种有若干套题,每个考场设考官两名,由两名考官逐一对考生进行单独口试,每个考生的考试时间为10分钟。

① 考前30分钟: 考官各就各位,拆封试题,进行准备;

② 考前20分钟: 考生到场;

③ 考前10分钟: 各考场第一名考生从多套考题中任意抽取一份,隔离进行准备;

④ 8:30分正式开考(开考后,考生完成第一部分阅读内容后,考官收回试题继续考试)。同时,各考场第二名考生从多套考题中任意抽取一份,隔离进行十分钟的准备;

⑤ 8:40分,各考场第一名考生考试结束(交卷后离场),第二名考生开考。同时,各考场第三名考生从多套考题中任意抽取一份,隔离进行十分钟的准备。考试依此顺序进行,直至结束。

(5) 成绩评定标准

① 口语考试评分实行100分制,满分为100分;合格分数线为60分。

② 口语考试根据考生的考试情况,当场将2名考官给出的得分相加,以两者的平均分为最终得分,并记录在册。

目前考试指定教材是由全国国际商务专业人员职业资格考试大纲编委会编写的《国际商务英语》和《国际商务英语口语》,考试大纲采用由全国国际商务专业人员职业资格考试大纲编委会编写的《外销员从业资格考试大纲》,以上三本书皆由中国商务出版社出版。

为了帮助读者更有效地通过外经贸英语考试,本教材以电子资源的形式向读者提供五份往年外经贸英语笔试真题,供读者学习和进行模拟考核。

参 考 用 书
Bibliography

1. 兰天.外贸英语函电(第五版).大连：东北财经大学出版社,2007.
2. 兰天,时敏,叶富国.外贸英语函电学习指导.大连：东北财经大学出版社,2009.
3. 赵银德.外贸函电(第二版).北京：机械工业出版社,2012.
4. 凌华倍,朱佩芬.外经贸英语函电与谈判.北京：中国商务出版社,2002.
5. 王俐俐.外贸英语函电与单证. 北京：机械工业出版社,2010.
6. 王金荣.贸易函电英文写作案例大全.北京：中国宇航出版社,2009.
7. 隋思忠.外贸英语函电.大连：东北财经大学出版社,2007.
8. 刘晓萍.秀漂亮的英文 E-mail.天津：天津科技翻译出版公司,2007.
9. 霍恩比.牛津高阶英汉双解词典(第四版).牛津：牛津大学出版社,1997.
10. 张其春,蔡文萦.简明英汉词典(第五版). 北京：商务印书馆,1995.
11. 李华驹.21 世纪大英汉词典(第一版).北京：中国人民大学出版社,2002.
12. 姚乃强.柯林斯高阶英汉双解大词典(第一版). 北京：商务印书馆,2008.
13. 刘超先.外贸实务单证与函电(第一版).上海：复旦大学出版社, 2008.
14. 熊伟.国际贸易实务英语(第一版).武汉：武汉大学出版社,2001.
15. 江运芳.外贸英语函电(第一版).重庆：重庆大学出版社,2007.
16. 林俐,鲁丹萍,陈俊.国际贸易实务.北京：清华大学出版社,2006.
17. 任丽萍,陈伟.国际贸易实务(第一版).北京：清华大学出版社,2005.
18. 王美玲.外贸函电. 北京：机械工业出版社,2010.
19. 朱佩珍.徐腾飞.外贸函电. 北京：科学出版社,2010.
20. 施士宇.外贸函电教程. 北京：中国人民大学出版社,2012.
21. 李金凤.外贸函电应用. 北京：清华大学出版社,2012.
22. 王妍,肖艳.外贸函电(第一版).北京：北京大学出版社,中国林业出版社,2007.
23. 仲鑫.外贸函电(第一版).北京：机械工业出版社,2007.
24. 张干周.国际贸易函电(第一版).杭州：浙江大学出版社,2007.
25. 李卫.外贸电子邮件的语境分析和写作特点——与传统外贸函电之比较.中国商贸,2011.
26. 熊玲.信用证各类有关问题辨析,现代企业文化,2012(3).
27. 王丽,刘红芬,王颖芳.国际贸易结算方式与收汇风险研究.工业技术经济,2005.
28. http://www.gslcn.org/knowledge/article.aspx? id=185.
29. http://125.46.79.98:8010/jasinda/html/20030929142014451/20031021155853175/2003102309482-3775_1.html.
30. http://baike.baidu.com/view/1473.htm.
31. http://blog.sina.com.cn/s/blog_62c347d50100o3ci.html 2013/9/7.
32. http://baike.baidu.com/view/105794.htm.
33. http://www.baike.com/wiki/%E5%8C%85%E8%A3%85%E6%A0%87%E5%BF%97.